PRAISE FOR *THE* EDITION

Second Edition

How People Learn

A new model of learning and cognition

to improve performance and education

Nick Shackleton-Jones

KoganPage

Publisher's note
Every possible effort has been made to ensure that the information contained in this book is accurate at the time of going to press, and the publishers and authors cannot accept responsibility for any errors or omissions, however caused. No responsibility for loss or damage occasioned to any person acting, or refraining from action, as a result of the material in this publication can be accepted by the editor, the publisher or the author.

First published in Great Britain and the United States in 2019 by Kogan Page Limited
Second edition 2023

2nd Floor, 45 Gee Street	8 W 38th Street, Suite 902	4737/23 Ansari Road
London	New York, NY 10018	Daryaganj
EC1V 3RS	USA	New Delhi 110002
United Kingdom		India

www.koganpage.com

Kogan Page books are printed on paper from sustainable forests.

ISBNs

Hardback	978 1 3986 0721 7
Paperback	978 1 3986 0719 4
Ebook	978 1 3986 0720 0

British Library Cataloguing-in-Publication Data

A CIP record for this book is available from the British Library.

Library of Congress Control Number
2022950008

Typeset by Integra Software Services, Pondicherry
Print production managed by Jellyfish
Printed and bound by CPI Group (UK) Ltd, Croydon, CR0 4YY

To my wife and the gods,
for whom we dance

CONTENTS

ABOUT THIS BOOK

This book is like those department stores where you can buy different kinds of things on different floors. In the olden days, department stores might have had an elevator with a person whose job it was to operate it, sometimes called a bellhop. The bellhop was usually dressed in a fancy outfit, a bit like a cross between a military and a circus uniform.

So these pages comprise three floors, and in this analogy I am the bellhop. On the first floor (the 'ground floor' as we say in the UK) you will find lots of useful tools and techniques for designing stuff that helps people to perform better at their jobs, and experiences that transform their attitudes and behaviour. You will find a detailed description of human-centred learning design, something I have called the 5Di model, and lots of tips on how to make your learning department efficient and effective.

On the second floor you will find a completely new model of learning and cognition; an all-encompassing general theory of learning that represents the first unified explanation of what we see when researching learning in human and non-human animals. It provides the foundation for the approach and advice offered on the first floor. It also contains a critique of education, and a clear description of the way education should work if it were to ever have anything to do with learning.

The third floor – ah, well, are you sure you wish to travel to the third floor, madam? The third floor explains what humans are, what thinking really is, and how you came to be the person you are today. It tears up 2,000 years of Western intellectual traditions, unseating those toxic conspirators Plato, Descartes, Wittgenstein et al along the way. It's the end of an era, and with it come a flood of radical ideas in areas such as marketing, entertainment, language, ethics, artificial intelligence, psychology, culture and decision making. If you are of a nervous disposition you might prefer floors one and two.

Some of you may wonder why I have departed from the self-important academic tone that you are used to in books that talk about how things work. Many people are impressed if you talk like a professor, so I hope you are not one of those people. It took me many years to unravel that particular conceit and to understand that playfulness – even childishness – is to be taken very seriously indeed. After all, it determines just how far you and I are able to travel. I hope that by the end of this book you will understand why.

PREFACE

Charles Darwin was not terribly smart. In fact, he was a college drop-out. Like many university students today, he was persuaded to study something that his parents thought respectable – medicine – but found it too tough and gave up. So they found an easier respectable degree for him to do (religious studies) which he managed to pass even though he wasn't much interested in any of it.

What he really cared about were rocks and pigeons, and it is likely that these rather geeky pursuits (not his trip to the Galapagos Islands) formed the basis of his theory of evolution.

You might also be interested to know that when he first submitted *On the Origin of Species* his editor advised him to leave out all the half-baked evolution stuff, and instead stick with the pigeon-breeding tips which he was sure would make for a popular Victorian coffee-table book.

But he stuck with the evolution story, and in return people laughed at him for decades and published cartoons of him as a monkey in the popular press.

The moral of the story is that it is *difference* that makes the difference. Human progress is the product of people who saw the world differently and – often by sheer luck and dogged determination – managed to popularize their ideas. Progress is not owed to the smart. Progress belongs to the peculiar. Indeed, one of the greatest *barriers* to progress is smart people who are nonetheless very conventional; they are excellent at coming up with reasons why things should stay exactly as they are. This is because today we call people smart when they are good at doing what they are told and passing tests to prove it.

So this is, I believe, a different perspective. One that will no doubt seem strange – ridiculous even – and which you will likely struggle to get your head round. In fact, so far I have not been able to find anyone able to fully comprehend what I am saying, even though I have tried to say it as simply as possible. Perhaps you will be the first.

In the unlikely event that you do grasp it, I should caution you that it will make you deeply unpopular. You will become a time-traveller, transported hundreds of years into the future then returned to the present day; someone who now looks despairingly at a world awash with medieval beliefs and practices. Almost nobody will understand what you are saying. You will often feel alone.

If you are still reading, I take it you have ignored my warnings – most probably because you don't believe them. Jolly good. We are going to start with cognition – with thinking – because learning is a cognitive process and unless I persuade you that thinking is not what you thought, we won't learn much about learning.

Cognition

01

Thinking is feeling

'*Thoughts are the shadows of our feelings – always darker, emptier and simpler.*'

FRIEDRICH NIETZSCHE, *THE JOYFUL SCIENCE*

The following passage contains an outline of experimenting on animals. If necessary, please overlook this boxed content.

He took them apart like machines – like a boy dismantling a watch to get at the cogs. He opened their skulls to take a look at their memories;[1] he sliced them up so he could feel their heartbeats with his fingers.[2]

Eventually, his neighbours complained about the screaming. He defended his experiments, explaining that they weren't really screams – just noises. Noises like the squealing of a hinge that hasn't been oiled.

If something doesn't have a soul, can you truly say that it 'screams'? Animals don't have souls, and so the sounds they make are just mechanical sounds – like those a rusty machine might make. Animals are merely complex machines; it's OK to take them apart. But though he persuaded his peers of this argument *intellectually* – his friends' sentiments betrayed them. The colleague who placed a kitten in a jar and then removed all the air, watching it slowly suffocate… well, he couldn't go through with it again. Though convinced by rational argument, his feelings made a more compelling case.[3]

Most people know René Descartes for 'I think, therefore I am' (*Ego cogito, ergo sum*) rather than his experiments on animals, but there's a profound connection between the two: Descartes believed that humans were fundamentally different to non-humans, and that the difference boiled down to our possession of rational souls, this being evidenced by language. His 'beast-machine' hypothesis proposed that animals were mere mechanisms, and much like the hydraulic statues popular at the time they moved around but lacked 'rational souls' – so you could do pretty much whatever you liked to them.

This idea, of the connection between soul and reason, goes back a long way. The Greek philosopher Aristotle believed there were three kinds of soul: the vegetative soul (that plants have), the sensitive soul (that animals have) and the rational soul (that we have). In his view, humans have all three, arranged a bit like Russian dolls. What sets us apart from animals is that although we have the soul of an animal which is somehow instinctive and emotional, we have this rational soul which is immortal and godlike, on top.

It does often seem that humans are quite different from other animals – just look around you: we have cars and iPhones, whilst they are still snuffling around in the dirt. Who could deny our differences?

What people tend to overlook is that until a few thousand years ago we were also just snuffling around in the dirt – just another type of monkey scraping a living with sticks and stones. Not even an especially successful monkey, as it happens.

Neither is it true that we have 'evolved' since then – evolution is a slow process and humans haven't changed much biologically in the last 70,000 years or so. For most of that time we were just groups of apes whose principal distinction was their complex herd instinct. Yes, we had big brains, but we were using that mainly to keep track of our social circles. So far as we can tell this is what modern-day chimps are doing with their big brains – together with most of the people on Instagram.

It's an intriguing thought, isn't it: that if we were to use a time machine to swap a child born 70,000 years ago with one born today, no one would notice anything unusual and both would grow up fitting perfectly into the world around them?

So what changed in that time? Hundreds of thousands of years ago we discovered a trick: telling stories. If we could make sounds that reflected our experiences, then we could pass them down and pass them around. This would mean that our relatives could benefit from our experiences, and (among other things) not make the same mistakes.

Telling a story is a remarkably altruistic thing to do. Information about food sources or danger is extremely valuable – you'd have to be a very self-sacrificing creature to tell a story, or to paint those stories on the walls of caves. But once everyone starts telling stories you have something like a collective memory – you have a *culture*. And a culture can be a useful adaptation.

Telling stories is not the only way a culture can spring to life – but it's certainly a big help. The ability that enabled humans to compose our stories and leapfrog other species was something like song: more specifically, a capacity for making sounds that reflected what we were feeling. And not just any feeling; an extraordinarily subtle kaleidoscope of feelings – feelings for every occasion.

In 2010 the psychologists John Pilley and Allison Reid published the results of their research with Chaser, a border collie, who had learned the names of over a thousand objects.[4] More importantly, they showed that Chaser was able to understand that words *refer* to objects[5] – rather than just being behavioural cues.

But while Chaser could use 1,000 words, a typical human uses around 30,000. Our amazing ability to tie a sound to a sentiment is the foundation on which our language and culture depend. It is also the reason why music plays such a big part in our lives today, across all cultures. In other words: a sound can make us *feel* something, and I can feel something and make a sound.

Because of this innate mechanism we can communicate – even with other species to some extent. I scream, you scream – we all scream, but whilst your dog will be alarmed by your screams, your computer most certainly will not. Your computer does not and never will use words, it can only ever appear to. In the chapter on language we will see that words do not actually refer to *things* – instead they are expressions of *sentiments*.

There are many species that do something like this, most notably birds. The humble honeybee also tells stories as a way of sharing information – only they do so in the form of dance. A single bee can share what it has experienced with other bees.

By the way, here's a big question: obviously our bee doesn't share *everything* it has experienced. So which bits does the bee share? The bits that matter, of course. Do different things matter to different bees? Probably not – probably what matters is 'hard coded', otherwise an eccentric bee might tell an entirely useless story about an unusual plastic bucket he spotted en route, and send his followers to their deaths. Notice how similar this is to what your friend does when you ask them about their weekend – they don't tell you about washing their pants on a 60 degree spin cycle, causing you to die of boredom. They tell you about the bits that matter.

Of course an oral tradition suffers from some problems: you need subtly different sounds for different things if you want to tell increasingly useful, complicated stories. Also, the stories tend to change a bit in the telling. Mostly this is OK, because the important things – the things that really matter, like 'There's a bear living in that cave' – get preserved.

Stories have a central role to play in human learning, therefore – something we will explore in the next chapter – but as an approximation we can say that stories are the default way in which humans store and share their experiences.

The storytelling ape

So humans became an odd storytelling type of ape, and though this was helpful it wasn't a dramatic advance at first. For millennia it seems we survived in small bands, telling our stories, and sharpening sticks. Stories meant that our discoveries could spread and accumulate. Eventually large, complex societies sprang up around shared stories and dense patches of food, and people began to specialize and trade – for example where one individual wanted to focus on making baskets then exchange them for food.

The remains of the Turkish city Göbekli Tepe date from prehistoric times, the oldest parts estimated to have been built around 9000 BC. The elaborate carvings and architectural construction suggest a temple and associated deities, with some authorities believing it to be a pilgrimage site.

Since the structure predates farming and the domestication of cattle in the region, it may be that stories took *precedence* over agriculture as an organizing principle, rather than stories being a means of organizing larger agricultural societies. The most plausible account seems to be that storytelling provided sufficient conditions for large-scale organization to occur.

Either way, the upshot was that not everyone had to be nomads, hunters and foragers. For the species as a whole this turned out to be a great strategy, even though living in hives made life for the lowly drone quite a bit worse: we lived longer, had more kids, but spent more time doing things that didn't make immediate sense.

This shift also precipitated a significant shift in our approach to learning. Up until that point – for millions of years – we had learned as all animals do: by observing our peers and parents, copying them, being guided on tasks of increasing complexity via feedback that made us feel better or worse. Having our peers laugh at us or our parents praise us are powerful motivations.

But in a complex society one might aspire to a different life to one's parents – one might need to be apprenticed to a different role. Apprenticeship was a kind of 'parent-swapping' scheme that made sense as activities diversified. Today we tend to think of learning as involving a lot of reading and writing – but this is merely a historical accident. A blip; a detour.

Writing was born of economic necessity, as an accounting tool: it was just hard to keep track of who owed you what otherwise. It was a way of externalizing stuff that we were poorly adapted to keep in our heads. As a secondary thing someone eventually figured out that you could also use writing to record stories.

But notice that some societies were doing just fine without writing: when Christopher Columbus landed in America, the Native Americans didn't have a writing system as such, but a rich oral tradition and a way of representing history artistically. They had developed complex societies without the need for writing – so whilst gossip is universal, gossip magazines are not.

Writing is important, but not in the way that people imagine it is. Plato writes that the Egyptian king Thamus was offered the gift of writing by the god Thoth as a '*pharmakon*' (a remedy). But Thamus rejects the gift, observing that it is more poison than medicine – and moreover something *alien*.

Today, writing has enabled us to shift from knowledge being something in our heads, to something out there in the world – for example in books and machines. We have become the people who know almost nothing but can do almost everything as a result. We like to think we are much more knowledgeable as a result of writing – but go back only a few generations and you will find illiterate people who knew far more than you: how to make clothes, build a house, maintain a steam engine, farm the land.

Don't kid yourself – they wouldn't have struggled with iPads. No, writing merely opened the way for machines. Writing is indeed a parasite.

In the world of learning, writing presented the opportunity for *learning elimination*: for example externalizing knowledge in the form of checklists or guides (there is evidence that such 'performance support' approaches were in use by the ancient Egyptians). Today, if you have to buy 15 things at the supermarket, you might make a list. The list prevents you having to learn them. Tomorrow your refrigerator will tell the supermarket what you need and you won't have to drive, read or write. You will just think 'I'd like a pizza' and it will appear by drone.

There is something I should tell you about humans and their stories. Just like other animals humans can make sounds that corresponded to what they experience: a dog will yelp in pain when you step on its foot, as will a human.

Animals can also make sounds that correspond to what they *have* experienced, or *expect* to experience. A dog can get excited when it anticipates going for a walk, for example (or whimper when a cruel master raises a stick). Our connection with our pets stems from feeling similarly about so many things.

However, unlike most animals humans can get excited about things they merely *imagine*; things they have concocted from other experiences – for example, the idea of a mighty human who is a bit like their chief, only mightier. These stories have a curious power to alter our behaviour: you can tell a person that there is a bear in a cave and they will stay away from the cave. But you can tell a person that there is a divine bear in a cave, and they will leave offerings for it.

As societies became more complex, these stories enabled social cohesion – otherwise the story is just: 'My family is better than yours', and that ends up getting pretty divisive.

'System 2': imagination

This ability does have something to do with brain structure (if not size). In essence, a simple creature can store what it experiences as feelings. The activation of these feelings (what we call 'cognition') can then be used to guide behaviour. We remember that some food with a certain appearance tasted bad, so we avoid it.

So why do I eat Brussels sprouts? The answer is that I can have feelings about *imaginary* situations, and I can use these to control my behaviour in a more sophisticated way. I might not want to eat my Brussels sprouts, but I can imagine how upset my mum will be if I don't, and my feelings about an imaginary situation can outweigh my feelings about a current situation.

Only more complicated nervous systems seem to be able to do this 'feeling about imaginary things' trick, but it's certainly not unique to humans. If you have a dog you will see them doing this quite regularly. They want to do something, but they know you will yell at them if they do. You recognize the feeling of conflict in their eyes.

Sometimes they give in, so you yell at them. Sometimes they don't give in, and you pat them on the head and say 'good boy' (this is also how we raise children, by the way).

It should tell us something interesting about our cognitive similarities that we can use the same approaches to training our pets as we do to raise our kids. If you're thinking 'Of course – this is just conditioning!', then keep reading. I hope you will soon see that conditioning rests on a much more profound learning mechanism.

There is a popular story we tell today, even among scientists, of the rational (pre-frontal) area of the brain, and how it intervenes to control the emotional parts of the brain (e.g. the amygdala). This story has found its way from Aristotle to Kahneman. I am saying that this story is wrong: we do not have 'rational' and 'emotional' faculties in some neo-Cartesian dualism – instead we are entirely emotional. Our complex behaviour comes from the interplay between the emotions we are experiencing right now, and emotions we can imagine.

You can think of us (or your dog) as having two 'systems' if it helps – but they are both emotional. One says: 'Eat the doughnut!' The other says: 'Think of how guilty you will feel later!'

In Descartes' time, body–soul dualism was the norm. Had you tried to explain to someone that there is no such thing as 'soul', they would have laughed to your face: 'Of course I have a soul! Who is it talking to you now!?' they would have scoffed. People readily accepted this dualistic view, since it conveniently distinguished us from other creatures.

Today we have abandoned this superstition, only to substitute another: the feeling–thinking dualism. We don't imagine that thinking and feeling are different in squirrels, of course (we are supernatural creatures after all).

This silly superstition still holds us back in areas ranging from ethics to language and artificial intelligence (AI). Learning experts will ask about the role of emotion in learning, and there are still respectable scientists chasing 'reason' and 'emotion' areas of the brain, just as there were once scientists looking for the source of the soul in our heads.

Let me repeat this point, since it is the central premise of this book, the foundation for understanding learning and cognition, and a radical rejection of thousands of years' worth of Western intellectual traditions: **you don't think. You have no thoughts. What you call 'thinking' is feeling; 'thoughts' are just fancy feelings.** We have them, animals have them, we are not supernatural creatures. Humans are better than most animals in being able to have complex feelings about imaginary things – such as the future, laws of motion, doughnuts and themselves – but none of our abilities is unique.

We used our ability to have feelings about imaginary situations to create stories that were not simply accounts of past experiences, and our ability to connect sounds to sentiments to share them. Stories started to have an evolution all of their own. The stories that made groups of apes more successful tended to survive.

One of the most influential stories, it turned out, was the 'we are special' story. The 'we are special' story took a variety of forms, but in essence the story told a group of people that they were better than everything else in creation in some qualitatively different way, and that they were therefore entitled to use everything as they wished.

By 'qualitatively different', I mean not just that they are stronger, smarter, more beautiful (although that is also quite an influential story), but actually a completely different, superior, class of being.

You know, it's pretty tough to maintain a story like this in the face of evidence when other beings seem pretty similar to you, so the story had to involve some supernatural element – some 'special essence' that made them different. Aristotle told this story, as did Plato after him, and more recently Descartes; it concerned rational souls.

The rational souls story entitled a specific people to do all manner of things that we find instinctively abhorrent: for example travelling some-where, finding people who looked a lot like them, stealing their land, killing them and selling them into slavery. Or just inhumanly experimenting on them to find out more about them. In their heads they had 'rational souls', so they could do whatever they liked to (what they deemed) 'soulless crea-tures', because they thought the people of the land didn't deserve better treatment.

In America and Great Britain, married women were considered property, by law, throughout most of the 19th century. People debated whether women had souls. To those people, it seemed they might, but in a crude ir-rational state – like those of children. The tacit rule of thumb was that the less of a 'rational soul' something or someone had, the more those specific people were entitled to do what they wanted with it.

Fast-forward to the present day – our entire way of life still revolves around one particular supernatural story that most of us continue to be-lieve: the story of reason.

Plato, Aristotle, Descartes and most of the philosophers in-between saw a close relationship between reason, the mind, and the divine. Man's ration-ality was what linked him to the divine and separated him from the beasts: 'I think, therefore I am'.

Notice that Descartes did not say 'I *feel*, therefore I am'. His argument was that although my thoughts might be wrong, there must be an 'I' that thinks them. But why couldn't we make the same argument for feelings? My sensations of the world might be wrong (I might, for example, be a brain in a jar), but there must be an 'I' that senses them.

There's a good reason why Descartes didn't make this argument: he was being a bit sneaky. Ironically there is actually no reason for the 'I think' bit of 'I think, therefore I am' to be there. It bears no logical relation to the conclusion.

Centuries before Descartes, St Augustine had argued that of all the things one can doubt, I cannot doubt that 'I am' – and Descartes was well aware of his writings. But Descartes was a (pathologically) rational man, good at rational things, who wanted to assert the primacy of reason and in so doing recreate the world in his own image. So he added 'I think' onto the statement like a bloke hitching his dinghy to Augustine's cruise ship. He could equally have said 'I feel, therefore I am.' What was the big deal about thinking?

As we saw, Aristotle believed that animals and humans alike possess a feeling, 'sensitive' soul. At various points it seems Descartes admits that animals have 'sensations'. So although 'I feel, therefore I am' makes just as much sense philosophically speaking – we can't have it. 'Feelings' cannot be linked to the soul, and to God.

And whilst we stopped believing in souls, we carried on believing in reason and thought – this, at least, separated us from the animals. We think, they feel. We are superior. Have another hamburger.

But in case you think I am making an argument for animal rights, let me remind you that that is not my central intention. I am trying to say something far more fundamental about people – something with implications for our understanding of learning, cognition, language, relationships, ethics, culture, politics, social media, marketing and AI (to name but a few areas): you don't think. You have never thought. You have only ever *felt*.

The affective context model

The theory that underpins this radical shift in our understanding of ourselves – in fact our understanding of all creatures – is called the affective context model. Yes, I know it's not very catchy. The heart of it is that **all cognition is a variation of affective response** – reaching all the way back to the earliest nervous systems and our primordial ancestors.

In case this sounds odd, I would like to ask: is it not much odder to think that humans have some special, entirely different type of activity going on in their heads that no other creature possesses?

Why do we talk about 'reason' and 'emotion' centres in the human brain? We don't describe the brains of rats like this. Do we think dogs separate reason and emotion? Has it never struck you as strange that we so easily accept that human brains separate reason and emotion, *in a way that no other animal's brains do?*

Oh dear. It seems you are the victim of an elaborate scam, and I expect that thought will take some getting used to. Animals have feelings, humans have feelings, we started calling some of the more sophisticated feelings 'thoughts' and then we fell into the trap of believing thinking and feeling were different somehow. An entire Western intellectual tradition based on the idea that thinking and feeling are distinct is mumbo-jumbo.

There is no logical reason or basis for thinking that human minds operate in a fundamentally different fashion to those of our close relatives – Darwin made that point convincingly, and neuroscience has provided abundant evidence to that end.

But this is not how persuasion works, even for philosophers; it's all about what I can make you *feel*. (Of course I can pretend that it's all perfectly logical, if that makes you feel better. In our culture strong feelings are attached to the notion that something is 'logical'.)

There's a very modern consequence of this confusion about thinking, which we will come to in a bit: imagining that humans were, in essence, 'thinking things' was the top of a slippery slope that led to us thinking that we were basically algorithms that could be reproduced by a computer or uploaded to the cloud. In this way, the popular religious idea of an immortal soul was smuggled into our technological present via familiar Hollywood storylines.

By contrast, had we stuck with the idea of humans as *feeling* things, it would be much less clear how the 'you' that feels could be transplanted onto a machine that doesn't. Ironically, one of our greatest fears is that AI will behave like a (Cartesian) psychopath – applying rules rationally, with complete disregard for emotion.

In the world of learning, this infectious lie had catastrophic consequences: thinking about people as if they were data storage mechanisms – like books or computers – legitimized all manner or tortuous practices; collectively called 'education'. Instead of allowing people to learn as they normally would (as all creatures do) – from their experiences – we set in place a global bureaucracy of unprecedented scale, profiting from subjecting our offspring to monstrous deprivations, forcing them to sit down, shut up and memorize meaningless information to prove their obedience.

We tried to turn them into machines. We tried to stifle their learning, crush their individuality. It never worked, but we found a way to make lots of money out of it, and damaged every last one of them in the process. Now the monstrous Cartesian machine seems almost unstoppable.

But I am getting ahead of myself. You may still be reeling from the statement that you don't think – it seems preposterous… doesn't it? As I said earlier, back in Descartes' day if you had suggested that humans don't have souls, people would have laughed at you: 'Self-evidently we have souls! If we didn't have souls we would be dead! We would collapse like a burst balloon, my dear fellow! Pah! I am most intimately acquainted with my soul – of that I can be certain!' people might have said.

In a curious way, our stories – our feelings – are the limits of our world. Not our language. Language is simply the sounds we make to express how we feel about the world. Notice that although the idea of 'soul' suffered from profound logical flaws ('how does a non-physical thing alter a physical thing?'), people loved the idea because it made us special and immortal, and many – to this day – continue to believe it.

'Thoughts' are exactly like 'souls' – they are a supernatural thing that we invented to make ourselves feel superior and which today we take for granted, but which in a few decades' time we will read about in history books as being indicative of our hopelessly primitive culture.

I know you are quite sure that thoughts are happening in your head right now – just as Descartes' contemporaries would have 'sensed' the activity of their souls. What you mislabel 'thoughts' are indeed happening – neurons are firing and forming connections – but they are *feelings*, complicated intertwined feelings about subtle imaginary things, feelings prompted by the words on this page, feelings that you can make into sounds, but feelings nonetheless.

But where did Aristotle get the reason story? Plato divides the soul into three parts (rather than two): reason, spirit and the appetites. In his allegory of the charioteer, reason (the charioteer) must command two horses, one pale and noble (spirit) the other dark and unruly (the appetites). Where is the charioteer headed? You guessed it: the heavens. From the outset it is the role of reason to conquer the passions and steer us towards the divine.

Much as we do today, Plato views the appetites as irrational reactions emanating from the lower part of the soul, to be conquered by the altogether more desirable power of reason. The Stoics took it a little further – seeking to eliminate the emotions altogether – but throughout Western intellectual history the emotions remained a rather shameful reminder of our animal nature, there to be conquered by the divine power of reason.

The philosophical battle between the Stoics and Aristotelians is acted out between Mr Spock and Captain Kirk in *Star Trek*. The Stoic Mr Spock has all but eliminated his pesky emotions, whilst Captain Kirk struggles to master his. As we watch their relationship play out over and over again, the moral of their story is that it is better to have emotions and to master them than to eliminate them altogether (echoing the Aristotelian line).

Today, this idea of 'thinking' as distinct from 'feeling' has developed into an entire cultural mythology. Business people will say things like 'we need to set our feelings aside and think objectively', as if that were something that were possible. Education people talk about the role of emotion in learning, as if learning weren't entirely a matter of emotion; imagine someone saying 'Cognition plays a really important role in thinking!' – you'd guess that they didn't understand thinking at all.

Science sporadically claims to have discovered the 'emotional' centre of the brain – only to find to their disappointment that emotional states are inextricably linked to every aspect of cognition. In her book *Emotions, Learning and the Brain* the neuroscientist Mary Helen Immordino-Yang writes: 'Learning, attention, memory, decision making, motivation, and social functioning are both profoundly affected by emotion and in fact subsumed within the process of emotion.'[6] Subsumed!

In other words, these things that we call cognitive processes are not simply *affected* by emotional processes – they *are* emotional processes! But we have grown so fond of this dualistic narrative that we can't quite comprehend what we are reading. I sense that even now you are struggling with what I am saying. Why is that?

We are deeply attached to the idea that humans are somehow superior to and different from other creatures. We immediately accept the idea that thinking and emotion are separate in humans – it seems so obvious. We even imagine that 'reason' and 'emotion' occupy distinct areas in the brain.

And yet when we turn to non-human animals, and their remarkably similar looking brains, it is not at all clear what that might mean. Do you think the emotion your dog experiences when seeing a squirrel is different from his thought of a squirrel? Do you think Fido's episodic and semantic memories are stored separately? Do you think we could identify distinct 'reason' and 'emotion' structures in the brain of a rat?

As a rule of thumb this is a good sniff test to apply to any learning theory that you encounter: can you easily apply it to other animals? Behaviourism checks out – but how about the andragogy/pedagogy distinction? Do we think young dogs learn differently to old ones? How about Kolb's learning cycle (that suggests learning requires reflection)? Do you think rats spend much time reflecting?

I can spot a visceral reaction in you right now: instinctively you feel that we can't compare humans and dogs because humans are fundamentally different from dogs somehow. 'We work differently', your heart wants to say. You don't have a rational basis for this view, it's counter-Darwinian and frankly anti-scientific, but it's a feeling you are attached to. You have been steeped in this story for decades.

You can quite easily make noises in defence of this view – and perhaps you will call them 'rational arguments' to give them more weight with people who are attached to the idea that they are smart and rational, but really they are just a kind of elaborate barking – a territorial defence.

Part of you probably wants to yell 'hypocrite!' – after all, if there is no distinction between reason and emotion, between thought and feeling, then why bother writing this book? But look more closely: these words are converted into their corresponding sounds in your head (using a system psychologists call the 'phonological store') – each word has a distinct *feel* to it, a set of emotional resonances.

Strung together, subtle emotions form complex patterns that we may call a 'story' or an 'argument', sometimes even a 'song' – all have the power to move us. My story can move you, just as the bee's waggle dance moves its fellow bees. Most likely I am not going to persuade you until I hit on something that resonates with you – or give an example you can relate to. Computers and Mr Spock operate logically; we do not.

An altogether more likely prediction is that you are not going to believe much of what I am saying until it becomes the popular view, i.e. when the people *you care about* believe it. At that point you will most likely say: 'Well, I thought it was obvious all along'. That is how new ideas are accepted, and that is the reason why.

But what about 'the science'!? We like to imagine that reason (in the form of science) elevates us above the level of the shaman – forgetting that the history of science is littered with imaginary phenomena: phlogiston, the four humours, learning styles and so on. Scientists, too, fall in love with ideas, and once you have become attached to an idea it is pretty easy to find some evidence for it.

Most people today have a very naïve notion of science, namely that we go about measuring and observing things, accumulating evidence that tells us how the world really is. Instead, science is about wild imaginative stories that we systematically put to the test. All ideas are proven wrong in time, in the meantime competing narratives battle it out across the decades. In our modern culture you are infinitely more persuasive if you can pose as rational, objective or scientific or can say the word 'evidence' or something with 'neuro-' in it. In Descartes' time you had to show that your arguments were consistent with scripture.

To some it may seem as though I am implying that the feeling that 2 + 2 = 4 and the feeling that 2 + 2 = 5 are equally valid – since both are sentiments. To be clear, I am not: whilst both are indeed sentiments, sentiments can be arranged in a way which resembles the world to a greater or lesser degree – one which is logical or not – just as pigeons can be trained to peck in a logical fashion or stones stacked according to size.

Logical relationships are features of our world, to which our feelings may or may not correspond. What makes us different from stones or pigeons is our *awareness* of this correspondence: i.e. our awareness that our feelings follow a pattern (logical, musical or otherwise).

Science is a methodical way of checking the extent to which the organization of our feelings corresponds to the organization of the world: for example, we might feel that lighter objects (e.g. a feather) fall more slowly that heavier ones. Science provides a means of bringing our internal feelings about the world closer to the way it really is.

You might think that it is a good thing if our internal emotional world is aligned with logical relationships in the external world. Most philosophers did. And to some extent it is: many creatures have a sense of 'fairness', for example, meaning that they feel the imbalance of rewards or punishments keenly. But as someone who once studied logic I can tell you it's not really much use in the real world unless you are programming computers. When your partner is upset, pointing out the logical discrepancies in their reasoning is unlikely to lead to a successful outcome (and this may be one reason why philosophers wish we were more like machines).

Throughout its history our planet has been dominated by creatures with no explicit awareness of logic whatsoever – including dinosaurs, bacteria and the insects that continue to vastly outnumber us. Evolution has consistently selected illogical creatures over logical ones – we are creatures *designed* to behave unreasonably. One might even say this unreasonableness is quite logical: our self-serving biases promote our survival.

All creatures are designed to care about stuff that *matters*, and logical relationships rarely matter much. Since life on earth is competitive, much of our own cognition is given over to second-guessing what the other lot are feeling. Will that bear attack me? Will that attractive female mate with me? Can I sneak up on that creature before it notices me? Where am I in the social hierarchy? These questions aren't mathematical in nature.

The exceptions to this are notable: our brains are great at figuring out if a projectile is going to hit us (without having to do all the calculations on paper). Some of the earliest uses of explicit reason and logic were for predicting seasonal changes – which of course *does* matter if you are growing crops.

Prior to that, our understanding of the world around us was often expressed in terms of the character of deities – which is actually a great way to think about the world if your mental mechanisms are based around sentiment. For example, we can say 'Maria, the goddess of weather, is sad in the spring and cries a lot' as a way of encoding the information that, statistically, precipitation is heavier during spring.

Once people began to trade, writing and mathematics became important for keeping track of things, but only because we had begun doing something that no other creature had done before. Isn't it odd how logic only became important once we had writing? Logic works well in an alien world – a technological one. Logic will make you a good computer programmer, but a poor hunter-gatherer. As I will argue later, logic and reason are not at all human but instead the way in which an external force acts on us, adapting us to its ends.

One of the consequences of our story about reason is that we began to worship logical people. We called them 'geniuses' and we thought of them as people with incredible powers of deduction – often capable of complex mathematics – who contributed to human progress. But this is a made-up story. Geniuses are often not super-smart, and super-smart people often lead dull, bureaucratic lives.

I'd like to finish this chapter by returning to the example I mentioned in the preface: Charles Darwin was definitely not that smart. He was a college drop-out. His father wanted him to become a doctor, but Charles found the studying too difficult so he quit. His dad – determined to make something of his son – enrolled him on a theological degree which was much easier, and which Charles managed to pass, but wasn't really interested in. This is a familiar story, even today.

What Charles *really* cared about were rocks and pigeons. He was a bit of a geek.

The whole *Voyage of the Beagle* thing was also a red herring. Charles was just there to keep the captain entertained with lively conversation – pretty much like the modern-day entertainers on cruise ships. He wasn't even the first choice. Since he was sea-sick much of the time, he probably sucked at that too.

The 'beaks of finches' story, though poetic, has little to do with his thoughts around evolution which more likely came about because of his interest in pigeon-breeding. You see, he spotted that he could significantly alter his pigeons by breeding them over the course of a few generations and began to wonder that if *he* could do that in a few years, what nature might accomplish in thousands.

In fact, the first edition of *On the Origin of Species* contained a great deal of discussion on pigeon-breeding, causing his editor to advise him to drop all the evolution nonsense – which was a half-baked idea in any case – and instead publish a book on pigeon-breeding which everyone would have liked. Charles refused.

Once more – it is not an abundance of thought that makes a person a genius, it is that they feel differently about the world. Darwin was a geek, fascinated by breeding birds and old rocks. The young Albert Einstein ruminated over travelling at the speed of light, and though he failed some of his college courses and was not the best at math (his wife was better and helped him with some of the trickier proofs), his wild ideas won him acclaim. How many young men do you know who are wondering about stuff like that?

And Marie Curie – the only person in history to have won two Nobel Prizes – was decidedly and unashamedly different. She once remarked: 'Be less curious about people, and more curious about ideas'. Certainly she was smart, but in a world where women were actively dissuaded from contributing to progress, it was her unusual and singular determination that won out: she cared deeply about things that most people don't even wonder about.

If you look at how the word 'genius' is used commonly today, you will notice that it is disproportionately associated with a particular type of thought – mathematical thought. Mathematics is deemed to be the bedrock of reason, hence 'geniuses' are identified principally by their ability to solve complicated mathematical problems.

America's smartest man (according to some journalists) is a chap called Christopher Michael Langan. His IQ is estimated at between 195 and 210 (based on standardized tests of intelligence largely centred around verbal and mathematical reasoning) – but you have probably never heard of him. That's fine, he hasn't made any significant contribution to society. In fact he spent 20 years working as a bouncer, and in 2008 won $250,000 on a game-show. Memorizing facts paid off for him, you might say.

It is not reason, but *difference* that makes the difference – differences in the way we feel about and therefore perceive the world. Geniuses may indeed be smart people, but that is not what makes them a genius; it is their willingness to challenge popular thinking that defines them. For this reason alone, they become the authors of our future. If we want progress, we must embrace difference.

If cognition is a thoroughly affective process, what does this do to our understanding of learning? In the next chapter we will find out.

Key points

- There is no such thing as thinking. Thinking is just a type of feeling, not a different kind of cognitive activity.
- Humans (and other animals) express their feelings using complex vocalizations, collectively called 'language'.
- The principal role of language is storytelling, a technique used to share feelings with others.
- Humans use the same mechanisms for learning as do other animals.
- Conventional educational practices are based on an incorrect understanding of cognition and learning.

Endnotes

1 R Descartes and A Kenny (1984) *The Philosophical Writings of Descartes: Volume 3*, Cambridge University Press, Cambridge
2 A C Grayling (2005) *Descartes: The life and times of a genius*, Walker and Company, New York
3 A Guerrini. The Ethics of Animal Experimentation in Seventeenth-Century England, *Journal of the History of Ideas*, 1989, 50 (3), 391–407
4 J W Pilley and A K Reid. Border collie comprehends object names as verbal referents, *Behavioural Processes*, 2011, 86 (2)
5 Or, as I will argue, the reactions those objects elicit.
6 M H Immordino-Yang (2016) *Emotions, Learning, and the Brain: Exploring the educational implications of affective neuroscience*, W W Norton & Company

Learning

02

Reactions that change us

'People will forget what you said, people will forget what you did, but people will never forget how you made them feel.'

MAYA ANGELOU

I would have been around 15. I attended a Quaker boarding school in the South of England. It wasn't exactly like Hogwarts, but if you've never been to boarding school that's not a bad approximation.

On Sundays we were allowed to dress as we liked and head into the local town, riding the bus into the town centre, spending our weekly pocket-money. It was terribly exciting for lots of reasons. One of those reasons was girls.

My boarding school was almost exclusively boys, with a smattering of girls in the sixth form. The local town, however, enjoyed something like a 50/50 split. If you are reading this book and not still a teenager, I suspect you can still remember how important it was to you as a teenager to be cool. In fact, as far as I can remember, the greater part of my teenage years consisted of trying to figure out how to be cool. Eventually I gave up. Giving up on being cool is called 'adulthood'.

At this stage, though, I was still very determined and working on a new hypothesis entitled 'colour co-ordination'. I will spare you the technical details, but broadly speaking the proposition was that being colour-co-ordinated made you more cool – and on this particular Sunday I was going to put it to the test.

I had purchased all the required equipment: I had green combat trousers, a green jumper and a green bomber jacket. Heck, I even had green trainers. There was no doubt about it, I was colour co-ordinated.

I can still remember the street where it happened. There were two girls – of a similar age to me. Perhaps a bit older. They were walking towards me. I was feeling pretty cool. I wasn't expecting them to audibly gasp with admiration at my ensemble, but I was definitely checking for signs of awe. It did seem that one was looking at me and whispering to her friend. What might she be saying? Perhaps: 'Oh my! He's so cool!'

They seemed to be blushing. It was understandable. Clearly the colour co-ordination was working. As they passed me I strained to catch what they were saying. One phrase I heard clearly:

'He looks like a gherkin'.

I bought a bus ticket. I returned to my dorm. I didn't wear green for the next 25 years (true story).

When you look back at your own life, you can probably still recall some of the more embarrassing episodes. Don't worry – I'm not going to ask you to share them. You probably prefer to remember the embarrassing incidents suffered by *other* people. But in the relatively sober world of work people live in fear of embarrassment – the unfortunate incident that in a single instant reduces a lifetime of hard work to an amusing anecdote.

In the BBC edu-comedy series *Horrible Histories* there is a sketch format called 'Stupid Deaths' in which the Grim Reaper taunts famous figures regarding the manner of their demise. Death literally laughs in the face of Heraclitus, the Greek philosopher who – as far as we know – died in a pile of cow manure.[1]

Heraclitus was, by all accounts, a towering figure philosophically – one of the pioneers and perhaps the first to go in search of a metaphysical explanation for the world around us. And yet generations of British schoolchildren will know him only as the bloke who died in a pile of dung. You've got to admit, it's a pretty good story.

People will sometimes say about learning that 'we learn best through failure', so it might seem surprising that we work so hard to avoid failing at things. But instinctively we are acutely aware of the possible price of failure: embarrassment and reputational damage.

As social creatures we are hard-wired to experience social failure in much the same way as we experience injury.[2] Social pain activates the same brain pathways as physical pain. Indeed it may be this hard-wiring that *makes* us social creatures: if we didn't care about what other people thought about us, we might just go off and do our own thing.

Even people who like to think of themselves as staunch individualists fear humiliation to some degree. Shame and embarrassment stick out in our memory like nothing else.

There is much more to learning than the transfer of knowledge. Like every other creature we are designed to remember what matters – and as *social* creatures what matters most is often the reactions of other people. But our schools restrict social interaction, as do our training courses. And yet – despite all our efforts – the social interaction is still the most valuable source of learning.

Education seems to have completely lost sight of learning, which at its very heart is about experiences, stories of experiences, and how they make us feel. We have fallen into thinking that learning is about remembering information. But our 'instructional' techniques for forcing people to remember information have turned out to be terribly ineffective and quite abnormal – and so we will have to start over. We will need to start with a very different set of assumptions about learning.

I argued above that human beings are storytellers. This is the kind of statement people nod in agreement with, but which nobody has been able to adequately explain. Why are stories so important? We tell stories all the time – on Monday morning we tell stories about the weekend, we tell stories about shocking things, great successes, great failures. Online we struggle to resist the urge to click on links to salacious stories. In the evenings we pay to watch stories. We take our experiences and turn them into stories; 'If it isn't a story, it didn't happen'.

In the 16th century the Earl of Oxford was reported (by John Aubrey) to have inadvertently broken wind in the presence of Queen Elizabeth. He was so embarrassed that he disappeared off travelling for seven years. On his eventual return, the queen greeted him saying 'Welcome back – I'd completely forgotten about the fart!' Today, it is one of the few things that we know about him.

None of this should come as a surprise to you. What should surprise you is that nobody has ever really got to the bottom of why you remember some things and not other things – not even close. Our collective failure to understand learning and memory has already had a profound impact on your life: in all probability you have spent more than a decade in an educational system where you are far more likely to remember embarrassing incidents, friends or inspirational teachers than you are algebra or history or chemistry. Sorry – we bungled 15 years of your life.

Today, billions of children are wasting billions of hours sitting in rows, wasting their time, because no one has understood the basic mechanism behind learning and memory. Volumes are published on weird and wonderful theories regarding how we might better store information. In the workplace, businesses around the world spend upwards of $350 billion each year training people, with very little evidence that any of it is effective.[3] In academia, huge amounts of misleading research are published every year, in support of a fundamentally incorrect understanding of learning; every day someone produces another paper arguing that the world is flat.

There are, of course, things that I remember from school – such as maths classes. Our maths teacher had a big jar of aniseed balls and if it was someone's birthday he would take out the jar and hand them round. Sometimes we would pretend that it was someone's birthday and he would play along. You could see on his face that he knew we were deceiving him and he would feign surprise – 'Really? Didn't Martin have a birthday a few weeks ago?' We knew he knew, and he knew we knew he knew – and the whole charade was delightful.

Like you, I remember lots of things from school. Almost none of those things are the information that I was taught in lessons. I remember no algebra. No differential calculus. I barely recall my times tables – I am still pretty shaky on 7x8. How many times must I have had to repeat that? 10,000? History, geography, biology, physics, chemistry and religious studies – all a big blank. Surely that should strike us as odd; that the formal periods where learning was supposed to be taking place seem to be far less memorable than the informal events that were not on the syllabus? Why is that?

What if I told you that everything you thought you knew about memory and about learning is wrong? Not just slightly wrong but completely and fundamentally wrong – wrong all the way back to Plato and the ancient Greeks?

Our basic understanding of learning goes something like this: learning is the process by which we store information in our heads. We take knowledge from one source (such as a book or a teacher) and we memorize it, so that we can recall it later.

In case you think I am setting up a straw man, Merriam-Webster defines learning (noun) as 'knowledge or skill acquired by instruction or study', and the Oxford English Dictionary defines memory as 'the faculty by which the mind stores and remembers information'.

But if we take a definition like this at face value and compare it to our school days it seems very peculiar: it is not at all clear to me what knowledge or skills I acquired. I still have a smattering of French, but most of what I remember isn't really what you would call 'knowledge', and the skills I acquired – such as how to interact with peers, dress like a cool dude or force myself to run on rainy days – don't seem to be the same skills that I was taught (things like dissecting frogs and titration).

In addition to that, I recently went back to my old school – for a school reunion – and was quite shocked at how inaccurate my memory of the school was. There was a whole set of tennis courts that I had forgotten existed. So some of the things I thought I had stored, it turned out I only imagined I had stored.

Where did we go wrong?

There's no single point, but in 1885 Herman Ebbinghaus did something incredibly stupid, committing a scientific blunder the consequences of which we are still suffering today.

He was researching human memory and, seduced by a trendy new approach called psychophysics, decided that it would be a good idea to create a 'pure' stimulus with which to experiment on memory; something for people to remember that had no special significance for them at all, so that their pesky personal experiences wouldn't interfere with the results. So he created nonsense syllables – three letter trigrams like RUP and SFH to give people to learn.

If you were a participant in his experiments you would be presented with these nonsense syllables, each for a set period of time, then later asked to remember them. Why did he deliberately create neutral, meaningless stimuli for his experiments?

His mistake was rooted in the intellectual conventions introduced by the ancient Greeks. You may recall that they viewed emotion as something to be overcome by the power of reason, and that later René Descartes deepened the reason/emotion divide, firmly establishing the mind-body duality, and equating the emotions with the misleading physical aspect of our nature and the mind with the true, divine side. Body=bad, mind=good. Reason=good, emotions=bad.

You can still see the impact of this age-old prejudice today in our stereotypes about men and women, with women traditionally perceived as more prone to emotional assessments of situations and men likely to assess them rationally. In Western society we celebrate the 'dispassionate' and 'objective' nature of business or scientific decisions (all of which turn out ultimately to be emotion in disguise).

So Ebbinghaus probably believed he was doing a *good* thing – by studying information in a 'pure' form, devoid of any meaning or emotional significance, he could get a more accurate picture of the way the rational human mind processes information.

Sadly, though, he achieved precisely the opposite. Human beings are storytellers; our minds are finely tuned to the emotional significance of events. On the other hand our memory is exceptionally efficient at getting rid of everything boring: stuff with no personal significance. Stuff like Ebbinghaus's trigrams.

Figure 2.1   The forgetting curve

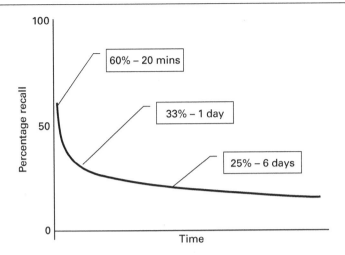

When Ebbinghaus plotted the results, he found (predictably) that the majority of the nonsense syllables were forgotten in a short space of time. What Ebbinghaus *thought* he had discovered was something called the 'forgetting curve', a steep curve that illustrated how information is typically lost from memory.[4]

But he hadn't. Although he didn't realize it, he had *actually* discovered something far more important: namely that memory is all to do with meaning. He had discovered that information without personal significance is just 'mental garbage' to the mind, and is disposed of as quickly as possible. You do this every day: as you walk along a street, each of the paving slabs, each brick, is distinct and different in some way – but there's nothing especially meaningful about any of them. Any visual impressions you have are quickly dumped to make way for stuff that matters.

At this point the sensible thing to have done would be to concede that personal significance is clearly integral to the process of remembering. Had he introduced meaningful trigrams into his lists – like, for example, FLY or TEA – he would have discovered that these were far more likely to be recalled than the nonsense ones, and our story might have ended happily.

But he didn't. Blinded by his convictions, he went on to investigate means by which the mind might be *forced* to retain nonsense. He discovered that by repeating the meaningless information over and over again, at intervals, some of it could be retained. He discovered a kind of psychological force-feeding method. In our paving stone analogy, this would be like forcing people to walk the same street over and over.

Figure 2.2   Meaningful versus meaningless trigrams

RFT	TOY	GBU	CAT	MJQ	TIE	VGR	EGG	FGS	HAT	BJK	MAP
JOB	GTR	POT	YHU	GOD	AKL	HIP	NJI	MOP	VGY	TIN	CFT
BHU	HUT	DFT	GUY	ZSE	FOG	XDE	SAD	NKP	HOT	TVF	MAD
TAP	GSF	GUN	ZXC	TIP	HBJ	GAS	QWE	KIT	DCF	GYM	JGF
NKL	PIG	GVQ	BAT	VCX	TEA	KNJ	PIT	NAU	HAM	SJI	BIG
YES	JUH	LEG	BTY	EYE	BCS	BIT	GHJ	GUN	YFT	LIP	NXV
JAJ	PIG	KSJ	WET	BHT	GAG	VFT	OLD	HRF	FAN	FTC	FOX
DEW	YGS	HUT	KCK	HEN	VSK	YUM	CTG	PUG	VGY	TEE	HFU
BCV	OIL	GJI	ROT	FWX	RAG	HWZ	BAD	TDE	ZOO	VGS	QUE

If you don't believe me, I would encourage you to try the following simple experiment for yourself: in Figure 2.2 is a list much like Ebbinghaus's, but with precisely 50 per cent of the trigrams meaningful words and 50 per cent classic Ebbinghaus trigrams. You are welcome to use this list or create your own if you prefer.

Either way, I would like you to find an experimental subject (children work well) and offer them a reward for remembering as many trigrams as possible in the space of one minute (for example, a cookie for every five that they remember). Give them a minute to look at the list, then ask them to recall as many as they can. I'm willing to bet that they remember hardly any of the meaningless trigrams.

Now of course there are a few different ways to explain the results of this experiment – there always are – but the simplest is that we preferentially store information which is meaningful to us, and ignore that which isn't. I suspect you would also find that this differs between individuals – that 'cat people' are far more likely to remember the word 'cat'.

So what Ebbinghaus accomplished was the metaphorical equivalent of discovering the best way to use a smartphone to hammer in nails: his research was simultaneously accurate and grossly misleading. In other words, whilst there probably *is* a best way to hammer in nails with a smartphone, if you're doing that in the first place you are a bit of an idiot. And what if entire volumes were published on hammering in nails with a smartphone – hundreds of thousands of research articles on the various ways to batter a nail with a smartphone? Would you find it at all reassuring that people say their technique is 'evidence-based', or would you feel inclined to say 'Stop that! It's ridiculous!'?

As is often the case with primitive psychology, the patent ridiculousness of the approach didn't prevent it from being widely accepted as a model for memory, learning, and ultimately for education. Today we still employ this barbaric technique in the method known as rote learning,[5] both at school and at work, forcing people to repeat things over and over so that they can memorize them just long enough to pass a test. And then forget them.

In our normal lives many important lessons are learned the first time. There are good reasons for this: a creature that had to be bitten many times by a tiger before learning that tigers are dangerous wouldn't last long. A child doesn't need to burn their hand on a hot stove repeatedly. Of course, some things take a few attempts: but as a rule of thumb, *the deeper the personal significance, the more reliably something is learned*[6] – we don't often repeat our more embarrassing mistakes (and our embarrassing mistakes echo through eternity). Conversely, if you have to repeat something over and over again in order to remember it, that's a good indicator that it doesn't matter much to you.

It makes perfect sense for memory to work in this way: your memory needs to be efficient, so it only stores the stuff that matters. But which stuff matters? Answer: the stuff that has an emotional impact. This is rather an elegant system, since what has emotional impact to you can be both programmed from birth (nature) and shaped by your development (nurture). As an infant you can experience pain, then life introduces you to a whole world of pain you didn't know existed.

Scientists use the expression 'homeostasis' to refer to the way in which creatures are set up from birth to seek out conditions that are good for them and avoid those that are bad; at the most primitive level, pain and pleasure, fear and attraction steer us in the right direction. As big-brained creatures we have the ability to elaborate and extend these reactions to an extraordinary degree, up to and including our choice of smartphone. We can experience shock on realizing someone at the party is wearing the same outfit.

If you wanted someone to remember something unimportant, how would you do that? Well, you might find a way to make it important. You might, for example, threaten them with pain (since pain matters to all creatures). In fact, pain is often used to condition non-human species. But humans are a special kind of creature – the kind that experience all manner of social anxieties. So you might threaten people with disgrace – or with parental disappointment. You could say: 'If you don't pass that test your parents will be bitterly disappointed in you.' Alternatively, you could just punish forgetfulness by forcing people to repeat information again, and again, and again.

It's also true that brute force methods such as forcing people to see something over and over again change the way a person feels about it. One version of this mere exposure effect,[7] the 'familiarity breeds liking' phenomenon, was researched by Richard Zajonc and explains why, for example, the population of Paris went from despising the Eiffel tower to quite liking it.

It may have occurred to the more enlightened among you that perhaps a more positive approach, such as relating information to some of the other things that people care about – for example, a desire to help others – would be much better. I suspect that some of you are reading this paragraph and taking it in, only because you can see an application to the people in your care. Alternatively, if you are a salesperson, it may help you to understand why taking the time to understand what matters to your customer is so important.

One law remains absolutely unbreakable: *one care always builds on another*. You may be using a carrot or a stick, but no one ever remembers anything except by virtue of its relationship to the things that matter to them. Our starting point for the design of any environment designed to help people learn must therefore be the individual, and those things that matter most to them. This, and only this, forms the basis of their learning.

Sadly, what Ebbinghaus ultimately encouraged was ultimately a form of abuse – he had discovered that you *can* fit a square peg into a round hole – if you hit it again, and again, and again (rather than, say, wondering why it didn't go in the first time). If you point this out to people who work in education they will usually get quite angry and defensive and come up with all manner of excuses for doing horrible things.

At heart – as we shall see in a bit – this is because people tend to get emotionally attached to conventions, and build a set of justifications around them.

Remembering versus memorization

One of Ebbinghaus's contemporaries was also deeply disturbed by his experiments. Frederic Bartlett had spent decades studying cross-cultural transmission of information – the way in which cultures store and pass on learning normally, for example through storytelling. In sharp contrast to Ebbinghaus he viewed memory as a *constructive* process, in which we continually 'recreate' what we know in the light of personal significance and our environment.

In every culture, people tell stories. In fact, this is typically a big proportion of the time they spend talking to one another – perhaps as much as 80 per cent.[8] In no culture are people routinely required to memorize lists of meaningless symbols. To imagine that one could discover anything interesting about learning in this way is quite perverse.

Bartlett pointed out that by stripping a stimulus of any personal meaning, Ebbinghaus had destroyed the very phenomenon – memory – that he was attempting to investigate.

Frederic Bartlett was an unusual chap. Born in 1886 in a small English town, Bartlett spent his first 14 years as a 'normal country boy', playing cricket and helping with the harvest, until the age of around 14 when he attended a private primary school. Due to illness he was unable to continue his schooling, but he began educating himself. At his father's suggestion, he signed up for a correspondence course and on completing his degree was invited to become a tutor at Cambridge, where he went on to take a further degree at Cambridge University.

He was an atypical student – a country boy mixing with the elite upper-class, his peers almost exclusively the product of private tutoring. Ten years later he was to become the director of the Cambridge Laboratory, the most prestigious centre for psychological research at the time. We forget that even in early 20th century England, education was still a luxury predominantly reserved for the elite; everybody else learned just fine without education.

Bartlett's approach to psychology was heavily influenced by his interest in anthropology. Whilst Ebbinghaus studied memory, Bartlett studied 're-membering' which as he saw it, is an *active* process in which people reconstruct meaning within their social context. In some of his early experiments he gave people drawings of military men to remember and questioned them about them at intervals of 30 minutes, then later, after a week or two.

He noted that things that were particularly interesting to people at the time (during the First World War) such as pipes, moustaches and cap badges were more likely to be remembered, and that the expressions on people's faces also made a big impact – for example whether someone was smiling or looked stern.

Bartlett was also interested in something he called 'conventionalization' – the process by which stories from one culture get passed on into another. He used a process similar to Chinese whispers in which people read a Native American folk tale entitled *The War of the Ghosts*, then told the story to someone else, who in turn told it to someone else.[9]

Here is the story that they read:

The War of the Ghosts

One night two young men from Egulac went down to the river to hunt seals, and while they were there it became foggy and calm. Then they heard war-cries, and they thought: 'Maybe this is a war-party'. They escaped to the shore, and hid behind a log.

Now canoes came up, and they heard the noise of paddles, and saw one canoe coming up to them. There were five men in the canoe, and they said: 'What do you think? We wish to take you along. We are going up the river to make war on the people.'

One of the young men said, 'I have no arrows.'

'Arrows are in the canoe,' they said.

'I will not go along. I might be killed. My relatives do not know where I have gone. But you,' he said, turning to the other, 'may go with them'.

So one of the young men went, but the other returned home.

And the warriors went on up the river to a town on the other side of Kalama. The people came down to the water and they began to fight, and many were killed. But presently the young man heard one of the warriors say, 'Quick, let us go home: that Indian has been hit.' Now he thought: 'Oh, they are ghosts'. He did not feel sick, but they said he had been shot.

So the canoes went back to Egulac and the young man went ashore to his house and made a fire. And he told everybody and said: 'Behold, I accompanied the ghosts, and we went to fight. Many of our fellows were killed, and many of those who attacked us were killed. They said I was hit, and I did not feel sick.'

He told it all, and then he became quiet. When the sun rose he fell down. Something black came out of his mouth. His face became contorted. The people jumped up and cried.

He was dead.

It's a curious story isn't it? I wonder how you would retell it if I asked you to. I'd be willing to bet you wouldn't forget that ghosts were involved somehow. Ghosts are quite an exciting topic for a story.

When Bartlett did just this, his findings were nothing like Ebbinghaus's – it didn't matter whether information was presented at the beginning or the end of the story, and reproduction didn't follow the forgetting curve pattern. Instead, with each retelling the story became simplified and conventionalized around its dominant features – such as the death of the main character. Things that people were largely unfamiliar with, such as seal-hunting, became things that people were more familiar with, such as fishing.

In short, Bartlett showed that people process information in terms of the things that are most meaningful to them. We take images, stories, and we store them in terms of what matters to us.

Unlike computers or books, living creatures have something at stake in the world. We are connected to the world via our senses, and by the reactions that those senses engender. Those reactions form the basis of our way of making sense of the world: they tell us what to care about. So humans do not store or acquire information in the way that inanimate objects do, as we have learned by trying to make machines function like people.

Somehow, scientists and laypeople alike acknowledge this feature of human memory: unlike computer memory or books, our memories are terribly unreliable. We only remember bits and pieces of the experiences that we have – and sometimes we even make things up. Mostly, this is fine – we joke about how poor our memories are – but once in a while it really matters. For example, when we are witness to a crime.

Steve Titus was a 31-year old restaurant manager, engaged to be married to Gretchen. One night they went out for a romantic meal and on the drive home they were pulled over. The police officer had identified their vehicle as looking similar to one identified as part of a rape case.

A photograph of Steve was shown to the victim, who remarked that, of the line-up, his was the photo that looked most like the rapist. When Steve later appeared in court, the victim asserted that she was absolutely sure he *was* the rapist, though Steve and his incredulous fiancée and family continued to protest his innocence. Steve was taken away to jail.

As luck would have it, an investigative journalist tracked down the real rapist, a man suspected of 50 or so similar crimes in the area, who subsequently confessed to the rape.

Steve was released and took the police to court. Consumed with bitterness, anger and the feeling of injustice, Steve lost his job, fiancée and savings. He obsessed over the case. A few days before the civil proceeding Steve died of a stress-induced heart attack. He was 35.

At Steve's trial, psychologist Elizabeth Loftus had argued that Steve had been a victim of false memory – something that Elizabeth knew a thing or two about. Prompted by a desire to undertake research in an area that would be of value to society, she had been studying memory since the 1970s, and what she had discovered was – frankly – shocking.

In her early experiments she had shown participants short films of a fictitious car accident in which two vehicles collided. After watching the films, she asked her witnesses about the accident, and she would vary the wording of the questions. Sometimes she would ask the question 'how fast were the cars going when they *smashed*?' and other times 'how fast were the cars going when they *contacted*?' Disturbingly, the estimates of speed varied by almost 10mph, depending on the words used.[10]

And then she went further. She asked participants about broken glass at the scene. Participants who had heard the 'smashed' question were significantly more likely to recall (non-existent) broken glass.

Over the next few decades Elizabeth went on to investigate a whole host of problems with human memory – she found that not only could memory be distorted, but *completely fictitious memories implanted* – for example, a memory about being lost in a shopping centre as a child.[11]

A bit like Bartlett, Elizabeth viewed remembering as an active process – one in which the memory is created. She proposed that two kinds of information – information stored at the time of an event, and information after the event are combined in a *reconstruction* of events.

I would like to suggest an alternative explanation of her findings – one which takes this idea a little further and lays bare what I am proposing:

Imagine that you were supposed to go on a school trip to the zoo. But, being the maverick teenager that you are, you decided to bunk off and go to the cinema instead. The Ferris Bueller wannabe in you knows you might be quizzed later on your whereabouts, so you hatch a plan. You ask one of your friends – who is going on the trip – to take notes, so that you can fabricate the whole experience if later subjected to interrogation.

Unfortunately your partner in crime turns out to be less than reliable. The scribbled zoo notes read as follows:

- Zoo is in some kind of freaky forest.
- Tigers rock!
- Food sucks, man!
- OMG! One kid got sick and he threw up in the trash.
- Reptile house had massive spiders!

As things turn out, your parents get a tip-off that you might have skipped the trip, and over dinner they are unusually interested in your day. You curse your lazy colleague – but your inventiveness knows no bounds. You tell a plausible story about a zoo in the centre of a spooky forest – pine trees as far as the eye can see – tigers, lions – oh, and a terrifying giant tarantula.

The cherry on the fabricated cake is the detail around the classmate – 'I've seen him around, but I don't know his name' – who threw up in the trash (probably as a reaction to the terrible zoo food). Your story is so convincing that you almost believe you were there yourself. In fact, years later, you actually believe that you went on that trip to the zoo.

The affective context model makes a radical claim about memory: **we don't actually remember any of the experiences that happen to us. Instead, we store our reactions to those events – how they made us feel – and these reactions are used to 'conjure up' a memory when needed.**

Let me repeat that: you don't actually remember anything, you just store how things made you *feel*, and you use those emotional imprints to create memories on demand.

This is different from Elizabeth's account, as it suggests that *no* sensory information about experiences is encoded at the time of an event – only our *reaction* to those experiences. Emotional reactions are the building blocks of your memories, and your thoughts. Every last one of them is nothing more than a complex pattern of affective responses.

You might think that this is a preposterous claim – how could you reconstruct all the detail that you do, just by using your emotional reactions? Well, for starters, are you really aware of just how much detail you actually store – or is your mind tricking you? Try this: draw a five-pound note (or ten dollar bill) from memory. Resist the temptation to look it up, or produce one. Just draw what you remember. Chances are, you will be shocked by how inaccurate your memory is.

Try something else with which you are intimately familiar – such as, for example, the front of your house. There is a good chance that you won't even get the number of windows correct.

In 2016 the company signs.com gave 156 Americans the challenge of drawing famous brand logos from memory – Starbucks, for example.[12] Again, you can try it yourself if you like. The results reveal shocking verging on obscene levels of inaccuracy for many of the participants. Pretty much the only thing they consistently got right was the colour green and the presence of a woman.

So how does the affective context model explain this?

In 1949 the neuropsychologist Donald Hebb make a remarkable discovery.[13] Whilst investigating neuronal activity, he found that when two or more neurons were activated simultaneously they tended to form connections. This is sometimes summarized as Hebb's Law: 'Neurons that fire together wire together.'

So you can imagine that as you move through the world, from home to train station, from train station to coffee shop, that your neurons are firing and wiring. Your brain changes in response to your external environment, and it seems fair to assume that the firing and wiring reflect your experiences somehow. Right?

All this is merely neuroscience 101 – but it begs the central question: what is all the firing and wiring encoding? You might guess that our neurons are encoding the way things look – or sound – or even a set of meanings (or 'schema').

Whilst it is clear that the visual cortex does map the things we see as we see them,[14] both the degree and type of error that we make strongly suggest that we don't *remember* the visual features of what we see. In other words, the complicated visual picture that registers in your visual cortex is quickly transferred into a far simpler pattern of emotional reactions, which can be easily stored and used to conjure up a picture on demand, by running this process in reverse.

FMRI[15] scans suggest that something like this does happen: when you are recalling a visual memory, similar areas of the visual cortex are activated as when you first experienced it. You can also disrupt a memory by altering a person's emotional state; people about to address a large audience may find that they have entirely forgotten their carefully rehearsed speech!

On the other hand, if you want to conjure up a memory all you need are a few words. String them together and you have a story. A story works by creating a series of sounds which cause a specific set of emotional reactions in the recipient, reactions which in turn activate the visual cortex, enabling a listener to picture the events the storyteller is describing.

Of course to maximize the effect, it helps to exaggerate the *affect*: dramatic gestures, pronunciation and faces will all help. And, of course, music. Why is the soundtrack so important to a Hollywood movie? Now you know why.

And while we are on the subject of movies, why do people go to the cinema to watch a movie even when they sometimes have the option to watch the same movie at home? Could it be that the presence of other people, experiencing the same thing, accentuates our emotional experience?

The affective context model says that what is being encoded – indeed *the only things that are being encoded* – are your *emotional reactions* to events and information – how these make you *feel*. These reactions are the things that thoughts and memories are made up of. By 'emotional reactions', I don't mean happy, sad, etc, but all the subtle and largely unconscious emotional reactions you have to events.

For example I imagine you would agree that you have different emotional reactions to different haircuts, or to the sound of a bluebottle, a bumblebee and a mosquito – but you would struggle to categorize these in simple 'happy/sad' terms. The sound of a mosquito is a very specific feeling – which is why you have a specific set of words for it: 'the sound of a mosquito'.

Once again, the affective context model proposes that as you experience events, the events themselves are not encoded; instead, your *reactions* to those events – for example to the colour green, or to the presence of a woman – are stored, and these feelings are then used to build a memory on demand. This emotional trace may then activate the same neurological regions involved in originally perceiving the stimulus – effectively 'recreating' a version of it.

These versions tend to have huge mistakes visually-speaking, but are affectively sufficiently accurate. This accounts for the context-sensitivity of memory;[16] we may not recognize a 'scary' schoolteacher at the supermarket, where they seem far less intimidating.

I believe this is a good account of memory function because all the sorts of things that you would expect to happen to a system that works like this do in fact happen with human memory. Emotions tend to fade over time (unless they are especially strong), they get confused with similar feelings, they are easier to retrieve when you feel similarly, when you retrieve them they are affected by how you are feeling right now, and, last but not least, they are vague and unreliable.

You might wonder why we don't remember more details of movies – which are invariably emotive. One reason is that we have stronger responses to experiences that are happening to us personally than those we are witnessing cinematically, but a more important factor is that our affective responses take into account what matters to us.

For example, we may watch a nail-biting account of an ascent of Everest, but unless we are planning on making the ascent ourselves it is merely entertaining. It is not a reaction that needs to be stored. You can see an actor behaving violently in a movie, and that impacts you very differently to seeing a person behaving violently in your train carriage during your morning commute. Our emotional reactions register relevance.

Strange as this idea may seem, there is a growing body of support for it from the realm of neuroscience. In his book *The Strange Order of Things*, the neuroscientist Antonio Damasio remarks: 'In the march toward the human cultural mind, the presence of feelings would have allowed homeostasis to make a dramatic leap because they could represent mentally the state of life within the organism.'[17] Antonio argues that creatures took a big step forward when they became able to represent what they are experiencing, with feelings.

I should point out that the affective context model is sometimes misrepresented as saying: 'Emotions are very important to learning', or, even worse, 'Make stuff fun if you want it to be memorable'. People say that because they still have this Cartesian idea of feeling and thinking as separate processes.

But this is not what the affective context model is saying at all – it states that as you move through the world, it is *only* your emotional states that are recorded, and that these emotional states are sufficient to reconstruct your experiences as memories. Your emotional reactions are to memory what letters are to words: they are what memories are made of, quite literally.

You wouldn't say: 'If you are writing a book, you should consider using some letters of the alphabet!' This would be nonsense – what you write *is* the letters.

Understanding the affective context model is a bit like looking closely at every object in the world and discovering they are all made up of Lego bricks (or atoms). Your affective reactions are the letters that your experiences, and your thoughts, are written in.

Putting this into practice

What this means in practice is not that we need to make everything fun or dramatic; it means that if we want people to remember things we need to take the time to find out what matters to them. We can't simply assume that every student will be equally enthralled by algebraic equations – we have to accept that they are different, and that for each individual, only what matters sticks.

We can, of course, make dull stuff matter to people by doing things like threatening them (with a test) but this is generally a nasty, primitive, ineffective thing to do. They will memorize what they need to pass the test, then forget it shortly thereafter (because it no longer matters).

If you are or have been a teacher you will recognize certain moments of tension in your work: namely, when your students want to talk about one thing but you feel duty-bound to press on with the lesson 'otherwise we won't get through it all'. This is the definitive tension in teaching – the difference between education and learning, one might say.

If you care at all about your students, you will probably experience some twinge of regret at these moments because at some level you realize that pressing on with the stuff the *system* cares about, at the expense of what your *students* care about, is the very opposite of learning. It is actively shutting down their learning.

We are so used to thinking of emotions as one of the things that happens in your head that we struggle to think of them as the *only* thing that is happening in your head. Imagine that you are standing with a friend watching someone play a sophisticated computer game. 'It's amazing to think,' you remark, 'that this program is all just 1s and 0s'. Your friend turns to you in astonishment: 'Well, I guess some of the basic maths might be 1s and 0s but I'm pretty sure the rest is much more complicated'.

But your friend is wrong: however complex a computer program may seem, it can ultimately be reduced to patterns of 1s and 0s. This is machine code.

It might seem that 'feelings' might not be complex enough to give rise to the richness of memory but just like our computer program – or our DNA (or vision) – amazingly complex things can arise from simple building blocks. Machine code is written in 1s and 0s; human code is written in feelings. There is no distinction between thought and feeling after all.

Some people imagine that we think in words – but we know for certain that this isn't true; people's thoughts are formed before they speak, and people with no language can still think.[18] Turns out, we think in feelings. Probably we have this in common with most creatures. Words are just how those feelings sound. Words are just the names we give to feelings. Our feelings are more flexible than most mammals', and so are our sounds.

Once again, the relationship between thoughts and feelings is like that between a painting and patches of colour. A painting is made up of patches of colour. A thought is made up of feelings. Words are like the names we give to paintings – like 'Mona Lisa'. We speak a word, and it summarizes and communicates a pattern of feelings that comprise a thought. I can do it now – I can say 'dog' and your feelings about dogs are activated, and your mind generates a kind of blurry mental image from them.

If we are thinking about memory and learning, we must accept that different people will remember experiences differently. No one is merely 'storing information'. We are not books or computers. We react to things. We store those reactions. Those stored reactions change our behaviour. We disregard this feature of human memory at our peril; merely exposing people to information risks them having no strong reaction at all – in which case they will most probably describe it as 'boring' or 'irrelevant' and will be unlikely to remember it, still less to act on it.

People struggle with the idea that our minds don't store information – it seems very counter-intuitive. They know that the brain rewires itself in response to external stimuli, and that memory somehow retrieves events from the past – so it seems logical to assume that the brain stores information. But it's important to be emphatic about this, because this is where education goes wrong: with the idea that the mind is like a box into which we can transfer knowledge.

To see where this idea leads us astray, imagine that a friend offers to store something of importance to you. 'I have a special storage box' he says. 'I can store something important for you'. You give him a spare house key. Some months later, you lose your own house key, and you turn to your friend for help. But, to your horror, when you open the special box, it is empty. Your key isn't there.

However, the box is lined with a kind of plasticine and, in the bottom of the box, the imprint of your key is visible. You take this to a locksmith and he is able to reconstruct your key. Did the box store your key or not?

This analogy is helpful in understanding other features of human memory: certain things are not going to be stored very well by the box – a feather, for example. A feather is simply too light to leave an impression. For you and I, this corresponds to boring events – they are simply too 'light' to leave much of an impression.

The box won't store paintings well – I mean it will store the outline of the frame, but not what is painted on the canvas. It isn't designed to do that. This is like long numbers – if a friend says: 'This password is really important', and then proceeds to give you 26 numbers to remember, then the chances are you will remember that he told you an important password – but you won't remember what it was.

In this analogy the plasticine is our emotional reactions to things. Unlike plasticine, our emotional reactions change over time, so that the sorts of things that leave an impression will be unique to you, and very subtle.

According to the affective context model we start out in life with some simple emotional reactions to things – for example smiles and faces, which delight us automatically.[19] We prefer attractive faces. Other things may scare us from the outset. But very soon we start to refine our feelings. We have a simple repertoire of sounds to reflect these feelings – when a child laughs or cries, everyone understands how it feels. Mothers can even distinguish the significance of different types of cries.

As social animals we have an in-built sensitivity to other's feelings[20] (and people across cultures have no difficulty recognizing some expressions).[21] Laughter is contagious, and public shame is painful. As an example, I was once at a comedy club where every joke the comedian used fell flat. After a few minutes, he started to go to pieces. For the first time I truly understood the expression 'to die on stage' – I was so overwhelmed with the feeling of embarrassment for him that I struggled not to get to my feet and drag him physically from the stage to avoid further humiliation.

This same mechanism works at a more subtle level to shape our personality. If, for example, we have a parent who flies into a panic whenever a wasp approaches, we quickly learn to react in the same way to buzzing objects – wasps, bees, even flies. Our emotional responses tend to mirror those of others. Over time we may come to refine our reactions – responding differently to bees than to wasps, for example.

This is presumably why infants are so attentive to faces; faces are the mirror in which they can see the world. Seeing the world is not really what's important to them – they need to see how people *react* to the world. That, and only that, will enable them to see it as they should.

To give another example, an infant might initially be startled by a dog. However, over time not only do they learn to react positively to dogs, they develop different emotional reactions to different breeds.

Pause for a second and consider my earlier question: do you feel the same when you hear the sound of a mosquito as you do when you hear the sound of a fly? I'm pretty sure you don't. How exactly does the feeling differ? If I say the words 'sausage dog' and 'German shepherd dog', you have different feelings in reactions to those sounds – feelings that you use to conjure up an image. Could you say exactly how those feelings differ?

If someone passed you in the rain with a bright pink umbrella with spots, you might remember it later. This suggests that you have a distinct emotional reaction to umbrellas, to bright pink, and to spots – but I imagine you

Figure 2.3 An illustration of the affective context model

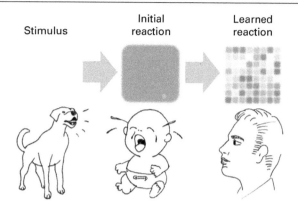

would struggle to put into words exactly how these things make you feel. And, frankly, you don't need to – you put those feelings into words by saying 'spotty, bright pink umbrella'. All our words are feeling words.

The affective context model suggests that we have subtle affective responses to all of the things that matter to us in the world. Once again, I am sure that you feel differently about different haircuts – but could you say exactly how these feelings differ or why? As we saw in the previous chapter we might think that we lack the words to describe the subtle variations we experience in our feelings towards objects – but in fact this is precisely what our vocabulary does – it describes sets of feelings: 'chair' describes the feeling that something might be appropriate for sitting. 'Mohawk' describes a particularly striking and non-conformist hairstyle.

One of the interesting consequences of this is that 'if you don't feel it, you don't see it'. As someone almost entirely oblivious to social cues, I routinely have the kind of conversation which goes something like:

'Did you *see* the expression on her face!?'
'Whose face?'
'The woman in the crazy hat!'
'Where? Where's a woman in a hat?'
'Oh, forget it.'

At face value it might seem difficult to understand how emotions give rise to the richness and sophistication of our mental life: here, again, a good metaphor might be the human retina. The human retina is configured to detect patches of light of different wavelengths. But as we develop, we learn to perceive these patches of light as objects, and our visual experience develops a richness and depth that goes way beyond 'patches of light'. So it is with our emotional reactions.

As I say, one consequence of the way in which our emotional reactions are conditioned is that different people 'see' different things, depending on what they feel strongly about. You and a friend may both take the same train journey – but if your friend is an expert in plants and you are an expert in architecture, you may recall very different things. You may tell an entire story about the intriguing variety of architectural styles (whilst your friend only saw 'buildings'). On the other hand, your friend may relate the shifting patterns of plant types in detail, while you only saw trees and bushes.

This point turns out to be very important in education: two students sitting in the same class may hear and remember very different things, depending on what they care about (their 'concerns'). The only way you could design a truly effective educational programme would be to start by understanding what *concerns* each individual, since this determines what they will remember.

We can confidently predict that students who are subjected to a barrage of information that they perceive as 'irrelevant' (for example, not on the test) will be more likely to forget it – and for this very specific reason, learner-centricity must be placed at the heart of any educational design process.

What are you concerned about?

Now it is also true that our concerns are shaped by our lives, and as parents and educators we will sometimes want to shape the life of a young person by creating a *new* set of concerns – ones which will play a role in the way they encode experiences for years to come. But, as is probably immediately obvious to you, we wouldn't accomplish this without stirring the emotions of a person. As above, new concerns are always built on the old.

If you want people to learn, you've got to start by getting them to care. If you want them to care, you've got to start with what they care about today. In our modern-day education system we accomplish this by frightening people. We tell them a story about the horrible things that will happen to them – the dire consequences, the parental disappointment – if they fail to pass a test.

But in an enlightened world we might place people in a challenging situation – one in which their status was at stake, for example – or (less directly) we might tell a story about someone who lost their life as a result of a poor decision. A child learns to react in the same way the people around them react; copying their parents and their peers.

We are curiously elaborate creatures: we start out like many mammals, caring about pain, food, sex, status, family and fairness – and we end up caring about recycling plastic. 'Learning' is the name we give to this shaping of our concerns. 'Education' might describe the intentional shaping of concerns, were we not busy trying to get people to memorize facts.

It's important to note that a person's 'concerns' are not the same as their 'motivations'. I've noticed, just as Bartlett did, that language has a curious 'conventionalizing' effect. If you try to say something new, you have to use new words or familiar words in new ways – like 'concern'. But people will quickly translate these into something more conventional.

So it is that some people come to the conclusion that 'affective context' is just a fancy way of saying: 'Motivation is important in learning' – whereupon they can nod sagely and say: 'Of course – but other things are important too'.

Motivations *are* important, but they are only a small part of our concerns. If I am standing talking to you, and I suddenly develop a nosebleed, you will remember that for a while and most likely tell a story about it. But it would be odd to say that you are 'motivated' by nosebleeds. You are *concerned* about them, for sure. The reason you remember that the Starbucks logo is green, is because you are concerned about the colour green (not 'motivated' by it).

Imagine a whole jungle of concerns in your head – an undiscovered continent teeming with life. 'Motivations' is just the name we give to some of the taller mountains. 'Concern' is a word I use to describe anything that you have a reaction to.

The distinction I am trying to draw is a bit like that between 'weather' and 'atmosphere'. When people talk about 'emotions' they are usually referring to gross emotional states – like anger or surprise. These states are like weather systems – typhoons or warm fronts. I am talking about atmosphere – the system that sustains all life, just as affect sustains all cognition. We can suppress a person's gross emotional state – but affective context is still the basic processing language that the brain uses.

In the days when I was teaching, I used to spend a lot of time telling students information that they would write down in their notebooks so that they could immediately forget it, and later memorize it for the sake of passing exams that they were scared about. Oftentimes they would voice this concern by saying 'Sir, will this be on the test?' Much of it seemed dull to them, I am sure.

On one occasion, I was working my way through the part of the curriculum that dealt with abnormal psychology. It was a hot summer day, and my students were bored and distracted. I started talking about bipolar disorders and treatments.

A hand went up. One of the quieter students suddenly had a lot of questions. They wanted to know about different treatments and side-effects. A conversation ensued. It turned out they had a close relative who had been diagnosed with bipolar disorder, and wanted to know much more about what might help.

The things that people care about shape what they remember and what they learn. Had I spontaneously combusted, all the students would have remembered that (people catching on fire unexpectedly is pretty much an innate concern), but it seemed a bit far to go to get their attention.

So now you know how memory and cognition work. It is hard to overstate the significance of this shift in perspective. It overturns a way of thinking that dates back to Plato – a world in which reason and emotion were considered separate. What I am saying is that every thought you have is comprised of emotional reactions. Thoughts are feelings, and our words simply summarize a complex pattern of feelings. When we use words, we communicate those feelings, and we know what they mean because we grow up together. In essence, we operate in the same way that rats and cats do: it is not that we have thoughts and they don't; it is just that our feelings are a bit more complex and malleable.

In sum: our thoughts are made up of feelings, our experience is made up of feelings, our memory is made up of feelings, our decisions are made up of feelings (yes even, and especially, 'rational' business decisions and legal ones, as we shall discuss later), our perception is made up of feelings. Thinking is feeling. Thinking *is* feeling.

From an educational standpoint, there is very little point in asking people what they think they should learn – or what they think other people should learn. They will likely come up with a list of topics and a plausible-sounding rationale, but the result will not be a curriculum that has the desired outcome.

A much better starting point is to understand what they care about: taking time to talk to someone (e.g. via a mentoring/coaching relationship), or to observe them, or to get them to tell stories are all approaches that are likely to reveal the things that matter to someone. This is the only effective way to start helping someone develop, by asking: 'What do you care about?'

It should be immediately obvious that this presents challenges to conventional classroom delivery: the people in your class all care about different things. If you are not going to 'steamroller' these differences by – for example – threatening them with a cane or a test, but instead relate information to their individual interests, then you are going to be boring most of the people most of the time.

Dumping content 'en masse' isn't going to work. Instead, you would have to find a way to personalize learning, and in order to do that a way to find out what matters to people.

And what does this mean for you every day? Up until this point you probably assumed that as you walked along the street something like this happens: you saw and heard things and some of those things made their way into your memory, so that you can recall them later. Now you know that this doesn't happen.

Instead: you walk down the street, some of the things you see cause an emotional reaction. You store your reactions, and you can use these feelings to recreate the experience later – for example by telling a story. If you are an adult, you will most likely fill in the blanks with sets of reactions that you have developed over the years. For example, if I say 'Imagine you are in a fancy restaurant' you will have this feeling that there are tables with tablecloths on them and chairs – probably made of wood – and lots of silver cutlery and glasses on the tables.[22]

You experience the world indirectly; through the way it affects you. Like a spider, sitting at the centre of a web of emotions, the world makes your finely tuned sensitivities tremble – and it is this that you call 'experience'. You live your life through an emotional kaleidoscope.

You make a decision to do something, and someone says: 'Why did you do that?', and you come up with some sensible sounding explanation, but in reality you did what felt right. We are rationalizing, not rational, creatures. Your entire life is like a piece of music that plays out, whilst you experience the illusion that you are writing it.

The rationalizing animal

One of the important principles assumed by the affective context model is that we are largely unaware of the complexity and sophistication of this process, which occurs at an unconscious level. Support for this comes from a curious experiment called the Iowa Gambling task.[23]

Imagine that you are a participant in this experiment: you are presented with four decks of cards. Your goal is to win as much money as possible. Each deck contains a mix of cards that will either reward you or punish you. What you don't know is that some decks contain more reward cards and some more punish cards. The question is – how quickly will you figure out which are the 'bad decks'?

Most participants pick cards at random, taking about 40–50 turns to figure out which are the bad decks. What's interesting, though, is that measures of galvanic skin response (similar to that used in lie detectors) show that participants are already nervous when their hands hover over the 'bad decks' – *after only ten trials*! In other words, they have unconsciously learned to feel anxious far quicker than they have consciously figured out the problem. The experiment suggests that at least some of our learning mechanisms operate at an unconscious, non-verbal level.

What if the way you feel about everything, and the relationship between those feelings, is largely handled at an unconscious level?

In 1998 psychologists Anthony Greenwald and Mahzarin Banaji came up with a way to test people's implicit (unconscious) memories, and the associations between memories that people weren't aware of.[24] They created something like a computer game in which you had to sort words into columns. A word would appear in the middle of your screen and – as quickly as possible – you would have to drag it to the column on the left (for example titled 'Women-Strong') or the column on the right (for example titled 'Men-Weak'), depending on where you felt the word best belonged.

What they found is that when the columns were titled in line with our biases (for example 'Men-Strong', 'Women-Weak') people sorted the items much quicker. The same method was used to check for all manner of implicit biases and stereotypes; for example, it showed that in an average sample around 70 per cent of adults have a preference for white people over black people.[25]

In the vast majority of cases, people who were shown to have implicit biases were not consciously aware of those biases.

The implicit association test suggests two things: first, the way that we feel about things may well be processed unconsciously. Second, there are relationships *between* the way we feel about things, of which we are not aware.

But I can understand if you feel a reluctance to accept a completely new model of how your mind works. People grow accustomed to a way of thinking, and have an instinctive defensiveness around the conventions that they have grown up with. People have a tendency to 'bark at things they don't recognize' – they just make more complicated sounds.

When it was first introduced, Darwin's Theory of Evolution was criticized as being 'just a hypothesis'. It was true – it lacked any evidential support whatsoever. People raged at it or laughed at it; it seemed ridiculous – was Charlie really suggesting that my great-great-great-grandmother was a monkey? How preposterous! Look at this cartoon of him as a gibbon! Ha ha ha!

But what Darwin's theory had in its favour was explanatory power: there were many peculiar things that evolution could explain – fossils for example – that the prevailing theory could not (although attempts were made: 'God put them there to test our faith', etc).

What makes the affective context model the best theory?

A good theory has explanatory power – so what things can the affective context model explain? It turns out a great many – here are just a few.

It explains why Elizabeth Loftus found the inaccuracies that she did in memory: people don't store 'episodes', instead a memory of an event is simply a memory of how you *felt*. As you reactivate your stored feelings, your current feelings will play a part. The feelings you have about a word like 'smash' are quite different to your feelings about a word like 'contacted', and will cause you to conjure up a different reconstruction.

It explains why music and stories are so important to humans across all cultures, at all times: in essence they are the same thing; a set of affective responses that are shared using sound. It is likely that without an ability to associate sounds with emotions, we could not have produced language.

It explains why, when you look back on your life, it will be the emotionally significant experiences that you are more likely to recall.[26] These don't need to be life-changing events (moving country, moving house, getting married, the birth of a child, a cancer diagnosis); they can also be something as simple as a single damning or inspiring comment. This also accounts for the finding that if we can make information more personally relevant to learners, they are more likely to remember it.

It explains why, when we describe experiences as 'boring', we tend to remember very little of them. As Ebbinghaus discovered, information without affective significance is almost immediately lost. By contrast, if we present people with a list of dull words and exciting ones, they are more likely to remember the exciting ones.

It explains why two people may have the same experience, but recall very different things. Psychologists have long known that memory is an active process, not a passive one, but have lacked an explanatory framework for describing the ways in which memory is active.

It also explains why memory is context-sensitive.[27] Computer memory isn't context sensitive: you can take your laptop back to your old school and it works just the same – whilst for you the memories come flooding back. This also hints at why students perform best when taking a test in the same room in which they learned, or why people who are depressed tend to remember negative events and not positive ones.

Your general emotional state can seriously affect your ability to remember things – you can even be so panicked that you can't recall how to do the simplest things. You can get up on stage to give a speech you've rehearsed a hundred times, only to have the whole thing vanish from your mind.

Recalling our school days, we can also begin to see why we remember enthusiastic teachers (or terrifying ones) and the people who cared about us. When a teacher makes an effort to relate information to something that matters to us – something that is relevant – this has been shown to improve recall.

Other mnemonic techniques that can improve recall for boring information involve imagining bizarre or emotive scenes – the stranger the better. When designing learning, we should bear in mind that if learning takes place in an emotional state very different to that in which recall may occur (e.g. emergency situations), then the individual may be unable to recall much in the heat of the moment.

It explains why, when we recall information, the mistakes we make tend to be 'affective substitution' – i.e. we recreate experiences with elements that 'feel' the same. We may remember tigers instead of leopards – and we might imagine that our most feared schoolteacher resembled Miss Trunchbull from the Roald Dahl *Matilda* story.

In an extension of this effect, metaphor and creativity involve affective substitution. When Wordsworth writes 'I wandered lonely as a cloud', it makes sense only because we can compare our feeling of being isolated with how we react to a cloud alone in the sky. It is important to note that these two things are not being compared on the basis of what they mean (semantic substitution), but on the basis of how they *feel*.

This, in a nutshell, is the essence of creativity – being able to compare things in terms of how they make us feel. It enables us to write poetry, tell jokes, match our mood to a piece of music – and it's the reason why computers will never be able to do these things. Sure, they can copy us – even fool us – but there will always be a difference between you and your shadow.

Gamification and why people cheat

Finally, the affective context model explains a mystery at the heart of behaviourism. Behaviourism is a psychological school of thought originating in the 1970s. Its proponents discovered that behaviour could be modified through 'classical' and 'operant' conditioning.

For example, if rats or pigeons were presented with positive reinforcement (such as a food pellet) when they pressed a lever, they would press the lever more. Equally, if they were presented with a punishment (such as an electric shock), they would stop. This amazing discovery opened the door to a universe of possibilities for behaviour modification.

Today, we tend to use the word *gamification* to describe this technique. You have probably been gamified today – you may have received reward points for your purchases, or used a loyalty card. If you have children at school, they may well receive gold stars for good behaviour. But the behaviourists left the most important questions unanswered: what, exactly, is a positive reinforcement? And, for that matter, what is a punishment?

The answer is: a positive reinforcement is something we feel good about. Rats don't learn to press levers for wooden pellets, after all. And a punishment is something we feel bad about. The irony, of course, is that *behaviourism needs a model of affective states to make any sense at all* – i.e. to avoid definitions of 'positive reinforcer' and 'negative reinforcer' being circular.

Behaviourism is, essentially, a set of techniques for applying affective significance to bring about behaviour change: if we know a creature likes food and hates pain, how do we use that to bring about a change in their behaviour? Creatures that learn like us, feel like us.

Now that we have a shiny new model of how people work, let's take it for a spin. Here's an everyday tale of ordinary folk – see if you can use the affective context model to understand what is going on inside Mary's head as she starts her day.

Mary is annoyed that the 7:05 from Bracknell is cancelled. By the time the 7:35 arrives there are twice as many people waiting for the train.

More people get on with each stop, and by the time they get to Richmond the train is horribly overcrowded. There are shouts of: 'Can you move down please!'

As the doors are closing, a man carrying a latte jumps on the train. He spills some on another commuter. A heated argument ensues, escalating to the point where one of the men shoves the other hard, causing him to fall backwards into a woman with a pram. A third man intervenes, and two other commuters attempt to calm things down.

When Mary arrives at work, she immediately re-tells the story to Joe. She likes Joe. 'You won't believe my train journey today!' she begins.

'They cancelled my train, so by the time I got the 7:35 I was absolutely fuming – then it got so crowded that peoples' faces were pressed up against the windows. We got to Twickenham and this bloke spilled his coffee all over this other bloke – I mean, he was drenched! – and then they were yelling and shouting at each other…'

'Oh my God!' says Joe. 'That sounds crazy! Did someone kick off?'

'Yes!' Mary continues. 'This bloke punched the other bloke, and then he knocked this lady's pram over – I mean, it was just horrifying…'

'Wow. Was there like a whole crowd of people involved?'

'Absolutely – loads of people – they were holding this bloke back and yelling… anyway, it was complete madness.'

I hear stories like this all the time – probably you do too. You might think that nothing especially remarkable is happening here; it's just a fairly mundane slice of morning chit-chat to start the day. But lift the bonnet on this engine, and what you will see is far more interesting.

As she makes her way to work, Mary encodes her reactions to events according to the extent to which they impact the things she cares about. She recalls that it was a cold day (so she decided to wear her coat). The frustration caused by the lateness of the train was memorable – but she couldn't have told you the number of the train. During the journey any number of things were visible through the carriage windows – none of which she encoded.

The dramatic events relating to the altercation were remembered by most people in the carriage, however; especially since in British culture such exchanges aren't commonplace.[28] They make for a good story, and people like to hear a good story. Like all of us, Mary is travelling through life, fishing for memorabilia.

In reconstructing the story, Mary uses emotional imprints and pre-existing affective models of fights on trains, discarding details that had no especial affective significance and making predictable errors: both Richmond and Twickenham are relatively enclosed train stations and one after the other – so they *feel* very similar (despite having very different names).

She exaggerates the severity of the incident – reflecting the shock that she experienced as a witness. Her reactions to events are guiding her reconstruction – which is also influenced by her emotional state at the time of telling: she wants to impress Joe (no one likes to tell a dull story), and he prompts her, using affective elements of his own stories.

Stories tend to 'grow in the telling', since the more emotionally impactful they are, the more likely they are to be remembered – a kind of 'affective selection' process. Mary is not deliberately altering her memory: her recollection is always a product of past affective imprints and her current affective state.

Mary's experiences, her reactions, her retelling and the reactions of her audience form a kind of interlocking song – each event that strikes her resonating in a way that reflects Mary's 'shape'. These notes, when re-sung, resonate with others, changing the song once more.

The affective context model is an attempt to correct a mistake that has dogged us since the beginning of civilization. It's a new theory, so it has some way to go in terms of experimental support. But a good theory is not merely one that has been put to the test – a good theory is one that explains and predicts.

So – to conclude – why is it a better theory than the ones we have today?

Firstly, it provides a unified explanatory framework for a wide variety of psychological phenomena, ranging from operant conditioning to the unreliability of eye-witness testimony. Our observations about cognition – whether we are looking at a sea-slug or a human being – are now accounted for by a single theory, rather than a multitude of proto-theories. It explains everyday learning and memory just as dependably as it does findings under experimental conditions, and provides a foundation for us to critique and improve education.

Secondly, it can account for many hitherto unexplained peculiarities, such as the roadblocks we have hit with regard to artificial intelligence, philosophy, and the curious human propensity for bias, storytelling and music.

Thirdly, it's easy to test. For example, you could mix up a list of four-letter words, some of which have strong affective context (like 'stab') and others weak (like 'pave'), and see which people are most likely to remember.

Finally, it makes good sense: contrary to popular belief, human memory does not store everything that you experience. In fact humans are known to be 'cognitive misers' – expending as little cognitive effort as in absolutely necessary. We remember only fragments of what we experience, reconstruct events, and in a fashion which is thoroughly unreliable.

The affective context model proposes a system which is highly efficient (entire events can be reconstructed from our reactions to them) and selective: what should we remember? The stuff that matters, of course.

I'd like to end this chapter with new definitions of learning and memory:

Learning: a change in behaviour or capability as a result of memory.

Memory: the encoding of an affective response to an experience, which allows that experience to be reconstructed.

One of the problems we have to solve before we go any further is the difference between the terms 'education' and 'learning'. They are radically different things – so much so that education is almost the opposite of learning. But people have fallen into using them as if they mean the same, and this has buried learning.

Now that we have an understanding of learning, we can see how far education has drifted from it, and what we might have to do to resurrect learning and re-introduce it to education.

Key points

- Learning is not knowledge transfer.
- The affective context model is the first general theory of learning.
- According to the model, we store our affective reactions to experiences and use these to reconstruct them.
- A person's motivations are only a part of their broader set of concerns.
- A learner's concerns (their 'affective context') will determine what they remember and how they remember it.
- This process is largely unconscious.
- Learning is defined as 'a change in behaviour or capability as a result of memory'.
- Memory is defined as 'the encoding of an affective response to an experience, which allows that experience to be reconstructed'.

Endnotes

1 Horrible Histories. Horrible Histories – Stupid Deaths | Compilation (online video), 5 September 2019, www.youtube.com/watch?v=LlIe1Ixtgo0 (archived at https://perma.cc/Q4SJ-676D) (Heraclitus appears at 11:46)

2 N I Eisenberger et al. Does rejection hurt: an fMRI study of social exclusion, *Science*, 2003, **302**, 290–2

3 TrainingIndustry.com. Size of The Training Industry, 29 March 2021, trainingindustry.com/wiki/learning-services-and-outsourcing/size-of-training-industry/ (archived at https://perma.cc/T75X-AY4L)

4 H Ebbinghaus (1885/1913) *Memory: A contribution to experimental psychology*, Teachers College, Colombia University, New York

5 A variant of which is called 'spaced repetition'.

6 J L McGaugh (1993) *Memory and Emotion: The making of lasting memories*, Columbia University Press, New York

7 R B Zajonc. Attitudinal effects of mere exposure, *Journal of Personality and Social Psychology*, 1968, **9** (2, Pt.2), 1–27

8 N Emler (1994) Gossip, reputation, and social adaptation. In R F Goodman and A Ben-Ze'ev, *Good Gossip*, University of Kansas Press, Lawrence, KS

9 F C Bartlett (1932/1995) *Remembering: A study in experimental and social psychology*, Cambridge University Press, Cambridge

10 E Loftus and J C Palmer. Reconstruction of automobile destruction: An example of the interaction between language and memory, *Journal of Verbal Learning and Verbal Behavior*, 1974, **13** (5), 585–9

11 E Loftus. Lost in the mall: Misrepresentations and misunderstandings, *Ethics & Behavior*, 1999, **9** (1), 51–60

12 Signs.com. Branded in memory: 1500 drawings reveal our ability to remember famous logos, undated, www.signs.com/branded-in-memory/ (archived at https://perma.cc/8KEV-GDFJ)

13 D O Hebb (1949) *The Organization of Behaviour*, Wiley & Sons, New York

14 S M Kosslyn, W L Thompson, I J Kim and N M Alpert. Topographical representations of mental images in primary visual cortex, *Nature*, 1995, **378**, 496–8

15 Functional Magnetic Resonance Imaging – a brain scanning technique used to monitor activity in the brain.

16 D R Godden and A D Baddeley. Context-dependent memory in two natural environments: Land and underwater, *British Journal of Psychology*, 1975, **66**, 325–31

17 A Damasio (2018) *The Strange Order of Things: Life, feeling and the making of cultures*, Pantheon Books

18 E Fedorenko and R Varley. Language and thought are not the same thing: evidence from neuroimaging and neurological patients, *Annals of the New York Academy of Sciences*, 2016, **1,369** (1), 132–53

19 T Farroni, E Menon, S Rigato and M H Johnson. The perception of facial expressions in newborns, *The European Journal of Developmental Psychology*, 2007, **4** (1), 2–13

20 T Singer, B Seymour, J O'Doherty, H Kaube, R J Dolan and C D Frith. Empathy for pain involves the affective but not sensory components of pain, *Science*, 2004, **303**, 1,157–62

21 C E Izard (1971) *The Face of Emotion*, Appleton-Century-Crofts, New York

22 This is not a restaurant 'schema' in the traditional sense, since a schema is a set of semantic relations. Instead it is something like an 'affective schema' – a set of feelings that go together (like balloons and jelly and presents at a birthday party).

23 A Bechara, A R Damasio, H Damasio and S W Anderson. Insensitivity to future consequences following damage to human prefrontal cortex, *Cognition*, 1994, **50** (1–3), 7–15

24 A G Greenwald, D E McGhee and J L K Schwartz. Measuring individual differences in implicit cognition: The implicit association test, *Journal of Personality and Social Psychology*, 1998, **74** (6), 1,464–80

25 Interestingly, it has been discovered that the strength of biases detected by the IAT varies significantly depending on the participant's state at the time of testing. This is consistent with substitution error effects that we will encounter later on.

26 D Reisberg and P Hertel (2005) *Memory and Emotion*, Oxford University Press

27 D R Godden and A D Baddeley. Context-dependent memory in two natural environments: Land and underwater, *British Journal of Psychology*, 1975, **66**, 325–31

28 We know that the brain is especially active when processing experiences that relate to our core values, such as standards of decency. See J Kaplan et al. Processing narratives concerning protected values: A cross-cultural investigation of neural correlates, *Cerebral Cortex*, 2016, **27**

Education 03

The great learning prevention scheme

'People won't care how much you know until they know how much you care.'

ANON

In the year 2045 – much to everyone's surprise – an entire civilization is discovered living beneath the surface of Mars. Even more surprisingly, the aliens bear a striking resemblance to us (prompting speculation about a common ancestor).

After first contact is made, delegations are assembled for the purposes of establishing a better understanding of our respective cultures and – as a learning expert – you are asked to go along. You are astonished to find that they too have an education system – one remarkably like ours. 'Younglings' sit quietly in rows while an instructor supervises them. They remain in this system for a period of 10 years, culminating in a final examination, before applying for employment.

Only the curriculum is different. The younglings spend 10 years memorizing Pi (3.141592...) to as many decimal places as possible.

The final examination tests their memory of Pi – the average student can recall Pi to around 10,000 places, and grades (from A to F) are awarded depending on how many decimal places they can recall. Great importance is attached to these grades and the piece of paper on which they are printed. Martian employers use these grades when deciding whether or not to employ someone.

You politely enquire of your host whether Pi plays a central role in their culture – to which they respond that it does not, and that in fact most students forget what they have learned shortly after the exam, with the average adult only recalling it to around 100 places. There are hardly any jobs that actually require a person to know the number Pi by heart (which after all they could easily look up), with the exception of the role of 'Pi instructor'.

It turns out there are many Pi instructors, as they are needed by the education system.

The more you investigate, the more things strike you as very odd about this system.

First, it doesn't seem likely that a person's ability to memorize Pi would be a very good way to choose them for a job. Second, if people forget most of their learning, it's not clear why it is worth teaching them in the first place. Finally, watching the younglings in the classroom it is clear that many really struggle with the tasks of memorizing Pi – and it is hard to escape the conclusion that what is going on is really some kind of torture designed to make the younglings dull and compliant (and that this is the true purpose of the system).

When you speak to the younglings, you find that a few of them do quite like memorizing Pi, some of them like the teacher, but the majority are much more interested in things like dinosaurs, dance and Mootball (a Martian game similar to football). The most common response to how they feel about school is that it is 'boring'.

Something else you discover is that in the alien culture there is lots of scientific evidence about the most effective ways to get younglings to memorize Pi; entire journals are published on the subject under the title *The Science of Learning*. It doesn't seem to you that this is really evidence about learning per se – since memorizing numbers isn't the kind of thing that learning processes evolved to do – in either our species or theirs. Storing information is the kind of thing that a book or a computer does perfectly, but a creature very badly. You wonder if the 'educational' research really has anything to do with learning at all.

At the end of your visit you make the mistake of mentioning your misgivings to your alien host. Somewhat miffed, they enquire: 'Well, how do *you* educate your younglings?' In a conciliatory tone you explain that the human educational approach is much the same, but that the curriculum is broader – algebra, chemistry, history, etc. It is only when your host asks how much of this *your* students go on to use that you realize your error. You realize that we do exactly the same thing.

These days there is no shortage of people who feel that there is something wrong with the education system – everyone from billionaire entrepreneurs to 20-something rappers can hold forth on how broken it is. But no one has a clear idea of how to fix it.

Worst of all, the people who think the system is broken often cling to this 'knowledge retention' assumption about the mind: they intuitively feel that the mind is a bit like a computer or a book or a slate on which you can store facts. So when you press these people and ask them to describe the way an educational system *should* work, they eventually fall back on something resembling the conventional 'knowledge transfer' model, since they are unable to imagine what else learning could be if it is not getting people to store information in their heads.

I'm not just talking about your run-of-the-mill celebrities; I mean the very best educational theorists we have to offer still think learning is something like memorizing facts.

Intuitively, letting people learn what they want to learn seems appealing – and some people have indeed experimented with 'exploratory learning' – but overall the education system has concluded that this approach is no better than having people sit in rows, writing stuff down.

You might wonder how they arrived at this conclusion – to which the answer is they had both groups sit traditional exams, which consist of recalling facts you have memorized. It's worth pausing to reflect on what a ridiculous thing that is to do: in our aliens example, it would be like saying: 'When we allowed people to learn freely, we discovered they didn't memorize Pi to as many places – so we concluded learning freely is not effective!'

You might challenge me here: 'So how *should* we assess learning?' To which I would respond that since we can't observe neural changes directly (for the most part), we should assess it the same way we do with other creatures, by looking at what they can do. We might then have a lively discussion about the sorts of things people should be able to do – but almost certainly none of these would be regurgitating information onto exam papers.

In essence, the problem is that people have accepted Cartesian thinking, in which we *should* be able to learn like computers, and therefore think that learning is all about storing knowledge in our heads. This hidden assumption surfaces in popular sci-fi movies, like *The Matrix*, where someone plugs a cable into the back of your head and instantly you 'know Kung Fu' – or where someone's brain has been boosted by a chemical and you need merely flip the pages of a dictionary to 'learn a language'.

This is how computers work, after all – you download the program, and instantly they can do something new. This philosophical aspiration, to be like a computer, runs deep. I am sorry to disappoint you, but this is never going to happen.

Why? Well, compare this with the description of learning I gave in the previous chapter, where every change in your neural wiring comes as the result of an emotional reaction to events around you. This is how children learn a language. An accurate sci-fi movie would therefore need to have you learn a language *by reliving the entire life of a child* (say up to the age of 12) growing up in a foreign country.

How would that work exactly? Compare the nutty idea that if you wanted to watch a movie and only had one minute, you could run it at 100x speed to watch it anyway. It doesn't work! The brain doesn't work like that. The idea that we might work like that comes from computers which we know have some kind of internal clock, that sometimes we can just run faster to get the same result in a shorter time.

Now, there's nothing wrong with the idea that one day you might have a device that you stick in your ear that does the language translation for you (like the Babel fish from *The Hitchhiker's Guide to the Galaxy*), but you haven't learned a new language – in fact, the opposite: the device has pretty much *eliminated* any chance that you will learn the language. It has eliminated the need to learn.

If that scenario sounds strikingly familiar, that is because that is precisely what technology does for us: it eliminates the need to learn, it externalizes knowledge and capability. You could even have a chip installed in your brain that contains all the content in Wikipedia, and the ability to use your brainwaves to navigate to the topic you are interested in. But you will still need to read it. It will be only marginally quicker than what we do today, on our screens.

Let me be clear: *if you don't live it, you don't learn it.* This is also true of learning a second language sitting in a classroom: language learning systems present us with 'echoes' of the emotional context that we would experience if learning it for real. 'You are in a *boulangerie*, you wish to order some croissants,' etc. There is no shortcut, any more than you can sleep with a French dictionary under your pillow and wake up a fluent French speaker.

Because people are stuck with the Cartesian knowledge transfer model, it is impossible for an educational revolution to take place – however many people are dissatisfied with the current system. Until we understand learning, we will be using the wrong yardstick for measuring success. People will continue to moan about the current system, without being able to offer up a sensible alternative – in fact, bad alternatives will continue to spring up like toxic toadstools.

This volatile mixture – widespread dissatisfaction with education, coupled with a near-complete lack of vision regarding alternatives – has created a space in which all manner of terrible ideas attract investment: virtual classrooms, massive open online course (MOOCs), e-learning, micro-learning…

Each of these supposedly new approaches shares the same fundamental flaw – they promise to be a more efficient method for dumping content into people's heads, but none is sensitive to the individual concerns that drive learning. Each time they are deployed, they are sold to investors and consumers as hyper-efficient knowledge transfer systems, and each time people buy this nonsense, and every time they fail.

And yet, the market flourishes: investors grasp that widespread dissatisfaction with the Victorian model and (sensing a killing to be made) throw money at anything that looks promising.

How did education get in such a muddle?

The first thing to know about education today is that there are no good reasons why we teach the things that we teach, or teach them in the way that we do. Did you ever stop to wonder why you learned geography, history, maths, science, English and things like that at school? No? That's just as well – as there isn't a decent explanation.

But before we get into that, let's start where all good stories begin: at the beginning.

For the vast majority of human history, our approach to education remained largely unchanged: young children (and other animals) would learn through play in which they experiment with their new-found capabilities, through their reactions to the things they do, and through observation – in which they learn by watching what happens to others.

Since humans are social creatures and therefore designed to experience echoes of other's emotions (through a system of mirror neurons, and by interpreting their reactions through their faces and movements) we can feel another's pain or pleasure as if it were our own (albeit attenuated). This also allows you and I to enjoy movies where the hero – with whom we identify, obviously – triumphs over adversity. Hence, we also learn through stories, in which important lessons are handed down via an oral tradition. Valuable information, for example about life-threatening situations we are unlikely to encounter on a regular basis, is transferred in the form of stories.

The story format preserves the affective significance of information, so as to allow people to accurately reconstruct it. If you are telling a story about a bear in a cave to small children, it really helps if you yell the 'RAAAARRGGHHH!' sound unexpectedly and make claws in the air with your fingers. Every parent knows this – and now you know why. There is even a quasi-scientific name for the phenomenon – 'Motherese' – which describes the exaggeration of word sounds when used (more commonly by mothers) in speaking to babies and small children. It is hypothesized that this has something to do with helping children to learn a language by emphasizing the phonemes.

What the scientists missed is that it is not just the sounds but – more importantly – the *emotions* that are exaggerated. This makes it easier for children to understand what words mean, since in essence the meaning of a word is the feeling that it conveys. When we talk to small children, we automatically exaggerate our emotional expression – take a look for yourself if you don't believe me.

So children make their way through the world, learning how to react to things via the reactions of people around them. 'Don't pick that up!' the anxious parent yells as the small child reaches for the discarded lollipop lying on the tarmac.

As children develop further, they are introduced into their culture via a succession of roles and activities which grow in complexity and degree of challenge. For example, small children may help with some elements of food preparation, moving on to gathering activities, then graduating to hunting activities where observation is eventually replaced with the activity itself. They are usually supported and mentored by more experienced individuals as they go through this process.

This primordial educational approach is vastly superior to the formal educational system that we have today. In fact, we still learn in this way, though formal education forces it to the fringes of our existence – i.e. education actively *reduces* our opportunities to learn. Education is a cuckoo in the learning nest.

Education is, on balance, a learning prevention scheme. It's true that some learning will take place during your time in education, but generally this is despite the content that is on the curriculum: you learn about friends, enemies and social interaction, for example. You learn after school from your favourite TV programme, or under the desk from social media. Sadly, since you are no longer spending much time with your parents, you learn next to nothing about how they earn a living – that is all hidden from you. You are systematically unprepared for life and will suffer doubly: once during school, and again from the development you have missed.

It is also the case that many teachers trapped in the education system care deeply about the development of young people. Often they have this palpable sense that they are 'battling the system' or that the real value of their efforts – inspiring, supporting and encouraging people – goes unrecognized. And this is true. It does.

So if learning was working fine before education, how did we end up where we are today?

There are very few drawbacks to the natural approach to learning, except one that turns out to be significant: as I mentioned in the first chapter, in recent human history the creation of large, complex societies (due in large part to high-yield farm crops) allowed for explosive diversification of roles. Prior to that, it might have been a problem for you if, say, you were a girl, your culture prohibited girls from being hunters, and this turned out to be something you were interested in – but overall the choice of roles was limited.

However, in modern societies the proliferation of roles meant that there was a good chance that you might want to do something other than your parents' chosen vocation. The obvious solution would be to swap parents and indeed this is more or less what started to happen, through a system of apprenticeships.

Apprenticeships were the dominant approach to learning in complex societies until a couple of hundred years ago. The essence of an apprenticeship is that you learn how to do something by working alongside someone who isn't your parents.

For those already in positions of privilege, the aristocratic class, actual labour was considered grubby and demeaning and to be avoided at all costs. Instead they devoted themselves to edifying intellectual pursuits. This has also remained true until fairly recently – consider that even Bartlett, whose 1932 *The War of the Ghosts* study we covered earlier, was considered an oddball at Cambridge; a middle-class farm boy among the rich and privileged.

In India, China and Greece the story was the same: normal people learned their parents' trade or found work as an apprentice. The social elite, with nothing better to do, studied things such as philosophy, military strategy, poetry, charioteering, music, dance, scripture, art or mathematics.

The Chinese believed that boys were ready to start learning writing at age seven (which modern research broadly supports). The Romans believed that, ultimately, it was a parent's responsibility to teach their children up to a certain age, later developing a system of further education which culminated in rhetoric and philosophy – intended to prepare the upper classes for law or politics. This is the origin of our modern-day liberal arts curriculum.

In England, apprenticeships were the norm until the late 19th century. In fact there was a law against practising a trade unless you had completed a seven-year apprenticeship.[1] As elsewhere in the world, what schools existed outside of elite education largely served the purposes of religious education, with monks being trained in Latin and later Greek.

The need for free schooling was in part brought about by Victorian era industrialization. Parents who went to work in cotton mills could not work alongside their children as they might have done in the fields or home. There needed to be somewhere they could go – somewhere that would prepare them for life in a factory.

To be clear, school was the answer to the question: 'How can we prevent children from being injured in factories?', not: 'What environment would be best for children's learning?' Education was essentially unrelated to learning from the outset.

Later, post-war, the demand for literate workers expanded the need for schooling. The curriculum itself was something of an organic affair: for young children it centred on the 3Rs (reading, writing and arithmetic) and later years education was adapted from the medieval classical curriculum – adding subjects such as science and literature.

At various points attempts were made to make the curriculum more practical, but these failed since they were more costly than simply teaching the 3Rs, and didn't work well in a system where one low-skilled person monitored many. In other words, the system was as much cheap daycare as it was education.

Today we have a school curriculum arrived at by a combination of historical accident, religious influence and cost considerations – delivered within an educational system largely devised to provide daycare and obedient workers for an industrial era (with a university system designed for the elite bolted on at the end).

For the most part we still sit in rows writing, much like monks. Despite all the self-serving research, it doesn't really have a scientific basis: professors of education ignore research showing lectures to be ineffective,[2] and continue the ritual. It's nice to be the centre of attention. The whole thing is a money-making hotch-potch – a self-sustaining bureaucracy.

But the historical accidents that led to the system we have today are not the root cause of our troubles. Whatever the educational method – whether people are sitting in rows or clicking their way through e-learning modules – the underlying thinking is the same and it is this thinking that corrupts every single approach to education that we take.

The thinking is 'knowledge transfer'. We fell into thinking that the human mind stores information, much like the pages of a book, and that there are methods of (forcibly) putting that information into people's heads: by talk-ing at them, by getting them to stare at the information, repeat it over and over again, write it down.

But people don't store information – they store their reactions to it then reconstruct it. They reconstruct it based on how experiences made them feel. And as we sit in class, or click 'next' through another e-learning module, we feel only bored.

What I mean is this: education (largely) comprises a series of anxiety-driven tests, in service of which we try to cram as much information into our heads as possible. The anxiety stems from the myth that our future success depends on our performance on these tests. We have engineered a world of punishments and rewards to preserve the illusion that learning is taking place, and that education delivers it. We teach people to concentrate on doing what they're told, and have built a global network of camps into which we force our children, reassuring each other that it is good for them.

Education is a terrible model for learning, and an even worse model for performance. I am not the only person who suspects this to be the case, but in the absence of an alternative model many education people don't know what else to do, and many corporate learning people are still trying to educate.

Being able to access useful stuff on your mobile device is a big part of why it is falling apart – people are now able to figure things out for them-selves. They are not 'educating themselves' (use of online educational plat-forms is still pitiful) – they are just getting things done. They use resources every day, but never courses.

We like TED talks about online academies, but almost none of us will have spent much time there. Leading academic institutions have generously made thousands of their world-class courses available online – for free! Have you ever completed one? The high priests of education rhapsodize about magnanimously offering Oxbridge lectures via video stream to folks in sub-Saharan Africa – as if this would do anything more than burn through their data allowance (and of course if you want a certificate it is available at a price!).

I still remember the days when we used to run workshops on the latest updates to Microsoft Office. Now we just get on with it. Unfortunately, some of the 'useful stuff' about your place of work (such as the best ways of doing things) may not be on the internet.

You would think that educators would be rushing to plug this gap – their reputation has suffered from decades of inability to produce a convincing case for the contribution they make to organizations – businesses consistently complain that education is poor preparation for the world of work. But they are not.

Instead, much of the education industry is busy dreaming up ways of using mobile devices to do the same terrible things that never worked before – pushing out little bits of content and testing people, rather than talking to people about the useful stuff they might develop (resources) to help them do their jobs (user-centred learning design).

Ironically the very things that give learning professionals their sense of identity – instructional design, knowledge transfer, learning theory – are preventing them from making a contribution. So it is this shift of perspective – towards helping people rather than dumping content on them – that needs to take place. No amount of technology or marketing will fix a broken model. Artificial intelligence (AI) and virtual reality (VR) will not prove more effective ways of dumping content. If we want to improve education, we need to understand learning.

Smart educators intuitively grasped that something was wrong, and found ways to make students care (by making information personal or relevant, through sheer enthusiasm, or by bringing it to life in other ways) – but the system as a whole resorted to violence: canings and threats, and when these things were prohibited – tests. Tests, whose sole purpose is to make people feel anxious enough to remember. A cheap way to make people care.

The upshot is that we have become utterly muddled in thinking about learning and education, when really the two are really completely different things. Education is to learning as homeopathy is to medicine. They might sound similar, but education is a merely a series of peculiar rituals – like dining etiquette – whilst learning describes the way we adapt, cognitively, to the world around us. In this analogy, learning is a bit like 'digestion'.

The reason education pays no heed to learning is precisely the same reason homeopathy pays no heed to medicine, namely: they think they are doing it already, and accepting that they are not (and never have been) would be too much to bear.

So whenever you hear the word 'learning' used, it is worth pausing to consider whether it is really being used to refer to learning, or to education. Ninety-nine times out of 100, when people say learning, they really mean education.

Today the problem is really chronic, since much of the research that purports to be about human learning actually turns out to concern something like memorizing things or passing tests – and so is really about education, so won't tell you much about learning at all. When you ask: 'Why on earth are you doing that!?' in an educational context, people can blithely trot out the

Table 3.1   Education versus learning

Education	Learning
Ritual	Natural
Fact-based	Reaction-based
Topic-led	Task-led
Lecture	Conversation
Instructor-centric	User-centric
Explicit	Implicit
Content-centric	Context-centric
Anxious	Playful

rationalization: 'It's based on scientific evidence', conveniently overlooking that the scientific evidence has nothing to do with learning (similar to the Ebbinghaus/Martian examples I gave earlier).

Very few academic papers consider storytelling, for example – unlike Loftus' and Bartlett's work (this despite storytelling being our default means of explicitly exchanging information). In the 'learning industry' we are awash with 'learning management systems' and 'learning conferences' and 'learning design' – all of which are actually about education, since their focus is essentially on ways of getting people to memorize facts so they can pass some kind of test. In fact if you tell your average employee that they are going to have to do some learning one of the first questions they ask is: 'Will there be a test?'

We kid ourselves that these rituals have anything to with capability development. Our conferences are a like a gathering of rain-dancers meeting to discuss tips and tweaks to our dance routines: 'If you shake your head from side to side, it rains a little harder'.

For my part, when I talk about 'education' it is sometimes unclear whether I am talking about the public education system or the private, corporate, education system – or what the difference is.

Today, the underlying assumptions are the same, but the delivery models are quite different: we are typically enrolled full-time in the public education system, and our progress is generally measured through milestone assessments.

Once we leave the public education system and enter the world of work, we usually leave all that behind. The vast majority of university graduates go on to work in unrelated fields – an extraordinary tacit acknowledgement of the redundancy of the system as a whole.

Thereafter, formal education is likely to be sporadic at best, and oriented around the role that we are to do or – more likely – the regulatory and compliance requirements that the organization is required to meet. Where this takes place, we often fall back on the public education model: people sit in rows of seats listening to a lecture or review screens of information online. Often there is a test at the end.

In a truly bizarre twist in the tale, corporate education largely ignores the educational research produced by respected academic institutions in the design of its learning solutions, only to find that those same respected academic institutions are now looking to them for models of innovative learning delivery (for example, use of e-learning or video content). Professors of education are gobsmacked to discover that the procurement team have purchased a learning management system that will efficiently regurgitate their lectures as a series of videos, all in the pursuit of financial efficiency, and based on some benchmarking comparison with Big Business.

Setting aside the turbulence, it seems likely that over time these two systems will merge into a continuous rather than discontinuous system as they become more about learning than education, and will instead operate along a kind of gradient. The main difference between learning at the start of the educational process and at the end of the process is this: at the start our concerns (the things we care about) are quite broad and still in a state of flux. Towards the end, we will often have a much clearer understanding of who we want to be and what we are trying to do.

This means that at the outset the focus is much more on 'push'-type learning design. This doesn't mean force-feeding people topics in the way that we do today, it means creating an exploratory environment where people can experiment (in a playful way) with a wide variety of challenges and simulated experiences.

At the other end of the scale, people are earning money for many of the challenges they complete, because they have achieved a level of competence, and so the emphasis is much more on 'pull'-type design – on providing an environment rich in the kinds of resources they might need to further their learning.

To put it simply, at the start learning tends to be more about exploring experiences and challenges; later on, it becomes more about access to resources.

It's important to note that these are not absolute distinctions; a person who is, say, an expert in cyber-warfare may still choose to spend some of their time exploring challenges where they don't have much capability – cookery, for example. As they work on cyber-warfare challenges they are likely to be earning money and sharing their expertise with people who are slightly less competent. As they work on cookery, they are likely to be paying for these experiences and tackling simpler challenges in the company of people more skilled than they are.

Education from a commercial standpoint

Today's educational model is something like a 'cash for certificates' scheme. A simplified version of the story goes like this: young people are told that qualifications are essential for success in later life. They spend over a decade taking notes and cramming for exams, then three years listening to someone talk about a topic, taking notes and writing essays. Shortly before each examination, they memorize as much of their notes as possible so that they can pass and receive a certificate.

Then, mission accomplished, they forget much of this information and start to apply for jobs, presenting their certificate to potential employers as evidence of their suitability for the role. It is unlikely that their study will bear much relation to their field of work, however the certificate suggests that they know how to sit still, shut up and do as they are told.

When they start work, they learn how to do their job through observing others, Google, asking questions and – to some extent – trial and error. Their employer may provide some form of formal training but (again) this bears little relation to the job they are required to do and is typically one of two types: compliance activity required to reduce corporate risk, or an opportunity to meet other employees and feel valued.

In this way it happens that almost all learning happens outside of educational contexts, and in an entirely different fashion. Indeed, education happens when learning should be taking place – it pushes learning opportunities to one side. After a long day at school, the small child wants nothing more than to play with friends.

It may seem that I am being melodramatic in my assessment of education. But perhaps we are insufficiently outraged by what is going on. In his book *Affective Neuroscience* Jaak Panksepp writes:

> If at least part of ADHD [Attention Deficit Hyperactivity Disorder] is caused by excessive playfulness, it becomes a profound societal issue whether it is ethical

to drug children for such traits. Obviously it is essential to maintain attention to academic matter in the classroom, but is it appropriate to induce compliance in children through pharmacological means?... This is especially important in light of the possibility that such drugs can produce long-lasting changes in the responsivity of brain catecholamine systems, as is seen in the psychostimulant-induced sensitization phenomenon.[3]

In my terms, Jaak is suggesting that we are prepared to brain-damage children in order to suppress the normal expression of learning, and force them to comply with the demands of a ritualized education system. Not only have we laid the blame with the child rather than the educational system, we have 'pathologized' playfulness in order to provide an institutional justification. Bring back the cane – it would be far more humane.

There are, of course, exceptions to this. Passionate educators are sometimes motivated by a desire to support the development of people in their care. At an intuitive level they recognize that there is something wrong with the knowledge transfer model of learning, and consequently they take the time to get to know students, to make material relevant, and to inspire passion for their field.

Whether in an academic or corporate setting, good educators quickly realize that the 'drill and test' approach is at best ineffective and at worst damaging. As a result they often quietly subvert the purity of the curriculum: by building experiences and activities that self-evidently benefit the learning experience, by taking an interest in their students and adapting the examples accordingly – without having any formal basis for their approach, but a conviction that they are doing the right thing. And they are.

Every so often one will stumble across a heartening testimonial from someone whose life has been changed for the better by a teacher. I would encourage you to listen closely to what is said: invariably phrases like: 'They believed in me', 'They were inspirational', 'They really cared about me' and 'They took time to get to know me' come up.

We have become so used to hearing these sorts of things, that we entirely overlook their significance: nobody talks about memorizing information; the impact made by good teachers is on how they made people *feel*, not what they know. The 'knowing' part people will do for themselves, once they feel a certain way.

Inspire a student, and they may go on to achieve great things – but are teachers taught how to make students feel? I mean to carefully analyse and map how they feel today, using those co-ordinates to chart a course to the future via a complex journey of interrelated feelings.

In recent years the finance sector has seized on an opportunity to harness the education system for ever greater returns – at least in the UK and US. Now, to add insult to injury, young people are required to take out enormous loans (circa £40,000) to pay for their higher education experience, on the promise that they will repay the money during their lifetime should they be fortunate enough to find themselves in a job that is well paid.

This really is a sneaky scheme, since it plays on the relative inability of people of this age to think about their future, and their desire to have fun and make friends. Education has become a form of financial indenture.

During the pandemic year 2020, it seemed the ruse might be up: students unable to attend lectures for fear of contracting the virus instead watched video recordings of lectures from their bedrooms.

Slowly it dawned on us all that borrowing tens of thousands of pounds for the pleasure of watching people drearily recite information which could easily have been obtained for free on the internet didn't seem... rational.

Attendance at online lectures plummeted, and it seemed the game might be up. The *reductio ad absurdum* was being played out: if the online video lectures consisted of little more than people reading from a script, why not simply send people the textbook and allow them to learn at their own pace? But would people pay £40,000 for a textbook and an online multiple-choice examination at the end? Oh dear.

So the government was complicit in encouraging the students to return to their universities despite the risks of infection – even if it meant that they would be confined to halls of residence – so that the money-making charade could continue.

Of course students grasped that what they had paid dearly for was really three years of partying and self-discovery (at a safe distance from their parents), and felt they were entitled to ignore the restrictions. And they did. Acts of rebellion had to be quashed. The whole thing descended into farce.

How should education work?

When you talk to people about education, a question that quickly comes up is: 'What is the purpose of education?' The problem with this question is it tends to polarize the discussion: on the one hand some people believe that education should be about 'edification' or 'passion', enabling the individual to be the best that they can be. On the other hand, more pragmatic educationalists feel that education should be about equipping people to play a useful role in society.

These two groups have corresponding perspectives on who is 'in control' of the process – in the first case the learner is in control, in the latter the teacher (or education system).

The answer, of course, is that these two things are not incompatible – you can do both. But today, neither is accomplished.

If we use our push–pull framework, we can get a clearer idea of how this should work: education should be more like a conversation than a lecture. In a conversation, it doesn't make sense to ask who is in control – since if someone is 'in control' it's probably not a great conversation. Often, it is not clear where a conversation will go at the outset – rather people share and explore their respective interests. A conversation where someone has in mind a number of points they wanted to get across at the outset is rarely experienced as a great conversation.

Education is sometimes talked about as 'instruction', but the word 'dialogue' would be a far better term to use, because when we use the term 'dialogue' we understand that it is not a formal process in which we memorize things, and that there is some ongoing interaction between participants which results in progress, where the dialogue is healthy.

So it is with education: it has both 'push' and 'pull' elements, and these need to be constantly balanced through a process that is reciprocal. It is not enough that a child should 'follow their passions' – these passions provide an initial momentum, but should be steered through the various avenues that society provides through conversation and exploration. Education serves to shape passion into fulfilling employment.

What I mean by this is that by the time a child enters an educational process, they already have concerns and interests that are driving their learning; they may be interested in animals, or trains, or ballet. It is true that there are only so many jobs for zoo-keepers or train-drivers or ballerinas, but at this early stage a child's interests are quite malleable and generalized.

It may be that someone interested in trains has a more general feeling for things mechanical, or that someone who posts pictures of ballerinas on their wall is interested in costume or choreography. Learning about zoos might teach you a lot about running a small business. It might be that what someone is really seeking is an opportunity to care for others, or a sense of security.

The idea that an education system faces a choice between allowing people to pursue their passions and shaping them into productive workers is a false dilemma. Whether you are a sea-snail or a human, there are just two systems to consider: the pattern of things that you care about, and the world you find yourself in. These two things interact, shaping each other through-out your life. That's what learning is for.

The best outcome is that you find yourself in a world aligned with your cares; the worst is that you feel trapped in a crappy job doing none of the things that really matter to you.

So the question is: how do the things a person cares about become refined and aligned with the world in which they live? The answer is: through the two 'push' and 'pull' parts of the process.

The 'pull' part of education involves understanding the learner and what drives their learning – their affective context. Affective context describes all of the affective features of something, in this case the individual. Here, it means the totality of their cares (rather than 'everything they know'). I will also talk about experiences which add affective context – by which I mean experiences that shift what a person cares about.

As a metaphor, you can imagine affective context as a painting of a per-son, where each point of colour corresponds to something that they care about. At the most fundamental level of analysis, affective context describes who someone is. It is what makes you different from me. This will continue to evolve and change over time so the process is ongoing.

The 'push' part of learning involves using methods that contribute affec-tive context – methods such as challenging environments, stories, simula-tions – all of which have the capacity to steer the learner in new directions.

Things have happened to you, during the course of your life, that have shaped what you care about. These things might be a fictional character that you idolized, friends that you admired – they might have been some awful experience, or merely a single comment. Each moved us, tilted us in an alter-nate trajectory.

Many of these may have been accidental, or largely unwitting: your par-ents will try to set a good example, movie-makers will consider the messages they are sending, but the precise interlock between the world and your con-cerns is still more magic and intuition than it is science and craft. Education presents the opportunity to change that, through understanding which ex-periences will resonate with which concerns.

This is really quite different to what we do today: it is about providing op-portunities to experience a multitude of different situations first-hand, tack-ling challenges of increasing sophistication in a supportive environment.

As I noted above – this is really not unlike the way that learning has taken place for thousands of years, with children helping their parents with sim-ple, then more complex tasks. However in today's complex society we can-not simply fall back on allowing parents to take their children to work.

This would actually be a pretty good solution, were it not for the problem that in modern culture the assumption that children want to follow in their parents' footsteps is probably not a good one. True, children might be bored in meetings, but then so am I. Maybe we would have better meetings. With crayons and Play-Doh.

As the neuroscientist Antonio Damasio notes in his book *The Strange Order of Things*: 'It turns out that the machinery of our affect is educable, to a certain extent, and that a good part of what we call civilization occurs through the education of that machinery in a conducive environment of home, school and culture'.[4]

But today school is not really conducive. In fact, quite the opposite – educators are not remotely concerned with the 'machinery of affect' as they plough through the standard curriculum in order that students can pass a test.

So how *would* you create a system where children get to experience and explore different roles? You might have a system of placements or apprenticeships – or you could create a learning 'ecosystem' which gradually blends artificial challenges in a supportive environment into real challenges in the workplace, for example by providing simulated or simplified learning environments. In other words, you could take the learning into work, or you could take the work into learning. Probably we will need to do both. If we accomplish this successfully, both learning and work will start to feel more like play and the distinction will begin to evaporate.

Such a model may well cost more than sitting people in a room and having someone on a low wage write things on a board; but it is worth bearing in mind that the proposed model integrates learning and work. That is to say, the simple challenges that people tackle at the start of the process (for example translating a few words into another language) may be purely a learning exercise, but as challenges grow in complexity they quickly become actual, paid, work. This is an education system that makes money.

One of the ill-effects of the current system is that it unnecessarily infantilizes individuals, preventing them from undertaking a great many tasks of which they are perfectly capable, until they reach a certain age. Technology is beginning to undermine this, for example allowing a young person to make money by streaming their game-play or earn advertising revenue from their comical dance moves, entirely outside of the school/work system.

A laudable desire to prevent child labour has therefore backfired horribly, preventing people from discovering the things they enjoy doing, stunting their development, and delaying their entry into society.

In the model outlined above, you might also wonder: why not simply focus on the 'push' side of education – why bother to understand and adapt to a learner's concerns? Why not simply use a combination of compelling approaches – enthusiastic teachers, storytelling and simulation, for example – to shape people as required by society?

In answer to that question, there seem to be two major problems with education today.

First, the things people learn at school or university are not well aligned with the world of work. This creates a tremendous strain on the individual. As previously mentioned, most college graduates go on to work in a field unrelated to their degree (a recent study found only around 27 per cent of US grads found a job in a related field).[5]

How can this be an effective system? Once again, it is in essence a 'cash for certificates' scheme in which students demonstrate that they are able to follow instructions, and are therefore deemed fit for employment (since 'following instructions' was the core competency in the industrial era). Almost all of their learning will therefore be on the job – i.e. picked up through real learning mechanisms such as observation and trial and error.

This might be fine, were it not for the fact that they have now been (for the most part) deprived of the opportunity to develop a passion for learning, and have missed out on the chance to learn the sorts of things that might have been useful.

The defenders of education tend to be people who did well at school, by which I mean they are on the one hand pretty good at memorizing information and passing tests and on the other quite comfortable with obedience to authority. In the early stages of their development this obedience amounts to 'doing what you're told'; during university something more sophisticated – such as listening intently to the professor's lectures and mimicking their professor's views in essays.

As a consequence of this system of rewards and reinforcements, their self-esteem becomes inextricably linked to passing tests and following instructions. This can leave them feeling frustrated and unfulfilled in the modern workplace, with the result that they turn to academia – becoming the kinds of teachers who emphasize 'doing as you're told', the importance of passing tests, and defenders of the educational status quo. In this and many other subtle ways, the educational system is self-sustaining.

Even where a degree does relate to practice, people who make the transition normally report that what they learned in the classroom bears little relation to what they actually needed to know to do the job (and subsequently around 90 per cent of their learning happens on the job).[6]

It's worth pausing for a second to consider the skills that are actually useful at work today. If we take an office job, for example, they might be things like: managing organizational politics, fitting in, building a reputation, coping with information overload, writing emails, attending meetings, building positive relationships.

Today, lots of people spend most of their time answering emails and attending meetings. True – that may not be the case in a few years' time, but medieval history is unlikely to become a vital skill whatever happens.

By the time most people join organizations, they have a jaded attitude towards learning. They have been conditioned to think that 'learning' involves memorizing some stuff, which they will later be tested on. In turn these tests present a risk to their future success. It then becomes impossible to say the word 'learning' without people thinking you are referring to 'education'.

In light of this, a simple way to improve education is as follows: we ask: 'For what purpose?', then say, 'So let's teach that instead.' For example:

'Children should learn to read and write'

'For what purpose?'

'So they can express themselves in blogs, respond to emails and read street signs.'

'OK. So let's teach that instead.'

'Children should learn maths.'

'For what purpose?'

'So they know when they receive the correct change in a store, so they can complete their tax returns.'

'OK. So let's teach that instead.'

And so on.

If we can't think of a purpose, then perhaps we shouldn't be teaching something. Now it may seem to some people that this is, once more, a narrowly vocational way to look at education. Not at all.

Rather, the point is that if there is no affective significance to teaching – if we can't find a reason why anyone should care – then we shouldn't expect students to learn anything at all. Defenders of 'the classics' (for example languages such as Greek or Latin) will sometimes argue that such subjects are edifying, but perhaps what they really mean is that they are useful for impressing a certain kind of person at dinner parties. In which case we should be teaching people how to impress certain people at dinner parties – and if they are interested in doing that, perhaps they will learn some Homeric poetry too.

But what about things that people don't care about but should? It may well be that many students aren't terribly interested in completing tax returns, for example. We should permit people to experience challenges that resemble real life and allow them to choose. The point is that people will learn about something when they care about it, and if they don't care (or we can't generate care) then there is no point whatsoever in forcing the issue. **One care always builds on another** – that's why we hurt animals or reward them with food when we want to train them.

Quite possibly people don't care much about tax returns until they have to complete one – in which case that is the right point to learn. My personal view is that I would rather never have to learn how to complete a tax return. At no point does this seem like it would be a 'playful' activity for me. So this is the kind of task that I would happily pay someone else to do – someone who enjoys it.

If we have created a system where people are free to learn, and confident learners, then learning can take place as required, driven by the challenges people face and the things that they care about.

Today, the vast majority of educational time and money is wasted through a failure to grasp this central characteristic of human learning. Whether in corporate learning or public education we try to get people to memorize things that we (the educators) think are important, or that our students *might* feel is important at some time in the future, but which they don't experience as important themselves, right now.

This problem is compounded by the fact that younger people tend to worry less about the future in general. It helps not a bit when they grow into adults who say things like: 'I wish I had paid more attention in school' – what they really mean is: 'I care about this thing now – I didn't back then'.

The solution is not to lecture young people. The solution is either to allow people to learn as they care, or to find a way to make them care.

This is why teachers may experience frustration when, say, a celebrity footballer shows up at school one day and inspires a new-found respect for mathematics in his adoring fans – instantly achieving what years of dedicated instruction could not. But the mechanics are really quite simple: what matters to your heroes matters to you.

The products of our current educational system are 'serious', not 'playful' people. There is very little that is light-hearted about them. They are measurably less creative than the people they were when they entered the system.[7]

In truth there is probably a biological basis for reduction in playfulness in adult humans, and if one is looking for obedient clones with which to staff a Victorian factory, then playfulness and creativity are hardly desirable characteristics. But in a modern economy companies and roles change rapidly, and many more organizations are looking for innovation, ingenuity and lifelong learning.

I have personally designed culture change programmes aimed at making senior executives in global companies more 'creative' and 'innovative', and I can testify to the fact that it is an uphill struggle. The child is buried a long way down. These are people who have been recruited for their obedience, selected for their gravity, discouraged from experimentation and rewarded for severity. And now, grey and grave, they want to play.

This will cause difficulties for people expecting to change roles and develop new skills on a regular basis. Unless they are able to extend the 'playful' mode of learning into adulthood, they will find themselves at odds with their environment – obsolete in their 30s.

Stop and consider for a moment how you feel about the word 'play'. Is it something childish? Is it something you feel belongs in the workplace? Can you easily imagine someone saying: 'Stop playing around and get on with your work'?

Play is important because in humans it denotes 'learning mode', i.e. it indicates that you have entered a state of mind where your openness to experimentation and new ideas is enhanced. In this mode you are experiencing a protective bubble of psychological safety – by which I mean you aren't afraid of making mistakes or of embarrassment. What happens during play is stripped of further significance – activities take place for the sake of learning alone.

If you built a robot that had a button for different modes, then the button for entering learning mode would be titled 'play'. In other words, the robot's learning button wouldn't cause it to go into a receptive state where it memorizes everything it hears and repeats it back; that mode would be titled 'education'.

The fact that for many cultures play has come to signify a childish, unproductive, fun activity reveals just how terribly far our understanding of learning has been corrupted. Learning should mean something very like play – and nothing at all like 'education'. Like Medusa, education has turned us into ossified adults; as incapable of learning as we are of play. As a rule of thumb, a successful educational environment should be one in which learning feels like play – and where individuals reflect this when asked.

The second major problem with education is this: it's mainly ill-designed 'push'. There is little or no adaptation to the specific passions and concerns of the learner. At best, students may be streamed or experience a limited choice of topics, but there is no systematic approach to finding out what they care about and modifying their opportunities accordingly.

Why is this a problem? The psychologist Daniel Levinson believed that there was an underlying structure to a person's life.[8] In particular, he believed that there were two periods in our life when we call into question the structure of our lives: the 'age 30 transition' and the 'mid-life transition'. As Levinson says, 'Adults hope that life beings at 40 – but the great anxiety is that it ends there'. What a depressing thought. Why should your life begin at 40? How have we managed to build a system where your life begins at 40?

In Western culture we are familiar with the term 'mid-life crisis', which broadly corresponds to Levinson's mid-life transition, and is often an unsettling period where people realize that they have more or less done what is expected of them up to that point, without stopping to consider what matters to them.

The story goes something like this: as a young person, your parents and society impress on you the importance of passing examinations, often with dire warnings about the fate of people who do not. Driven by a concern to please their parents, and within a system of anxiety-based learning, students pass examinations, eventually receiving a certificate that indicates their suitability for employment.

Having not had much opportunity to explore vocations, graduates will often take whatever job happens to come their way, driven by the need to meet their financial commitments and service the considerable debt which they have now amassed. They then begin learning how to do this job, at the same time grappling with the complexities of adult life for which they are almost entirely unprepared.

Before they know it, they have children and bills multiplying at an alarming rate and the next opportunity they have to reflect on their life choices is when their own children are about to embark on this same journey. They may well experience a deep sense that their true passions have not been realized, accompanied by a feeling of panic.

In 2011 the UK's Office for National Statistics asked a sample of 16-to-21-year-olds what work they would like to do as adults. Six years later, when they checked back, only one in 50 were working in the career that they wished for.[9]

This is not a good story. That we are systematically inscribing this narrative into people's lives is not a good thing. We have to put an end to this. It is hard to know whether a system which allows people to become the person they wish to be will result in a more productive society, but it cannot be a worse society than one in which people are used in this way.

From educational institutions to learning organizations

Let's sketch the outline of how a good educational system might work. The two processes described above should be reflected in two interlinked systems:

1 A process in which the concerns of the individual are 'mapped' in an ongoing fashion.

2 A process in which individuals are exposed to challenges of increasing sophistication, which resemble real-world environments (i.e. from an affective perspective).

I'd like to explain these two things in order.

When I sit down with my youngest daughter's teacher at parents evening, her teacher has been instructed (by the education system) to share with me a scientific-looking progress chart which indicates her progress against a number of measures of literacy and numeracy and which projects her likely scores at some time in the future.

I know the whole thing is bogus, the teacher may also suspect as much, but my daughter is nine – and she is already worried about tests – so as long as we play along, we are doing a good job of making my daughter feel anxious about passing tests.

If I were to ask her teacher: 'What are the top five things that my daughter cares about?', what do you think her teacher would say? On the one hand, her teacher probably doesn't especially enjoy the rather stale and scripted conversations that she is obliged to have – but equally, she would probably be entirely incapable of identifying the top five things that each of her students cares about.

If the affective context model is correct, then it is our concerns that drive our learning, so it should strike us as odd that someone tasked with supporting our learning is completely unaware of our concerns.

Now you may think what *I* am saying is odd, but consider this: Facebook understands your concerns very well, as does Google. In fact, enormous investments are currently being made into designing systems that use your online activity – such as your social media presence – to accurately map your concerns to the tiniest level of detail. Such as what kind of latte you like to drink on a Monday morning. Why? Because if we know what you care about, we can predict what you will buy.

How can it be that we have developed sophisticated systems for mapping concern in one area of life, but completely neglected them in another?

What I am saying is that at a very basic level, an educational system should have some way of mapping the totality of concerns that each individual has (their affective context). At a primitive level this could simply be a mentor – someone who takes considerable time to understand each individual in their care. But one would hope for much more.

Ideally we would see an integrated system (the kind that marketing is building) that comprises digital and personal elements, which provides a much more comprehensive picture of the learner and their progress. And by 'progress', I most certainly do not mean test scores – I mean the changing kaleidoscope of their concerns and passions and their developing capabilities. In short, a system that knows who we are, and where we are.

I don't think it is controversial to suggest that some of the best teachers that we have working in education today are those who take the time to understand what matters to their students, and to make the material relevant to the things they care about. The great shame is that we have neither recognized the central significance of this activity, nor built any sophistication whatsoever into how it is carried out. It's just a 'nice to have'.

Picture a world in which your nine-year-old child's enjoyment of debates has been nurtured, developed into an interest in legal cases, and they are now preparing to defend their client in a simple legal simulation. This is not a narrowly vocational agenda; instead it is about matching the concerns of one party (the individual) with the concerns of another (society), in such a way that both are happy.

The second process that I have outlined above is exposing people to challenges of increasing sophistication. The aim here is to blend learning and work seamlessly. By this I mean that at one end of the scale, an individual is purely learning and not undertaking any actual work (and may be paying for this experience), and at the other end is working, teaching and learning very little (and may be earning from this experience).

An example might be language translation. At the very beginning, when a person knows very little of a new language, they are learning and not capable of doing any actual translation work. As they grow in proficiency, they are presented with translation problems of increasing complexity and will start to earn money from the translation work they are doing, depending on their level of proficiency.

There are some important features of this model worth pointing out:

- It doesn't start or stop at a given age. Instead it carries on throughout a person's lifetime. When people talk about 'lifelong learning', check that they aren't talking about 'lifelong education'. Lifelong education is more often than not a discussion about how higher education institutions can make more money by selling certificates to older people. Lifelong learning is about how you can be exposed to a wide variety of challenges at any time in your life. Today the closest thing we have to this is computer gaming consoles: at any point in my life I can purchase a flight simulator game and hone my skills. The game will track my accomplishments.

- Learning institutions are not a 'place' that you go to, where you are separated from the world of work. Instead, the education system is distributed throughout our environment like veins throughout the body. I imagine there will be both physical and digital spaces that you can experience simulations of work, and places within work where you can practise in a supported way. We should be able to make learning far more accessible and far less exclusive. Our current education system continues to discriminate against capable individuals from a lower income bracket.

- An individual will likely have a portfolio of areas of learning – they may be highly proficient in, say, cyber-attacks (and earn money from this activity), and far less proficient in cookery (and pay for this activity). It is likely that a learning portfolio is a good strategy in a fast-moving employment market, and also helps protect against mental decline in later life.

- The learner can change direction at any time. Whilst the concern-mapping process suggests areas for exploration, they are free to explore any area of learning.

- Learning is not organized by topic, but by classes of challenge. These classes of challenge are more general at the lower levels (e.g. relationships), but become more specific at higher levels of proficiency (diplomacy or politics). Mapping out the 'phylogeny' of concern is a big step on the road to making education scientific. Though it's hard to envisage this now, it might be helpful to think of it a bit like the maps of musical genres produced by popular streaming services. These maps allow the provider to confidently predict: 'If you liked this and this… you might like this.'

- As a person successfully completes challenges they earn badges that reflect their accomplishments. These badges tell other people, such as employers, what that individual can do and form part of their personal profile. The current education system is a bubble whose bursting is entirely prevented by a tacit agreement with employers. So long as employers continue to buy the idea that a degree is a good predictor of future job success, then the education bubble is intact. But, increasingly, they don't. There isn't much evidence to support the link, much effort on the part of academic institutions to establish a link, and in large part the relationship is only there due to a lack of alternatives. A simple badging system, with proven predictive power, would send the whole system tumbling.

- Topics are drawn in around the challenges rather than being the focus of attention. So, for example, a person who is passionate about alleviating developing world debt might study elements of international law, economics, agriculture, history and anthropology as required.

- Real and simulated, virtual and physical challenges are blended across the learning gradient. In an important sense, work and play are also blended (with the result that the challenge of work–life balance largely disappears).

- The system is inherently meritocratic: people are paid according to the value of their contributions, in terms of the work they do and the help they give others to develop. This means that a younger person can easily earn more than an older person. Today, our hierarchical model tends to reward older people with higher salaries even as their capability declines, in a way that actively discourages learning the older we get. Our proposed model would more likely encourage experienced people to make an income through developing others.

Let's imagine how this might work in practice.

From an early age, Larry was interested in three-dimensional structures. He explored a number of different areas (sculpture, structural engineering, game design and architecture) where he could work with structures of different kinds and eventually settled on architecture, joining a group of more experienced individuals in this field.

In studying architecture he picked up elements of history, mathematics and physics as they applied to the challenges he faced. He also developed presentation skills, computer aided design (CAD) skills and the ability to pitch his ideas persuasively.

He is now sitting in a coffee shop, working on some plans for a new proposal, for which he will be paid. Some of the more difficult questions around materials he has to refer to his peers – for which they are paid – but Larry was also earning a fair bit from providing support to the group below him.

In recent months Larry has also started earning a little money from drone flights. He started out with the drone simulator game – part of his simulation subscription options – but he enjoyed it, and after he earned a few badges he was able to fly the pizza delivery drones. It didn't pay much, but it was fun, and pretty soon he would be able to fly some of the high-value package delivery drones over greater distances. Eventually, if he improved, he would be entitled to pilot the commercial multi-passenger drones. He'd need to complete a large number of simulated runs first, though.

Finally, conscious that drone-piloting may be fully automated at some time in the future, Larry was just starting out in circuit-board design. There was a local business offering some hands-on experience once a week and his skills with a soldering iron had come along quite a bit.

Overall, education should average out as a gradient with more opportunities to play, explore and experience at the outset, when a person's concerns have yet to come into focus. As the individual begins to develop their capability, the challenges should increase in sophistication, and the available resources to match. However, across the gradient learning is driven by challenges which, as they increase in complexity, merge naturally into work.

One question begged by this model is how to organize early education. Specifically, what kind of curriculum to put in place, since it is impractical to expose children to every conceivable type of role and we want to avoid the kind of patchwork that comprises the curriculum we have today.

Individual differences and the role of badges

As children enter the system there should be a thorough and comprehensive analysis of their concerns: this might include interviews with the child, with the parents, observations and an analysis of data relating to historical activity. More importantly, they should be introduced into a world where they can explore challenges and environments reflecting the sorts of environments outlined above.

As a general principle, wherever there is a challenge to be tackled or an environment to master, there should be people of a significantly higher level of capability present, so that individuals can learn not only through play but through observation.[10] Children should be free to roam these different environments, supported by someone who regularly observes and engages them in conversation regarding their reactions and discoveries.

The implication of this system is that teaching, in line with other professions, vanishes. The people who teach are the people with experience who chose to earn at least some of their income this way. It is not that teaching itself is singled out for elimination, rather one imagines all jobs will go this way, i.e. they will be broken up into their component tasks to be picked up by the people with the capability to do them.[11]

In the industrial era, progress was made by breaking the work of a craftsman into distinct roles, enabling the 'production line'. In the next progression, a role is broken into its component tasks, to be undertaken in a distributed manner. You might quickly imagine pros and cons of this model: on the one hand it would largely eradicate the problem of teachers not really knowing how to do tasks in the real world.

Today – a bit like our Martian system – education mainly exists in a kind of bubble in which it is not actually expected to interface directly with work. As a result, being out of touch with the world is tolerated if not tacitly encouraged among academics.

On the other hand, you might worry about whether people who are good at doing something would be good at supporting others to learn how to do it – and probably you are right to worry.

But let's start by dispelling the myth that a teaching qualification makes you good at supporting learners; it doesn't. Like most qualifications, having a load of content dumped on you doesn't actually help much with the job to be done. Most teachers will tell you that the stuff you learn on a teaching programme doesn't bear much relation to the challenges you face in a classroom.

In our model, people will learn by doing. If they develop the ability to support learning, it will be reflected in the badges they earn. People interested in computer science may therefore choose a mentor who not only has impressive accomplishments, but badges for the quality of their support. Of course there will be resources available to people who wish to develop their ability to support learning.

Once again, what I am describing is a system of tiered challenges, an environment where at most points one is simultaneously learning and working, paying and earning, teaching others and being taught oneself. Not unlike the way we have learned for millennia, in fact.

Once a pattern begins to emerge – not necessarily a pattern of what a person is good at but a pattern of their concerns – then it should be possible to begin to steer the process, suggesting areas for further exploration. This point is important – it is not a child's capabilities but their *concerns* that steer their development. If we were simply to focus on what people are good at (but don't care about), there is a good chance that learning will be inefficient and the individual miserable.

In this model there is nothing to stop a child specializing early – for example, quickly climbing the ranks of challenge complexity to become an accomplished and high-earning cyber-attacker at the age of 12 (or a commercial drone pilot). Equally, children can continue to explore – indeed, adult learners may well be accomplished in some areas but relative novices in others.

Once again, there is no sharp distinction between learning and work; instead each person has a set of badges reflecting their accomplishments and a portfolio of activities where their capability ranges from novice (learning) to expert (working).

The idea of badges that reflect our accomplishments is also a significant departure from educational orthodoxy in which we earn certificates for the tests we have passed. By contrast badges are very much more about what you can *do*, rather than what you *know*. This is a much better system for all concerned; someone who is considering whether or not to pay you to do something can immediately assess your level of capability and task fit. Indeed, it would make sense to do this using an algorithm which automatically identifies the capable, available people for a task.

Each individual would have a portfolio of tasks from which they earn an income, matched to their level of capability across a range of interests. And consider it from the perspective of the individual – in deciding whether or not to take on a piece of work, a key consideration will be the opportunity to learn new badges. Businesses will be incentivized to provide assignments that provide opportunities to learn.

A system of badges would require a portable profile. Currently a record of your achievements and learning is often held by the organizations for whom you have worked. This is becoming increasingly problematic as people move from one organization to another with increasing rapidity.

Organizations will either need to configure themselves to offer a wide variety of short-term assignments, or accept a more 'plug and play' approach to resourcing. In this world an individual will own and maintain their own record of achievements, which will be a central, visible record of their accomplishments and evidence of their capability. In fact, this is already starting to take place; sites such as LinkedIn providing a unified marketplace for talent and recruitment.

What is missing here is the 'tree structure' of vocational development that we have described, together with an accrediting authority. I can record, for example, that I have 'successfully led' teams of a certain size within a Fortune 100 company, but this is like recording that I have 'successfully completed' a computer game – it doesn't say very much at all about my specific accomplishments. A proper system of badges would identify very specific achievements and a credible measure of my success. This could well involve ratings by other, credible, people.

The nature of challenges means that topics and capabilities respond to the gravitational pull of the task – mastery of computers might well involve learning to write script and to use numbers, but only in ways that relate to the learner's concerns. It is not that geography and history and so on are no longer taught, it is just that they are taught in a way which is relevant, which relates to the thing that someone is trying to do.

Overall, the structure of the system resembles something like a tree, with a few branches at the base, each of which divides again and again as challenges become more specific and complex. People can advance up the structure as they demonstrate capability and earn badges for their accomplishments, but they can equally move back down the structure and explore other branches.

The system is organized not around content and curricula, but challenges and concerns – around the things people care about, as these are reflected in the world of work. And this, because learning is affective.

What I have outlined above is consistent with a free-market approach to education, where work and learning are atomized at the level of tasks, and a blended marketplace for both created in which an individual can balance what they earn from work with what they pay to learn.

Free-market thinking has not always delivered the utopia we might have wished for in other areas, however, so what is to stop this descending into some dreadful money-making scheme?

In my view, public bodies should retain tight control over the system of badges and accreditation if they are to prevent the emergence of a kind of labour-market racketeering. By ensuring a common standard for accomplishments and the way in which these are assessed they can reduce the risk of a 'cash for badges' economy emerging to replace the 'cash for certificates' one that we have today.

Even as I write, though, private sector organizations such as LinkedIn are quietly assembling the component parts of a central record of accomplishments, and this should concern us, since it is already possible for me to pay to make myself more visible to potential employers.

I'd like to end this chapter by defining the purpose of education:

Education should support learning by providing a process that allows individuals to discover a sense of purpose, and to make it part of their working life.

In the next chapter I will talk about language. Language is central to thinking about learning because so much human learning takes place via language: the things that we read, the stories that people tell, the content people consume. If we understood language, we could use it more effectively.

Key points

- Our modern education system is largely based around historical accident and the demands of an industrial era for daycare and obedience.

- An education system based around learning would require two basic mechanisms: ongoing mapping of individual concerns, and freedom to explore challenges of graduated complexity.

- A well-formed education would integrate work and learning along a gradient, with activities at one end purely learning (and paid for) and those at the other end largely working (and earning).

- The integration of learning and work extends throughout a person's life and across all contexts, so that an individual has a dynamic portfolio of learning–work activities.

- Learning is task- and not topic-centric. It is organized according to classes of challenge which relate to real-world activities.

- Teaching becomes a task, not a role – one of the many activities that individuals may add to their portfolio depending on their concerns and capability.

- Recognition is given according to accomplishments, where an individual has successfully completed a challenge. An individual's record of accomplishments forms the basis for employment decisions.

Endnotes

1 The 1562 Statute of Artificers and Apprentices.
2 National Science Foundation. Enough with the lecturing, 12 May 2014, nsf.gov/news/news_summ.jsp?cntn_id=131403 (archived at https://perma.cc/2SZ7-HXVF)
3 J Panksepp (1998) *Affective Neuroscience: The foundations of human and animal emotions*, Oxford University Press
4 A Damasio (2018) *The Strange Order of Things: Life, feeling and the making of cultures*, Pantheon Books
5 J R Abel and R Deitz. Do big cities help college graduates find better jobs? Liberty Street Economics, 20 May 2013, libertystreeteconomics.newyorkfed.org/2013/05/do-big-cities-help-college-graduates-find-better-jobs.html (archived at https://perma.cc/WF8C-E2R7)
6 M M Lombardo and R W Eichinger (1996), *The Career Architect Development Planner*, Lominger, Minneapolis
7 K H Kim. The creativity crisis: The decrease in creative thinking scores on the Torrance tests of creative thinking, *Creativity Research Journal*, 2011, 23 (4), 285–95
8 D J Levinson, with C N Darrow, E B Klein and M Levinson (1978) *Seasons of a Man's Life*, Random House, New York
9 S Coughlan. How do career dreams really work out?, BBC News, 27 September 2018, www.bbc.com/news/education-45666030 (archived at https://perma.cc/5ZVQ-XEZ5)
10 Fans of the learning theorist Vygotsky will note that this is not unlike his 'zone of proximal development'.
11 This is sometimes referred to as the gig economy.

Language and learning

04

Sounds that express feelings

'To use the same words is not a sufficient guarantee of understanding; one must use the same words for the same genus of inward experience; ultimately one must have one's experiences in common.'

FRIEDRICH NIETZSCHE

Back in the 1950s, following the Second World War, people were eagerly awaiting their robots. The war effort had spurred huge advances in science and the first computers, initially created for code-breaking, entered popular consciousness. Isaac Asimov's 'Three Laws of Robotics' appeared in his collection of short stories *I, Robot,* and Robbie the Robot strutted onto the cinema screen in the 1956 science fiction film *Forbidden Planet.*

The 1967 episode of *Star Trek* entitled 'Tomorrow is Yesterday' featured a 'female' computer, and the following delightful dialogue:

Captain Kirk: Engineering officer Scott informs warp engines damaged, but can be made operational and re-energized.
Ship's computer: Computed and recorded, dear.
Captain Kirk: Computer, you will not address me in that manner. Compute.
Ship's computer: Computed, dear.
Captain Kirk: Mr Spock, I ordered this computer and its interlinking systems repaired!
Mr Spock: I have investigated it, Captain. To correct the fault will require an overhaul of the entire computer system. A minimum of three weeks at a star base.
Captain Kirk: I wouldn't mind so much, if only it didn't get so... affectionate.
Mr Spock: It also has an unfortunate tendency to giggle.
First officer: I take it that a lady computer is not routine?

Could there be anything worse than an affectionate computer? We had better fix that fault pretty soon. Sentimental or not, it seemed obvious to consumers that it was only a matter of time before a robot butler would be added to our TV and microwave as an everyday household appliance.

It wasn't just us simple-minded consumers who were thinking along these lines: artificial intelligence researchers confidently predicted swift progress. Marvin Minsky, a technical advisor for the 1968 movie *2001: A Space Odyssey*, judged the AI features of HAL 9000 to be a conservative estimate.

So... where's my robot?

It turned out to be a bit harder than anyone thought. Computers just didn't 'get it'. To take an example from machine translation, the phrase: 'The spirit is willing but the flesh is weak' would become: 'The vodka is good but the meat is rotten' in Russian. And there were other things just as bad.

Computer scientists had assumed that people speak in words, and that each word has a sound that you could train a computer to recognize – only, when they tried to do this, they discovered that people usually speak in a fairly unbroken pattern of noises, where the breaks don't even correspond neatly to the breaks between words. Worse still, the same word may sound very different in the mouths of different people – or even the same person – depending on the context. In the technical jargon there were no 'invariant features'.

This is why, even today, we often struggle to get Siri or Alexa to understand us, even when speaking with artificial clarity. I routinely lie in bed, shrieking 'Alexa! Bedroom. Light. Off!' to my intelligent assistant. I have no idea what the neighbours think.

Vision was worse. It turned out that computers couldn't recognize objects from what they looked like – they had to know what those objects really were. What I mean is this: we might *think* that we can feed a picture of a cat to a computer and say 'This is a cat', but actually the cat picture is just a pattern of light and shade – in some contexts a similar pattern may not be a cat, and in others a very different pattern may actually be... a cat.

There was a strange circularity to it all – you had to sort of know what you were looking at to know what it is. Sights and sounds were all about context – you couldn't pick up one small element without discovering it was attached to everything else that a person had learned. The only things computers could do well were the things most people did terribly poorly – logical things, like finding big prime numbers, or chess.

So people expecting results got very disappointed, investment dried up, and the expression 'AI winter' was coined to describe our deep disappointment in the boffins and the corresponding lack of cash for AI projects.

Put simply, the reason we entered AI winter is that we thought that we understood ourselves, so we incorrectly assumed it would be easy to get computers to do what we do. But we actually had no idea how humans work, and we found this out the hard way by getting computers to process stuff the way we *thought* humans were processing stuff – and discovering that didn't have anything like the results we were expecting. In a sense the philosophers and psychologists with their Cartesian baggage, not the boffins, were to blame.

One of the more intractable problems – a problem that we are still unable to solve – is language processing. In the early days of AI the reasoning went something like this: 'Language is made up of words. Words have definitions. If we feed the computer a dictionary and some stuff on grammar, it will be able to understand language.'

Theorists such as Noam Chomsky fed this delusion. Chomsky was a rationalist, one of a great many smart people doomed to failure by erroneous assumptions. He argued for the existence of a universal grammar that followed a common set of rules, and for a 'Language Acquisition Device' in the brain that somehow contained these rules.

It was a nice idea; if it were true, then it might be possible to discover these rules, transcribe them as a computer algorithm and type it into the Amstrad 64.

It was a spectacular failure. Not only did people's use of language stubbornly refuse to conform to rules, somehow no matter how much information we fed the computers they couldn't understand what we were talking about.

This is still true today. As I write, *Wired* magazine states: 'GPT-3 [a new type of AI programme] is learning our language.' But it is not, for the same reason that your shadow is not learning to dance. Like all AI programmes, it is merely a statistical approximation to what a human being would say – a very good one – but ultimately a shadow cast by billions of people sharing their sentiments online.

As the technology gets better and better, it can make better guesses at what a human would say – but at no point does it *understand* what is being said. The process of creating better and better approximations to what people say does not culminate in understanding, just as the process of creating better sound recordings does not result in a singer.

In 2015, an article claimed that IBM's AI system – Watson – could read and understand Bob Dylan lyrics.[1] But what the computer claimed to understand (that Dylan was talking about 'love fading') was not what Dylan was actually singing about. Dylan was singing about other things – like the war in Vietnam. But Watson didn't understand this because Watson was, in essence, just counting the words and adding up the ones that occurred more frequently. Human beings don't use words like this at all.[2]

So how *do* human beings use words, and why is this important?

I'd like to talk about how you feel. I'd like you to think back to a relationship break-up – if possible, to a time when you were in love with someone, then something happened and you went your separate ways. If you have experienced this, then you will probably still know how awful that can feel.

When relationships fall apart, other people use words like 'upset' to describe the way you are feeling. But to you, words like 'upset' probably don't do your feelings justice. What you feel is more like a hurricane – ripping things up, tearing through your life, wrenching at your insides. 'Upset' doesn't begin to cover it.

When talking about our emotions, it sometimes seems that we lack the words to adequately describe how we feel; that the range of words to describe our feelings – happy, sad, angry – is just too small.

But I'd like to show you that we have many more words to describe our feelings than you imagined. Let me introduce you to a few. Here's the first one: 'home'.

Now, you might think that the word 'home' describes a building, not how you feel, but hear me out. Imagine trying to define 'home' for a computer. You might draw a picture of a house, or of different kinds of houses. A small child might show you a picture of a snail shell and ask if this is its home, and you might say 'yes'.

Fairly soon you would realize houses can look like pretty much anything. You might define it as a place where someone lives. But consider this: people whose houses have been burgled sometimes complain that it doesn't feel like 'home' any more – and maybe as a result they move. The same house that felt like home one day doesn't feel like home the next.

Equally, when people move into a new house they often say something like 'it doesn't feel like home yet'. How would you explain this to a computer?

How would a computer understand the song lyric: 'Wherever I lay my hat, that's my home'?

When you think about it, it becomes clear that the word 'home' is not really about a building at all. It is a word to describe how you feel. A place where you feel you belong. You can feel 'at home' in different places, and sometimes not at home in the same place. You can stand on a beach and say 'Finally, I'm home!' We even imagine that our snail has some kind of feeling attached to being curled up in its own shell – and probably it does.

Here's another feeling word: chair. You probably aren't used to thinking about the word 'chair' as a word like 'happy', 'sad', etc – as a word that describes how you feel. But it is.

The odd thing about words like 'chair' is that although logicians have tended to think of them as describing a certain class of objects, we have never been able to explain the definition in such a way that a computer can reliably identify chairs. Why is this?

It turns out that when you say 'chair', what you really mean is 'something that makes me feel "chair"'. To see this, consider that exactly the same object can feel like a chair in one setting but not in another (say, an art gallery).

There is no common set of features to all chairs – all they have in common is that they are things that you feel are appropriate to sit on. You could quite easily travel to another culture, sit on something you felt was a chair, then feel embarrassment when told that it is actually a ritual chopping block. Now you feel that it isn't a chair.

What we mean when we say chair is actually something more like 'I feel like this is the kind of thing that is appropriate for sitting on, in this context.'

This is how children learn about chairs: not through dictionary definitions, but through refining the way they feel about things through experience – a sort of extension of homeostasis. A young child might well sit on a chair sculpture in an art gallery – but their parent's shocked reactions change the way they feel about objects in this context. Children are constantly clambering on things, and their parents constantly hissing: 'Get down from there!' through clenched teeth.

Here's what I am saying: **all of our words are feeling words**. All of them. From the word 'home' to the word 'chair'. They all describe how we feel about stuff. They do not describe a class of things in the world; instead they describe how things and experiences make us feel. Every one of the tens of thousands of words you know describes a subtly different feeling.

This means that our words are always fuzzy and changeable to some extent – and I am never 100 per cent sure that what I mean by a word is the same as what you mean.

It's worth taking some time to let this sink in. Sometimes people object and say things like 'Well, surely 1066, the Battle of Haystings, isn't a feeling – it's a fact'. If you are British, then you will probably have been taught that 1066 is a special date – the date of the Battle of Haystings, in fact. Thinking of it conjures up memories of sitting in history class, the lurid image of Harold with an arrow in his eye perhaps.

How about 1812? How do you feel about that? If you are Canadian, you probably don't feel like 1066 is any more special than, say, 1842 – but you probably have strong feelings about 1812. Every Canadian knows that Canada won the war of 1812. 1812 is memorable precisely because it feels special.

How about this: what do you think about the number 7? And the number 18? Can you tell me exactly how your feeling about '7' differs from your feeling about '18'? How about the number 3,712? I suspect you have very different feelings towards 18 than you do towards 3,712. Unless '3712' is your password – in which case you are shocked that I brought it up. Why is that? Computers don't feel differently about numbers.

So now imagine the problem that presents for AI. Every time the computer asks, 'What does this word mean?', the honest answer is: 'It just describes the way we feel about stuff'. What does 'chair' mean? Answer: it means we feel like something is a chair.

We don't have a computer that thinks like we do, because we don't have a computer that feels. The only way to get a computer to understand the word 'chair' the way we do would be by repeatedly yelling at it (or something similarly aversive) as it sits on the wrong things. But we don't do anything like this, and until that changes AI will never be remotely like human intelligence.

You might wonder how computers today manage to translate language. The answer is: they don't. What they do is search around for human translations of phrases and 'copy and paste' the results together. In effect, they don't understand the problem, so they copy our homework. Even the most advanced AI systems we have today are merely elaborate statistical approximations; they predict what a person would say based on what lots of people before have said.

This is not to say that computers can't be intelligent; they just solve problems in completely different ways – logical ways. For example when it comes to identifying pictures of cats, instead of looking at a picture and thinking: 'Does this feel like a cat?', the computer looks at all the pictures that *we* have identified as cats and compares it to those. And of course you can see why this would go wrong.

This is a problem that has foxed philosophers since Plato. They got confused because they assumed that words somehow refer to things in the outside world, rather than expressing feelings inside of us. One person who learned this the hard way was the philosopher Ludwig Wittgenstein. He developed a particular fascination for language.

In his early writing he starts out with a really clean, logical description of the world. A world in which words refer to things, and where the logical relations between words reflect logical relations between things in the world. He says things like:

> The existence of an internal relation between possible states of affairs expresses itself in language by an internal relation between the propositions presenting them.[3]

That almost sounds mathematical, doesn't it? But the more he thinks about this, the more his system falls apart. In his later writings he starts to sound quite mystical. In *On Certainty* he writes:

> But more correctly: The fact that I use the word 'hand' and all the other words in my sentence without a second thought, indeed that I should stand before the abyss if I wanted so much as to try doubting their meanings – shows that absence of doubt belongs to the essence of the language-game...

He has started to think of language as a 'game', and of words as things that can't exist independently of the way people use them. To ask: 'What does a word mean?' is to enter into a whole world of doubt, for the later Wittgenstein.

But Wittgenstein is wrong that language is like a game: he used the expression to describe his feeling that language is based around a tacit agreement between people to use words in the same way (and that therefore there is no such thing as a language that you can invent for yourself). But the problem is that games have rules, and language doesn't have rules because fundamentally whether or not a word is the right word is about whether or not it feels right. Just like ethics, as we will see in a bit.

There's a very specific reason why we 'use words without a second thought': *it's because words just express how we feel*. We don't think about the appropriate word to use (except in unusual cases), we just speak the words that correspond to how we feel.

We literally use words without thinking most of the time. Take a look at how you participate in an everyday conversation: the other person is saying something – feelings start bubbling up inside you (for example 'That reminds me of an experience I had!') – and before you know it, words are tumbling out of your mouth. It's very rare (even for us introverts) to formulate exactly what you wish to say in advance.

When this does happen, for example when someone is reading from a script, we can generally immediately detect that what they are saying is unnatural and scripted somehow. It takes a lot of skill for a movie scriptwriter to script speech, and for the actors to deliver it, in a way that doesn't come across as pre-meditated.

You may have noticed that I endeavour to write in this way – lots of dashes and obvious jumps – somewhat spoiling the deliberate and quasi-logical rules of grammar, but more closely reflecting the way expressions come to us in the moment – bubbling up from our sentiments.

Wittgenstein's mistake was simple: he thought that words were about things, not feelings. As long as he believed this, he was screwed. It strikes me that Wittgenstein was a far smarter person than I, but **his basic mistake illustrates the dilemma we face today with understanding human beings: it doesn't matter how smart you are – if you start with the wrong assumptions you won't be able to get to the answer.** Words don't refer to things, they express feelings. It is the feelings that are about things.

In the field of AI people assumed that humans store factual data about events, rather than their reactions to events. In education, this same error led us to imagine that we can create environments in which people memorize information, rather than environments in which they experience a reaction.

The role of words in learning

But the nature of learning doesn't change much as we age, or from one species to the next – it just gets obscured by educational ritual. At school we are told that learning consists of memorizing stuff in order to pass a test; but learning proper continues in the margins as we learn how to fit in from our peers: what's cool, what's not (and you won't learn much about that from the teacher standing in front of you).

As adults, this pattern continues: we join an organization and are given educational modules to complete – but the real learning takes place as we observe the reactions of those around us to the things that we do. The induction programme may tell you about the standard operating procedures and company values – but what really matters may be a very different story – one that you will discover for yourself in the ensuing months.

Many people will report taking six months to a year to 'find their feet'. 'Finding one's feet' is an expression that means knowing what the right thing to do is in a given culture, and human beings determine what is the right or wrong thing to do by observing the reactions of those around them.

For example: imagine you join a swanky London-based legal firm. The induction programme tells you the company values 'authenticity' and 'inclusivity'. One day the zany new intern decides to wear his Hawaiian shirt to a meeting with a senior partner. You wonder what will happen. Judging from the partner's facial expression, you conclude that wearing a Hawaiian shirt to important meetings is *not* a good idea and not an acceptable expression of 'authenticity' or encompassed by the term 'inclusivity'.

Since this kind of implicit knowledge is rarely written down, and since learning experiences are not designed with this in mind, it can take a long time for people to be confident about what they are doing.

Our philosophical biases have led us down a blind alley; we imagined the human mind to be like a blank page, on which words could be inscribed. We built machines that replaced the book, faithfully storing whatever information we inscribed, all the while overlooking that humans store their *reactions* to the world (or even their reactions to facts) rather than the facts themselves. We designed an educational system in which people were expected to memorize information, rather than react to experiences, and it all turned into a terrible mess.

Let me give you a simple example: some of you may have noticed that I misspelt 'Hastings' as 'Haystings' when describing the 'Battle of Hastings' earlier. If you did notice it, what was your reaction? Were you surprised – perhaps a little shocked? Was there a hint of outrage or a shift in your perceptions of me? I suspect it is the sort of thing you might remember, and perhaps even remark to a friend 'I'm not sure how credible the author is – I mean, he can't even spell Hastings!' Maybe you even looked it up.

Surprise and indignation are the way we react to things that violate accepted norms. These reactions help such peculiar events to stay with us, and are more likely to make their way into gossip as a result. Each reaction signals an adjustment to your mental model of the world – an investment of additional effort on your part. Of course not all the unexpected things that happen in the world drive a change in your thinking: only the ones significant enough to elicit a reaction.

How could a system of noises like this possibly work if we all feel differently about things? The answer is, it couldn't. Fortunately we are set up, biologically, to feel similarly about things (people will yelp in pain, just as dogs do), and then we go through a long process of maturation and socialization where we learn to make similar sounds in response to shared experiences. When it is rainy and cold, for example we say: 'Ugh! I hate this weather', and other people say: 'Me too', and we feel a sense of connection at feeling the same things, because we are making the right noises.

In this way our personality, reactions, memory and culture form an interlocking mechanism. Our culture determines what we react to: what we perceive, consider and remember. Over time, our reactions determine the type of person we become (and vice-versa). The stories we tell about ourselves reflect the things that matter to us, which in turn connect us to the broader library of stories about things that matter that makes up our culture.

As far back as the human story goes, the story format has been, and continues to be, the central mechanism for learning and knowledge transfer. In 1969 the psychologists Bower and Clark showed that if you had people convert unrelated words into a story, it improved their retention seven-fold.[4] This is one of the largest memory effects known to cognitive psychologists.

It works, because in creating a story, we add emotional significance to words that are otherwise unconnected; we convert them into a format we are designed to store. Your body is a vehicle for carrying stories around, stories which in turn connect us to each other and a shared sense of meaning.

Wittgenstein was misled because from the outset he tried to create a logical description of the world. What he missed is that logic and mathematics are not a natural language – they are an artificial language. Unlike human language, which describes the way things in the world make us feel, mathematics and logic *are* languages recently created to describe the logical relations between things in the world.

As such they are almost impossible for humans to use. The vast majority of people struggle with complex maths, and the psychological literature is brimming with the list of ways in which human thinking deviates from the logical.

To see this, consider the number 3,756,981 – how does that feel? Probably it doesn't feel much different to 3,684,782. But here's the thing: they both feel like 'a lot', don't they? (And of course beyond a certain point any number – no matter how big – just feels like 'a lot'.) This is why you will later struggle to recall which of the numbers you heard – because they both feel very similar. You probably have a distinct reaction to the number '3', so you might remember that 'it was a big number starting with a three'.

'Feeling like a lot' is how humans react to really big numbers. Mathematics and logic are, however, languages perfectly suited for use by computers – enabling computers to do things that we can't, but equally ensuring that computers will never be able to understand the world in the way that we do.

This is the reason why humans struggle to understand the difference between one hundred billion and one trillion – because despite the fact that they are dramatically different numbers they *feel* very similar to us – they both feel like vast numbers. This is not a bias or a flaw in our cognition, it is simply a consequence of the way that we work: we store our reactions to things, and where our reactions are similar our memory will be muddled.

So generations of philosophers have made the same basic error and tied themselves up in knots as a result: they have assumed that words refer to things, and that the relationships between our words corresponds to the relationships between things in the world. But this is wrong: words refer only to our *feelings*, and it is our feelings that are about things. This accounts for the weird inexactitude and marvellous poetry of words – our feelings are blurred at the edges and can change depending on the context.

Of course the reason one becomes a philosopher is the pursuit of truth (and you can be sure there is always an emotional reason behind that), and so saying: 'All cognition is a form of emotion' is immediately deeply troubling to some people – it seems to imply a sort of reckless relativism. But nothing could be further from the truth: our feelings are based on our physical connection to the world, and because we are physiologically similar creatures, our experiences have a common root.

Our cultures then determine what we see and what we do not, according to what matters: in one culture a person might say 'Did you see that Rolex!?'; in another people might not notice the type of watch someone is wearing, and in a third 'watches' might have no significance at all.

Our experiences of the world are built on a foundation that extends all the way back to our single-celled origins: our homeostatic roots. When two people say: 'This sand is hot', it is because they are designed, physiologically, to experience it in the same way – to feel the same way about it. This is why the philosopher Friedrich Nietzsche writes: 'All evidence of truth come only from the senses'.[5]

And so two scientists will be able to make the same observations, only because the way a person feels about things does not 'float free' but is hardwired into our physical experience of the world. Our diversity as individuals extends from our similarities as humans, much as the branches of a tree extend from the trunk.

Once you begin to understand that words – all our words – simply refer to the way we feel about things (the reaction they cause in us), some of the difficult problems in AI and philosophy start to unravel. Words don't ever have precise meanings. Their meaning can change in different circumstances or depending on how we feel. The word 'dog' means very different things to people who love dogs and to those who are afraid of them. Consider the phrase 'The dog bounded towards him' – is that a happy thought or a frightening one?

We learn to use a word as we grow up, not from reading it a dictionary. How a word feels in one culture may be very different from how the (translated) word feels in another. People who are bilingual may feel like different people when they speak each language (and perhaps they really are).[6]

So words express feelings, and feelings are reactions to the world. Of all the philosophers I have read – from Heraclitus to Zizek – only Friedrich Nietzsche seemed to have truly understood this. In *The Gay Science* he writes: 'Thoughts are the shadows of our feelings – always darker, emptier, simpler'.[7]

In all likelihood, the word 'gay' caused a reaction in you, altering your perceptions and expectations significantly. When Nietzsche wrote his book, the word was innocuous, synonymous with 'joyful'. Our thoughts are the traces of the sentiments that accompanied our experience, and our words are merely vocalizations of the complex emotions to which they correspond.

When I say 'dog', I refer to my lifetime's experience of these creatures. Some elements you and I will have in common, for example the distinctive barking noises that they make, but on another level you and I may feel very different things when we say the word 'dog' – just as two people may both use the word 'love' but remain worlds apart.

When we use words to describe our world, we are describing how our experiences made us feel. This is *why* humans are natural storytellers – words reflect the emotional impact of experiences, and when we string them together we create a story. Because we grow up in a shared culture – by which I mean a culture in which people, to some extent, react in similar ways to similar things – I can learn to use words. I can use a word that describes a set of feelings in me, and be reasonably confident that it describes a similar set of feelings in you.

With words, I can make you feel what I feel. Interestingly, music also has this power, something to which we will return later on – but, if it helps, think of words as being much like the notes in a song: they are noises that express how you feel, and when you sing them someone else feels something similar.

We have become so used to our cinematic experiences being accompanied by a soundtrack that we overlook the question: 'Why?' Why do movies almost always have a soundtrack? A good soundtrack complements the storyline, deepening our emotional experiences, accentuating our reactions.

You can begin to see more clearly where education goes wrong: when parents read stories to children, the ones who do it well use exaggerated expressions, gestures and intonation to do so. This is a critical part of the process, since it is the *reactions* that the story causes that are stored.

But education doesn't understand learning: lecturers are rarely storytellers – they don't explicitly recognize the importance of dramatic expression in encoding information. Often learning is reduced to mere facts. Picture a parent whose bedtime story approach is a PowerPoint show summarizing Goldilocks and the Three Bears in a series of bullet points. You are far more likely to remember those teachers who conveyed genuine enthusiasm and passion for their subject, and who told stories that brought things to life.

The relationship between feelings and thoughts is similar to that between colour and paintings: a painting is made up of patches of colour. There are no paintings that are not made up of patches of colour – because that is what a painting is. There are no thoughts that are not a pattern of emotions – because that's what thoughts are.

The colours themselves (like our feelings) may be relatively simple, but through combination and complexity they give rise to elaborate, meaningful patterns. We give names to paintings – names like 'Mona Lisa' – just as we give names to thoughts – like 'chair' or 'home'. These are our words. There is no point in wondering if we shouldn't have more words to describe our emotions – every word we use describes a distinct emotion. Every word describes a feeling (yes, even the number '42').

Our minds are also remarkably good at imagining how we would feel; in the future, or in a different place.[8] I don't mean *accurately* predicting how we would feel (we are actually quite bad at that); what I mean is that you can sit on a train and easily imagine what it would feel like to sit on those rooftops that are passing by – or be the person walking in the rain, struggling with an umbrella. You might be wrong, but there is no doubt that you can easily imagine it.

It seems that human beings imagine feelings by default – not as something they learn to do later on. I have often wondered what it is about soft toys that makes my daughter want to purchase them wherever we go. So I asked her. She said: 'I can talk to them about things I would feel silly talking on my own.' The mind of a child automatically ascribes feelings to everything, and has no trouble at all with cuddly toys.

If you have some small children to hand, try this experiment: ask them how a tree would feel if you were to kick it. Or how a house feels when everyone in the family leaves to go on holiday. You will be surprised at how easily they answer these sorts of questions. If you ask an adult these sorts of questions, they might think you are suffering from stress – or they might think that you are rather poetic. This is because our society contrives to obscure what is really going on in our minds (thanks to Plato and co).

This way of encoding the world, i.e. according to the reactions that experiences create in us, opens us up to possibilities that are closed to computers – like poetry and metaphor. It also works well with parallel processing – the kind of processing that networks of neurons do. When we see something, the visual features trigger a set of emotional response and – Bam! – instantly we feel what it is (of course we can be wrong).

We usually use the word 'know' in this sentence, but it would be more accurate to say that we *feel* what something is. This process takes place before we are consciously aware of it; our nervous system will prepare us for 'fight or flight' when we encounter threatening stimuli before we can even say what the threatening thing is.[9] What we absolutely do *not* do is go through a protracted search process where we compare what we are seeing, one by one, to things stored in our memory. That would be silly and would never work.

Of course, if you had enough processing power and a big enough database, you could create the *illusion* of a system that does something similar – for example translating a phrase by looking at millions of similar human translations and calculating a best guess.

When humans describe things for other people, we chain together sets of feelings, using words to describe those feelings. But because two very different things can evoke similar feelings in us, we are able to make creative leaps. The poetic line: 'I wandered lonely as a cloud' only makes sense because we are able to link the feeling of being alone with a feeling that we have when we see a cloud alone in the sky.

In fact, because words describe feelings, not things, we can say all manner of things that other people can understand but computers never will. I can say: 'He was like a bull in a china shop during the meeting' and you can understand it, because I am comparing the feelings that underlie both – not because the person in question looks like a bull, or because the meeting was held in a china shop.

Of course we can tell a computer that 'bull in a china shop' means reckless, but if you had said 'a kangaroo in a glassware store' I would have understood you (and possibly thought it was quite amusing), and the computer would not. The reason we are able to make this comparison is that both situations evoke a similar sentiment – not because of their semantic features.

In summary, we use words to describe our feelings, and when we speak them other people have similar feelings. That's why people are natural storytellers – everything is encoded as feelings, and words evoke those feelings.

If you listen closely to people having a conversation, something like this is usually happening: one person tells a story, then another person tells a related story and so on. If you look *really* closely at this exchange you will see that what binds the conversation into a whole is *feeling*: the reason I chose to tell you one story rather than another is that your story made me feel something that I have felt somewhere else. This is what we mean when we say 'reminding'. We might say: 'Looking at the birds in the blue sky reminded me of that time on the beach' and what is really going on is that one feeling is activating another similar feeling.

The building blocks of thought are not 'facts' or 'knowledge'; instead they are 'reactions' and 'stories' and 'experiences'. Because of the way that different people react differently to events, it is important to establish a connection to someone if you wish them to change in some way.

'Establishing a connection' is the kind of thing that people tend to feel is important in lots of contexts, without quite being able to say why, so I would like to be quite precise: establishing a connection means understanding what matters to a person, and communicating that you feel the same way. You meet a girl at a party. You say: 'I love this song', she says: 'I love it too', and in that moment you both smile.

Language is one way in which we share the things that matter. Understanding what matters to a person is essential, since these psychological features determine those things that they will react to, and a person's reactions determine the way in which their experiences are encoded. When we interact with anyone we are either responding to the things they already care about ('pull'), or we are building new cares on top of the old ('push').

In the next chapter we will look at what this means for learning design.

Key points

- Words don't refer to things; instead they express the way we feel about things.

- A thought is a pattern of feelings (or reactions) to something we experience.

- When communicating with others, we express a number of related feelings in the form of words, and this activates corresponding feelings in the listener.

- In designing learning we aim to create an experience that will cause a reaction in an individual.

- We cannot confidently predict the reaction that will be caused in someone unless we understand what matters to them.

Endnotes

1 M Swant. Ad of the Day: IBM's Watson Talks Love and Loss With Bob Dylan in Advertising's Oddest Pairing, *Adweek*, 7 October 2015, www.adweek.com/brand-marketing/ad-day-ibms-watson-talks-love-and-loss-bob-dylan-advertisings-oddest-pairing-167420/ (archived at https://perma.cc/D22Q-E4M9)

2 My thanks to Roger Schank for bringing this example to my attention.

3 L Wittgenstein (1922) *Tractatus Logico-Philosophicus*, Routledge & Kegan Paul, London

4 G Bower and M Clark. Narrative stories as mediators for serial learning, *Psychonomic Science*, 1969, **15**, 181–2

5 F Nietzsche and W A Kaufmann (1989) *Beyond Good and Evil: Prelude to a philosophy of the future*, Vintage Books, New York

6 P Athanasopoulos, E Bylund, G Montero-Melis, L Damjanovic, A Schartner, A Kibbe, N Riches and G Thierry. Two languages, two minds, *Psychological Science*, 2015, **26**

7 F Nietzsche (2010) *The Gay Science: With a prelude in rhymes and an appendix of songs*, Vintage Books, New York

8 S K Langer (1967/1982) *Mind: An essay on human feeling (Vol 1)*, Johns Hopkins University Press, Baltimore, MD

9 N Burra, A Hervais-Adelman, D Kerzel, M Tamietto, B de Gelder and A Pegna. Amygdala activation for eye contact despite complete cortical blindness, *Journal of Neuroscience*, 2013, **33** (25), 10,483–9

Learning design 05
Push or pull?

When I left my job as a psychology lecturer it was, in part, because I was growing tired of telling people how they could change the world if only they took the time to apply some of the theory I kept banging on about. I wanted to try it for myself.

A few years later, I was running a team of developers, and 25 years ago we were creating digital training that would still look futuristic today: dynamically generated AI characters that interacted with learners in randomized simulations, virtual environments to explore and so on. We were both excited by, and proud of, the work we were doing.

We had developed an instructional approach we called the See–Hear–Do model (not to be confused with the Scooby-Doo model), based loosely on Jerome Bruner's Stages of Representation theory[1], according to which people encode information in three formats: enactive (by doing), iconic (through images) and symbolic (through language). By ensuring that learners used all three encoding modalities, we were greatly enhancing the effectiveness of our learning content. Or so we thought.

I think I imagined it would be nice to appear on the conference circuit, pointing to a bar graph showing how much more effective our approach had proved to be. As luck would have it, we were host to a work placement – a visiting Dutch research student called Marguerita – and together we designed an experiment.

In our experiment the same information – information about the solar system – was developed into five formats. Each format was different: the most basic version was simply plain text, other versions integrated more media – audio, video, culminating in a version incorporating audio, video and interactive exercises. All the modes of representation. Groups of university students were then given one of these different formats and the same task: use the materials for 30 minutes, then take a test to see how much they could recall.

Our hypothesis was that the richer encoding formats would produce superior recall scores. It helped that at the time the received wisdom was also that interactive learning was better than cheaper, less interactive formats.

We ran the experiment. We added up the scores. The results were clear: there was no significant difference in the effectiveness of the various formats. In fact, the students who had studied the text-only format performed slightly better, on average. Imagine that: realizing that perhaps an entire industry based around the production of online content could be replaced – with text documents.[2]

Our research wasn't published or peer-reviewed. I could see that there were shortcomings in the size and representativeness of our sample. A university cafeteria was hardly a controlled environment. But I had supervised enough student psychology experiments to know that our research design was fundamentally sound, easy to replicate, and that if our instructional design approach was even half as effective as we believed it to be we should have seen an effect.

As it happened, the results also tied into an observation that had been bothering me for a while: the internet was booming and fast achieving recognition in its own right as a learning tool. But the vast majority of information that was being served up was just – well – plain text. And people didn't seem to mind. In fact, if you were looking to find something out, you probably *preferred* plain text over other formats.

Even as the learning and development industry were busily handing out instructional design accreditations to each other, it was becoming clear that instructional design was not significantly improving learning in the real world. In fact, people would actively *avoid* formats (such as e-learning modules) that incorporated instructional design, and *prefer* formats (such as the pages served up by Google, or videos served up by YouTube) that had none. Instructional design, I realized, is mumbo-jumbo.

Today, billions of people are learning things on TikTok while avoiding all those free-to-use learning libraries whose sprawling course catalogues gather digital dust. Education just doesn't get it. Education doesn't get learning.

Even a superficial glance at TikTok reveals that what makes all that learning so sticky – whether it is learning about celebrities, dance moves, fashion or trainspotting – namely that it is either that it's the kind of stuff that *excites* us, or that the people talking about it are very *excitable*. The stuff that moves us bubbles to the top. Yesterday I learned that 50 rubber bands is enough to stop a sprinting human being. Bizarre indeed.

Your reaction is probably that these are not the sorts of things one *should* be learning about – and there lies the problem. Much as we might *like* people to function like computers – to do exactly as they are instructed by an authority, they don't and never will. Central nervous systems are not designed that way.

Education is content-centric, not human-centric. It's Ebbinghaus through and through. It is based on forcing people to try and remember stuff that doesn't matter to them, and instructional design represents a set of techniques for doing this. We have created all manner of organizations, systems and techniques for bending people out of shape, rather than understanding how they develop naturally.

There is, of course, a great deal of research in support of instructional design. But rather like the forgetting curve, this research is both accurate and misleading.

Many people struggle with the idea that scientific research can be both accurate and misleading – but in reality this is generally true. The history of science shows that one theory is eventually replaced by another, better, theory. It is always the case that the old, incorrect, theory is well supported by research, and usually the new theory has little or no support (at first). In other words, it isn't hard to find evidence to support an idea that, ultimately, turns out to be wrong.

So how *does* a theory with little or no support replace one with plenty? Through explanatory power. Invariably there are things that the old theory just never quite explained. The new theory accounts for these.

It is surely a legitimate challenge to instructional design that learners generally prefer formats *without* it to formats *with* it, when faced with a real-world task. Give me Google over an e-learning module any day. Instructional design research often repeats Ebbinghaus's mistake: in trying to determine the best learning formats, it overlooks the fact that in the real world we learn about the things that matter to us: how to fix a router, when to plant petunias, how to bake chocolate brownies.

In experimental contexts, real-world phenomena are often excluded, with the consequence that the findings reflect minor variations in cognitive processes – and completely miss the things that really matter. Put simply: people tend to find the evidence they are looking for, but may miss the bigger picture.

Learning researchers are often like people studying the corner of a dark room with a torch. They can tell you a lot about little bits of fluff, but have yet to notice the table, chairs and chandelier in the middle of the room.

The students in our own experiment learned equally well from each of the formats because they *knew they were going to be tested* – and were therefore motivated to consume the information, whatever the format. This variable – their concern – vastly outweighed the significance of anything else that we were testing, such as variations in content format. We had given them a reason to care.

So let's start by laying the foundations for learning design with a learning design model. There are many models for learning design, but only one that reflects the reality of learning as described by the affective context model: the push–pull spectrum.

As I have stated above, the affective context model proposes that we do not, in fact, encode 'knowledge' in our memories: instead we encode the pattern of emotional reactions that we have to experiences, and use these to later reconstruct experiences.

The important thing from a learning perspective, however, is that people are not blank slates: what they react to is partly nature, and mainly nurture. Some people will be astonished by architecture that others don't even notice – moved by classical music that leaves others cold – or left speechless by a work of art that leaves others unmoved. Some people even like country and western songs.

Learning design can therefore rest soundly on this conceptual foundation: since our learning is governed by our concerns, which in turn determine whether or not something has affective significance for us, **in any context we are either responding to the concerns that a person already has ('pull'), or we are trying to create new concerns ('push').**

This means that there are two grand classes of learning design that we can undertake:

1 **Pull.** Where people care about something, we do not need to provide affective significance. We can simply provide the resources they need. This is why plain text or simple video is preferred by people using Google or YouTube – because there is something they are trying to do. Something they *care* about. The vast majority of our learning is driven by the things we are trying to do, and which we care about. This is the 'pull' condition.

2 **Push.** Where people do not care about something, we need to provide affective significance. We cannot simply provide information and expect learning to take place. If someone is uninterested in safety, then providing procedural guidance will do little to alter their behaviour. If a student cares neither for history nor for the outcome of the history exam they are soon to take, then providing more textbooks will be of little use. We need to provide an experience, such as a challenge, experience or story, that will *add* affective significance to a situation. This is the 'push' condition.

It should immediately be obvious that these two approaches go hand in hand. If, for example, a young person cares greatly about a particular computer game, they will quite happily consume encyclopedic tomes on game strategy without the need for encouragement. Teenagers concerned about their appearance will demonstrate impressive attention spans as they sit through hours of hair and makeup tutorials in order to achieve the desired result.

If we can make people *care* about something or other, they will use the resources we give them (whether or not they commit them to memory is a separate question). Hence the learning is not something we 'do' to people – we just support it or create the conditions for it to happen.

This is why, in an important sense, there are no 'learners' – because people are generally just trying to get something done, and learning is a way to do that. Describing people as 'learners' is a bit like describing people as 'breathers'. Learning is a by-product of pursuing the things we care about. There is no 'learning centre' in the brain any more than there is a 'capability development centre', this is just a term we use to describe the way an organism changes.

You can probably already imagine how our modern world presents huge challenges for education: on the one hand, students are increasingly saturated in a hyper-charged diet of things they *do* care about and are primed to learn – sex, status, trends, relationships, comedy, shock and gossip – on the other, they are expected to function in a perversely rationalized environment where they are required to regurgitate information that has little or no significance to them. It's hard to imagine a more radical pattern of psychological stress – rather like feeding someone on a rich diet purely to deepen their suffering during starvation.

In normal life, our interactions with the world and with other people are often somewhere in-between 'push' and 'pull'. Take conversation, for example: in a good conversation people take a little time at the outset to 'establish rapport'. What does this mean?

It means people try to understand what the other person's particular concerns are and to find some common ground. For example, two people may start out by remarking on the inclement weather, then a little later on discover a shared passion for food and for local restaurants. Each person 'pulls' recommendations from the other.

At one point, one person remarks that the fish at a local restaurant is exceptional – to which the other responds that they don't much like fish. Their conversational partner then shifts into push mode: 'Oh, but you really must try the monkfish – I mean, if you haven't tried it you are missing out on one of the most incredible flavours!'

It is now clear that one person is trying to make the other care about something that they didn't before – to try something new, and to change the way they feel. If they have established sufficient rapport – if the other person now cares what they think – then this push attempt might be successful. Notice how similar this is starting to look to the way education should be.

A conversation really is a good metaphor for learning, since a conversation is one of the oldest learning methods we have. Conversation is first and foremost a vehicle for stories. If one person has nothing to say that interests us, then it isn't a good conversation. If a person takes no time to understand us, and simply 'pushes' their concerns the whole time, then that person is a bore and the conversation will feel, literally, like a lecture. Finally, we cannot enjoy a truly great conversation with someone who is exactly like ourselves – it seems comfortable at first, but eventually we crave a different perspective.

In this light we can make sense of the enduring appeal of coaching, which reliably features on the wish list of people asked about their development. Coaching (or more accurately mentoring) is a format that can be both experience and resource – both push and pull, depending on the circumstance. Sometimes we turn to a coach for help, sometimes they challenge us. They take time to understand our concerns and to address the things that we care about.

What may not be immediately apparent is that neither of these two classes of learning design – pull or push – is 'learning' in the educational sense. What I mean is that neither of these two classes has as their objective that someone should store knowledge in their heads. In fact, the former is more often 'learning elimination' – by providing resources we may actively *reduce* the amount of learning that takes place.

We will return to this topic later on, but first let's have a look at some examples of learning activities that fall into each category.

'Push' approaches to learning

First, if you wanted someone to care about something that they don't currently care about – and money was no object – how would you do it?

I'm guessing that you already know the answer. If I wanted you to care about poverty in the less developed world, then flying you to a country where people were living below the poverty line, allowing you to spend a month with a family whose children were dying of malnutrition – I imagine that would make you see things differently.

You might instinctively react against the thought of having this kind of 'concern' thrust upon you by another person, but life has its own way of shifting our concerns: people who don't think much about illness may find one day that they, or a close relative, have cancer. Suddenly they are Googling everything there is to know about cancer and learning at a voracious rate. We hear about people who have survived their battle with cancer and gone on to found charities; or to experience a complete transformation of their outlook on life. They might be the person standing before us, telling their story – and sometimes it makes us care. One day that person might be us.

Designed experiences

So the most effective way to get someone to learn (if they don't already want to) is by designing an experience. Creating a moment that matters. But what *kind* of experience? It is often said that we learn most from mistakes. This is not strictly true: people are making mistakes every day, all day long. But they don't change. A person may spend a lifetime failing to appreciate the feelings of others, being an insensitive twit, for example.

In fact, people learn from the mistakes that they *suffer from*. Humiliation is deeply felt. Rejection is painful. Losing a lot of money stings. If we want to design an experience, for example in which we 'engineer failure' in order that someone can learn a valuable lesson, then we need to start by understanding what they really care about. Otherwise, there is a good chance that our experience will have no impact – or have too much impact!

Equally, a powerful experience, such as first-hand experience of extreme poverty, does not need to be an experience of making a mistake. What matters is that it impacts us at an emotional level – otherwise we won't care any more after an experience than we did before. But how do we know what will impact someone and what won't?

If it were you, how would I design an experience that would truly transform the way you feel about things?

There are two answers: I could design the kind of experience that would transform *anyone* that went through it – just by virtue of them being human. Having to make life-and-death decisions is pretty impactful for most people, for example. Or, more constructively, I could find out about what matters to you, and base my designs on that.

This latter point is a central theme and will come up time and time again: *you cannot design effective learning experiences without understanding the people for whom you are designing them.*

While this might sound like common sense, it is the single greatest mistake in learning design today – namely, we focus on defining the content/

topics that we want people to memorize and the mechanism that we will use to get it to them, instead of analysing the concerns and context of the audience in question. We assume that knowledge can somehow be decanted into people like water into a beaker – when in reality it is a fabric woven from the threads of an individual's concerns.

We need to shift from content to context. For this reason, I will call this conventional approach to learning 'content dumping'.

Content dumping is the greater part of what we do to children in classrooms, and to adults enrolled in organizational learning programmes – we take some 'topics' that we would like them to know about as we spray them with knowledge in the hope that some of it sticks. Very little does, and still less translates into behavioural or capability change – but we carry on because we don't know what else to do, and we are hooked on the idea of learning as knowledge transfer, and of people as blank slates.

What I can confidently predict is that when we do engage in 'content dumping', what little sticks will tend to be that information that relates to something someone cares about (even if that just happens to be the instructor) – but it goes without saying that such a 'shotgun' approach to education, whether in school or in the workplace, is grossly inefficient.

I will talk more about designing experiences in a later chapter, but first I'd like to describe some of the alternatives before diving into the detail.

The effectiveness of experiences as a means to learn has led some to champion 'learning by doing' as the definitive approach to learning design. While first-hand experience is indeed a powerful way to learn, it owes its potency to the true basis of learning: learning by *feeling*.

This might sound like an odd thing to say – until you realize that storytelling and observation are also effective ways to learn. A child who sees his friend fall into a fire can judge from the screaming and panicked reaction of her parents that falling into a fire is a bad thing – without actually having to do it themselves. Equally, we can hear a story about someone who fell into a fire and learn not to do it ourselves.

Storytelling and observation

Since observation and storytelling don't involve much 'doing', it is clear that what all these mechanisms have in common is their affective elements. When we do something for ourselves, the emotional impact is first-hand and personal, hence 'learning by doing' has a special appeal – but any format that changes how we feel can result in learning.

In reality, we aren't always able to give people first-hand experience of things. That may be because it is too costly, too risky, or simply too difficult to organize. Examples range from 'being attacked by a bear' to 'engine failure'.

In such cases we may use storytelling to pass on important lessons. Human beings are storytellers – a statement that refers to both the enduring appeal of stories across time and cultures, and the significant role that storytelling plays in everyday life. Not only do we flock to cinemas to watch stories, we spend the greater part of our conversational time sharing stories. We call it 'gossip'.

Stories are important because they reflect the way in which we naturally share and encode memories. When something happens to us, it creates an emotional reaction. These emotional reactions are what get stored. If the event was significant enough, we will likely try to share it with other people – there is considerable social value attached to sharing good stories.

The way that we do this is to use words, which are a method for summarizing the feelings we experienced. A story is only as good as its affective dimension, however; a completely dull story, for example of how we completed a load of washing at the weekend, is not considered a story at all.

In fact, if someone did start telling you a story about doing a load of washing, you would instantly imagine that there is going to be something unexpected or surprising ('and then I realized that the cat was in the washing machine!') – it's simply inconceivable that someone would say: 'And 40 minutes later the washing was done' (end of story). So much so that if someone actually did this it would become a story in its own right, by virtue of being so bizarre.

Our words serve an important purpose – because we have grown up in a shared culture, our words create similar sets of emotions in the listener. The listener has now 'remembered' the story and is able to tell it themselves (although, as Bartlett discovered, when they recreate the story they will likely alter it subtly to reflect their own concerns).

So we like to hear stories. People at learning events will swap stories at the bar later. After-dinner speakers can make a living out of telling stories, if their story is sufficiently exciting. People will tell stories of their experience of battling illness, of going to war, of sailing the Atlantic Ocean single-handed.

One can also be a good storyteller. What is a good storyteller? Someone who knows how to express emotions powerfully, and connect to their audience. A bad storyteller can take a great story and make it feel boring.

In an educational setting, however, stories have suffered terribly from the corrupting idea that learning is knowledge transfer. In practice this means that so-called 'subject matter experts' will try to tell you *what* they learned, rather than *how* they learned it, because they have been misled into thinking that the 'learning point' is what needs to be transferred into your head.

Point a camera at a safety expert and ask them to talk about safety, and they will tend to say things like: 'Safety is very important', or 'You must always do such-and-such'. What they tend not to tell you is *why* safety is important, or why you must always do such-and-such. It is often quite arduous to get them to a place where they can say: 'Well, when I was first starting out in my career…', or 'This one time we were working on this piece of equipment and…'. This is all because we have become fixated on the idea that brains store information, and information transfer is what learning is all about.

Once again, what stories should one tell? Answer: stories that *matter* to people. How do we know what stories matter to people? Find out what they care about.

If we are thinking about designing a learning experience, this is one of the best ways to start the design process: ask yourself: 'What story will people tell about this experience?' Pause to consider how alien that idea is to conventional education: can you imagine that instead of lesson plans describing the topics to be covered, an educator wonders what story the students will tell? One of the stories my youngest daughter tells is of the day they were taken to a local museum and allowed to try on vintage clothing. It's one of the few things she remembers.

When you listen to the stories that people tell, you will notice interesting themes. As an example, people will often talk about meeting famous people – and often the things that the famous person had to say will have a big impact on the individual. They will say things like: 'I once met Muhammad Ali. He shook my hand and I asked him what his secret was, and he said "It's not how fast you move your fists, but how fast you move your feet." That advice is how I run my business today.'[3]

When you hear things like this, it is easy to wonder why these encounters are so memorable – why it isn't nearly as memorable to watch the same person say the same thing on TV, or to have the same advice imparted by a non-famous person. Our knowledge transfer model can't explain that: the information is the same regardless of from whom it comes. Computers do not store information differently based on whether the person typing it in is a celebrity.

I once worked for a large telecommunications organization, whose CEO made a point of attending every staff induction session and answering questions put to him by new starters. But as the organization grew, a decision was made that the CEO would no longer be able to attend these sessions and instead people would be able to choose from a number of pre-recorded videos of the CEO responding to frequently asked questions.

At an intuitive level, you can probably sense that this is a step backwards – but why exactly? Having the CEO answer frequently asked questions is clearly better than a pre-prepared speech (since at least some of the responses will address the concerns people have), and from a knowledge-transfer perspective the same 'learning objectives' are covered. So why is it a very different learning experience?

Status-dense situations

Imagine that you are given a choice between attending a talk given by Nelson Mandela, and a talk given by one of your training team about the life of Nelson Mandela. Which would you prefer?

In order to understand these situations, we need to know that humans are both social and hierarchical creatures. Celebrities and other important people (such as chief executive officers) are held in high standing. For this reason, any encounter with them is what I will call a 'status-dense' situation. Because of their status, your interaction with them is high stakes in a social sense.

It is like scaling a cliff: if your interaction goes poorly, you risk ignominy and public shame. If it goes well, your self-esteem and reputation enjoy a sudden boost. Because these are highly emotional situations, they remain in our memories a long while – and grow in the retelling!

This may help us to understand another aspect of the teacher–student relationship: if the role of teacher (and the teacher themselves) is admired and respected, they can more easily influence the memory of students. Teachers who care deliver better educational outcomes.[4] But students should also care about their teachers: if the profession falls into disrepute, their effectiveness suffers too.

At the start of conference speeches, speakers will often spend quite a bit of time establishing their legitimacy by talking about their experiences, their accomplishments, their qualifications, their publications – why? Why should it matter?

Because social status impacts how we encode information. Sometimes we will invite celebrities or sportspeople to talk about things they know next to nothing about – education, politics, leadership – for the simple reason that their status makes what they have to say memorable.

More legitimately, it is often helpful for trainers to have significant experience of the job – or to rotate from training to practical roles – in order to retain the respect of organizational learners. It's hard to take a leadership trainer seriously, for example, if they have never been a leader.

From a learning design standpoint we can engineer 'status-dense' situations in the interests of improving learning – for example, if people are set a developmental challenge that culminates in a presentation of their work to the 'board of directors' or to a local celebrity, this can make quite a difference to what people learn.

Formal education will sometimes create similar situations, for example graduation ceremonies where parents are present to witness the culmination of one's accomplishments.

Simulation

On the evening of 4 April 1968, Jane Elliott, a teacher in a one-room school in the small US town of Randall, was ironing a tepee when she turned on the TV and learned that Martin Luther King had been assassinated.[5] She was ironing the tepee in preparation for a lesson about North American Indians, but she was troubled by the suspicion that her children wouldn't really understand discrimination unless they experienced it for themselves. She was reminded of the Sioux prayer: 'Oh great spirit, keep me from ever judging a man until I have walked in his moccasins.'

So the next day, she decided to do something different. She talked with her elementary class about the assassination of Martin Luther King, and then asked her pupils if they would like to feel what discrimination was like. They agreed.

So she divided the class according to eye colour. Blue-eyed children, she told the group, were superior. They sat at the front, and they got to place fabric collars around the necks of the brown-eyed children so as to more easily distinguish them. The blue-eyed children received extra privileges – second helpings at lunch, access to the new jungle gym, more play time – and they were discouraged from fraternizing with the brown-eyed children.

The blue-eyed children quickly adopted an air of superiority, while the brown-eyed children became timid and withdrawn, preferring to isolate themselves during recess. In the space of a single day, academic performance improved for the blue-eyed group, just as it deteriorated for the brown-eyed children. The following day she reversed the experiment.

By all accounts the experiment had a profound effect on the children, though it didn't necessarily make Jane popular in her local community. She went on to repeat her experiment, and years later many of her students would recall the lesson they learned.

This kind of 'push' approach is simulation. Simulation is used to create an environment that operates and feels like the real thing, so that people can learn. A simulated environment can be as simple as a role-play of a difficult conversation or as complex as a flight simulator.

People sometimes make the mistake of assuming that a simulator is something that merely looks or functions like the real thing – but the critical thing is that it is *affectively* similar. I once completed a training course for people intending to travel to offshore drilling installations. Since these journeys typically involve a helicopter ride and the possibility of ditching in the sea, the training involved escaping from a helicopter fuselage. Several times. Upside-down. Wearing copious amounts of gear and sitting next to the HR director.

Today, of course, it might be easier to recreate this experience in virtual reality (VR) – with modern games technology providing a very high degree of accuracy – but I can assure you that this would feel nothing like the real thing: the disorientation, the rising sense of panic as you grapple with the seat-belt while holding your breath, heavily gloved hands struggling with the mechanism. If there is a significant affective dimension to a situation, overlooking this in the simulation can render the experience near-useless.

This gives us a fair idea of the sorts of things that we can legitimately simulate on a computer: if, for example the thing you are trying to simulate is 'completing a budget spreadsheet', then a computer simulation will probably work well, since the real activity and the simulated one feel very similar. But we should be sceptical of a computer simulation of leadership – unless, of course, the team you are leading are entirely virtual.

Finally, this is why VR is a promising learning technology – the power of VR is precisely that it 'feels' as though you are there, and it greatly extends our ability to simulate how things would feel in reality.

So far I have been talking about 'push' learning and all the ways in which we can make things that people experience meaningful for them, so that they will be able to reconstruct them (to some extent) later. The thing that all these approaches have in common is, of course, affective significance. We remember what we care about.

Anxiety-based learning

But say you had some really dull information – information that you know people don't care about – and you wanted to force it into people's heads somehow. How might you do that?

One obvious approach might be to hold a gun to their head, or threaten to injure someone they care about. How would this help? Well, these kinds of threats would likely generate anxiety in the individual, and this anxiety would provide affective significance for the information.

If I think back, I can still remember the bright-red face of my prep-school Latin teacher, inches from mine; small flecks of spittle on his lips as the veins in his neck bulged and he shrieked at me for not knowing the declensions of the Latin word 'war'.

'*Bellum, belli, bello, bellorum, bellis, bella.*' To this day, I remember the corner of the oak-panelled room in which I was made to stand until I could recite it accurately. In the event that the school is still standing, I could take you there and point it out.

This kind of approach I will call 'anxiety-based' learning and, sadly, it pervades our education system. Indeed, it is the dominant mechanism that education employs. These days it is not deemed acceptable in many countries to use corporal punishment in schools, so instead we have resorted to testing. Testing works only because it is a way of creating a kind of artificial anxiety, which serves as the affective context for otherwise unimportant information. A test is a kind of threat.

As a result, modern education (largely) comprises a series of anxiety-driven tests, in service of which we try to cram as much information into our heads as possible. The anxiety stems from the myth that our future success depends on our performance on these tests. Obviously it helps if society and parents collude in sustaining this myth, working in harmony to create the impression that if you don't pass various tests, you will end up working on a production line, chopping the heads off fish.

To some extent this used to be true – there existed a kind of 'cash for certificates' economy in which employers would offer you an HR job on the basis that you got a history degree from a reputable university – even though you had forgotten almost everything and the degree bore no relation to your work – and defenders of the system will point to the fact that people with degrees earn, on average, more than those without them.[6] Today, some companies (such as Google) are beginning to explicitly recognize how ridiculous this all is.

The overdependence on anxiety-based learning is driving education to the point of crisis: on the one hand, presumably out of sheer intellectual bankruptcy, governments are placing more and more emphasis on tests, forcing them further down the age range in an attempt to bolster their standings on increasingly publicized international test comparisons (such as the PISA rankings). While this serves political agendas and brings commercial opportunity for testing companies, it is to the detriment of learners and businesses.

How so? Anxiety-based methods of pushing content have negative side effects. The most damaging of these is that they create a deep association between learning and anxiety. If a person's experience of learning is that it typically comprises a challenge in which you are required to memorize information so that you can pass a test – and that the test is likely to be competitive, with significant potential risk to your self-esteem, reputation and future prospects – then the majority of people will learn that learning is a negative thing.

This is quite evident when you take adults who have been through this experience and propose that they do some 'learning'; they immediately interpret this as meaning 'education' and ask: 'Will there be a test?' You can see the relief on their faces when you say: 'No', and a voice in their head says: 'Great! So I don't have to remember any of this.' How can this be a good thing?

There are a great many reasons to avoid the test as a learning design approach – but we will return to these in the chapter on education.

Behaviour modification

Here's another learning challenge: if you wanted to train your dog to fetch a stick, how might you do that? I have a suspicion that devotees of testing in schools would be more likely to suggest electric shocks – but I would guess that most people would suggest something along the lines of dog treats or the more economical 'Good dog!' approach.

While you may not be aware of the exact principles that you are applying, you may be interested to know that your approach was called 'operant conditioning' by psychologists who investigated ways of modifying behaviour in the 1970s.

The man who is most often credited as the father of operant conditioning is Burrhus Frederic Skinner, who went on to become a Harvard professor. He is perhaps most famous for the invention of the Skinner box. The Skinner box is a chamber, typically about the size of a large cardboard box, in which all distractions can be removed except for the things the experimenter wishes to control.

If you were a rat – or a pigeon – placed in a Skinner box, you might find a lever and a light. Pressing the lever might cause a food pellet to be dispensed, or the floor to become electrified. In this way it was possible to exclude all stimuli and all behaviours except the ones being investigated, and see how one affected the other.

Skinner also invented something similar called the 'teaching machine'. The teaching machine worked a bit like the Skinner box in that the learner would see just the information they were supposed to learn, then they would have to give the correct response. If they gave the correct response they would be rewarded; if not they would repeat the exercise until they got it right. So, for example, you might be given a rhythm to reproduce (by pressing a lever) and when you correctly reproduced it you could move on to the next exercise.

Because of the emphasis they placed on behaviour, psychologists like Skinner were called 'behaviourists'. In part, the movement was a reaction against psychoanalysis – the approach pioneered by Jung and Freud, which placed great importance on the inner workings of the mind and in particular the unconscious. Psychology was still relatively new and struggling to gain acceptability as a science, and some people, such as the behaviourists, were really uneasy about all the mental stuff that couldn't be measured. 'Let's just focus on behaviour,' they said: 'We can measure that. It will all be very scientific.' And so it was.

They made important discoveries: they found that you could take a reasonably intelligent animal, such as a dog or rat – or pigeon – and get it to do pretty much anything you wanted through conditioning. The kind of conditioning I am talking about is called operant conditioning, as mentioned above.[7] Operant conditioning works in the following way: a creature does something (usually just through trial and error) and one of three things happens as a result: something bad happens, something good happens, nothing happens.

For example, a rat might bumble around a cage until it accidentally presses a lever – at which point a pellet of food is dispensed. A dog might find that every time it crosses over to one side of the room it receives an electric shock. You can guess the rest – rats learn to press levers, dogs learn not to cross over to one side of the room.

Operant conditioning is a tremendously powerful way to shape a host of behaviours since human beings are not so different from other animals and respond in a similar fashion. For example, it can help explain addiction: the most powerful 'schedule' of rewards is one that is unpredictable – you are never quite sure if the next press of the lever will be the one that gets you the food pellet. This can enable us to understand why people become addicted to gambling, or stay in abusive relationships.

It also has obvious applications in the areas of education and consumer behaviour. It turns out that animals can learn to feel good not just about rewards, but about things that 'stand for' rewards – such as gold stars or points, for example. When a parent offers to pay their child for every A that they get in their exams, they are using operant conditioning to modify their child's behaviour. The money isn't strictly a reward – but we all know that it can be exchanged for rewards. Likewise, gold stars for good behaviour in school, points for purchases, and badges for accomplishments at work can all be used to push our behaviour in the desired direction.

In an organization many people complete programmes – such as MBAs and lesser types – mainly to receive a certificate. The certificate can be pinned to a wall, or added to an online profile and traded for respect and self-esteem. This is why offering certificates has always been an important part of organizational learning programmes.

In recent years this approach to behaviour modification has sometimes been called 'gamification', which confusingly implies something about playing games[8] – due in part to the fact that many modern games incorporate operant conditioning in order to get their players to spend money.

The behaviourists showed that many of the same behavioural conditioning mechanisms that could be demonstrated with animals could also be applied to humans: punish a dog and it learns, punish a human and they learn.

But the refusal of many behaviourists to consider internal mental states (since these couldn't be directly measured) left gaping holes in their explanation. One of these holes was observational learning.

Observational learning

If you have children, you probably sometimes worry about what they are learning from watching television or, more likely these days, online video.

Back in the 1960s, Albert Bandura conducted a now-famous experiment into observational learning. In essence, he showed young children (girls and boys, aged between three and six) a video of an adult kicking and punching a large inflatable toy, and found that they were likely to imitate what they had seen. Most interestingly, though, he found that whether or not they would imitate the behaviour depended, in part, on what happened to the person they were watching.[9]

I guess this will probably not come as a surprise. If your friend strokes a dog, and the dog bites him, you will learn the lesson without having to suffer the same fate. What you may not know is that even chickens can learn from watching other chickens on film. Admittedly the chicken film industry is fairly niche, but there it is.

Again, knowing that we are able to learn from observing others leaves unanswered the question as to how this process works. The affective context model suggests that we automatically mirror the emotional states of things that we feel emotionally connected to[10] – so, for example, if we go and see a film in which the hero (with whom we identify) is brutally beaten, we experience anxiety and stress.

Note that this identification is not based on appearance alone. If the hero happens to be a dog (and we like dogs), that also works just fine. We even mirror more subtle affective states; as we pass people in the street we pick up on their gait and expression and automatically imagine how it feels to be them.

This means that when, for example, we are training people on a procedure by getting them to watch the procedure, it's tremendously important to demonstrate the consequences of getting the procedure wrong, otherwise it is much less likely that a person will remember how to get it right.

A simple example: you can demonstrate the correct way to stop at a red light, but really you ought to show (or describe) the consequences of not stopping at a red light if you want people to learn to do it correctly. This has enormous implications for safety and data protection training, for example.

By mirroring the process that storytelling uses (for example, stories of awful things that happened to employees who screwed up), we can have far greater impact.

Another consequence of this characteristic of human learning is that the enthusiasm can be infectious. We probably all remember teachers who were really passionate about their subject, and some of this enthusiasm can transfer to us, and the way we feel about the same topic. Without the affective context model, it is hard to explain why enthusiasm should be so important in a teacher, though people do generally feel that enthusiastic and inspirational teachers have had a big impact on their lives.

But note that we wouldn't expect an enthusiastic maths teacher to necessarily produce the best test results (since test results aren't a good measure of learning in the real world). What I mean is that an enthusiastic maths teacher may produce students who feel good about maths and go on to work in that field – but it may well turn out that students who feel terrified about exams get the best scores (and go on to avoid maths like the plague in later life).

If you have ever been to a conference, you will know that, as a delegate, you would much rather attend lectures given by someone who speaks passionately about a topic and that these seem to you to be more memorable. There are, of course, exceptions to this: a very dull speaker might be talking about something that is terribly relevant to your line of work. This happens to me regularly.

Having established that both humans and chickens can learn in a similar fashion, you may be left wondering if there is anything special about human learning at all. I would argue that this is a good sign – a lot of learning theories assume that there is something fundamentally different about human learning, and this is likely to betray a deeper bias, for example towards building models based around rationality.

Anticipatory learning

While there is nothing qualitatively different about human learning, we do seem to be better in two important areas: sharing our feelings and imagining how we would feel. If there is anything that we seem to be able to do better than our evolutionary relatives, it is picturing the future and – most importantly – how we will feel in future.

This means that there is a relatively special kind of learning that humans can do: anticipatory learning. You can, for example, tell someone that they will be playing the part of Romeo in a stage production of *Romeo and Juliet* in three months' time and they will go into a panic and start learning lines as fast as they can, just at the thought of being onstage and not forgetting what to say. I'm pretty sure chickens don't do this, though I haven't actually tried it.

One of the interesting things about this ability – the ability to project a future state – is that it seems to mature quite late in humans, perhaps because it is one of the more sophisticated cognitive functions relating to developments in adolescent perspective-taking.[11]

This may mean that learners who have not yet reached adulthood struggle to really care about their future selves. Since they can't really imagine the consequences of having to spend their 30s chopping the heads off fish, they find it hard to develop the motivation to study hard right now. Equally, if they can't clearly picture how it will feel to be totally unprepared for an exam in three months' time, they may leave revision to the last minute.

This suggests that if you are going to frighten people with the prospect of exams as a way to force them to memorize stuff, if the people are young you should inflict exams every couple of weeks, rather than at the end of the academic year. I am not actually advocating this; I am just pointing out that if you are going to bully someone, there are probably more and less effective ways to do it.

For adults, however, anticipated challenges can work quite well, especially if, as suggested above, there is a status-rich dimension to the challenge – for example having to present to a panel of highly respected individuals. In addition, if we are able to make anticipated outcomes 'real' for people – for example using simulations, VR, or just people who can tell a compelling story – then we will stand a better chance of shifting concern.

Trial and error, and play

Two other 'push' approaches worth discussion are 'trial and error' and 'play'. 'Play' is probably the best way to think about learning as it occurs naturally. It's also a great starting point for early years education. Lots of animals play; it's not difficult to guess that play and learning are closely related – the question is *how*?

From an affective perspective, play is all about consequences. You can imagine 'playing' on a flight simulator – and this being a good way to learn about flying a plane – but you would be uneasy if you thought your pilot was just 'playing around' on your transatlantic flight.

Equally, if you have children (or have ever been a child), you will be familiar with the excuse: 'But we were only playing', which is used when the consequences turn out to be more serious than you were expecting and now there is 1) a valuable object in pieces, 2) a small child in tears, and 3) an angry adult yelling at you.

Play is something we tend to do a lot less of as adults, which is a bit of a shame, because it is a great way to learn. I suspect that this happens for a number of reasons: as adults we become more capable of imagining and anticipating potential bad outcomes, and also society discourages us from 'playing around' and instead looks sternly at us as if we should 'know what we are doing'. Looking as if you don't know what you are doing is often considered a bad thing, and so to avoid embarrassment we stop doing it.

Play occurs quite naturally in a wide range of species – such as rats, for example[12] – and tends to decline as animals enter adulthood. This suggests that it is not a social construct peculiar to humans, but a natural part of our development.

It also suggests that it plays a central role in learning, since young animals (including humans) spend large amounts of time engaging in play, and it would be very odd indeed if this huge expenditure of energy served no useful purpose. It may be that play declines due to biological changes that take place during the transition into adulthood, and on the assumption that the organism is now sufficiently adapted to its environment.

This raises the intriguing question as to whether continuing to play would be a good thing for adults to do, where their environment was subject to ongoing change. In the United States, around 43 per cent of people aged 60-plus play computer games every day,[13] suggesting that the appetite for play is not simply extinguished as one enters adulthood.

Play is a condition in which we can express our desires without the consequences being too serious. A simple example might be the 'tickle game'. One person might tickle another person. This might be an expression of a desire for physical contact – or to influence others – and the other person might laugh, up to a point when they say: 'Stop it! That's enough now!' in a serious voice, which signals the end of the game by indicating that the consequences are now serious.

How does a lion cub know that their parent is now tired of playing? The answer can only be a change in the affective consequences: where previously they were batting them about playfully, they are now inflicting significant pain.

In playing, a person learns about the consequences of expressing their affective impulses and the point at which the world 'pushes back'. Individuals may vary in their reaction to the consequences – even within a play environment. Some people may find that the sense of accomplishment in successfully taking off in a flight simulator outweighs the sense of disappointment when they crash.

Other people are hyper-sensitive to negative consequences – even in the game environment – so play needs to be carefully calibrated to the individual's tolerances. Once again, individual differences in a person's pattern of concerns are surfaced through play.

If we are setting up a 'play' situation for learning purposes, we need to ensure on the one hand that the consequences within the play environment resemble those in the real environment, and on the other that the consequences are not too serious – because if they are, it will cease to be play. For example, we might create an online game where if you do something reckless you die in the game, and maybe lose some of your virtual possessions or status – but probably not suffer a heavy financial penalty.[14]

People may react very differently to role-play; for some of them the risk of making a mistake in front of colleagues may seem as great as (or greater than) the risk of making the same mistake in real life. Others may be less concerned.

It is interesting to compare play as a learning approach with the traditional approach in familiar training contexts: for example, you might compare conventional classroom training with an aircraft simulator in pilot training. Or learning how to use a drilling rig. Probably you would be well advised to start with a simplified play environment: the cockpit of a single-seater aircraft, for example, rather than the overwhelming complexity of a 737, and then allow people to master one after the other.

The advantage of play over classroom training is this: in a classroom we struggle to give the information any affective significance – so it doesn't stick. In play, the affective significance comes naturally with the consequences, so we learn more efficiently.

Second, classroom training tends to focus on storing information which we can then *apply* to our behaviour. But (as explained above) we don't actually store information – just a reaction to that information that we can use to reconstruct it – so this makes the whole process terribly inefficient, as opposed to just storing the affective outcome of our behaviours. This is why 'learning by doing' is much better – because the feelings aren't two steps away.[15]

Of course, there are situations where we might be worried about people learning by just 'playing around' – surgery, for example. Or cyber-attack. Here our challenge is twofold: to create a play environment where the consequences sufficiently resemble the real world (so playing the game *Operation* might be fine for eight-year-olds but not for your heart surgeon) and, second, to 'de-risk' those environments so that learners feel comfortable trying things out. I confess, there are some board games I just don't like to play – Monopoly for example – just because people tend to get quite upset when they lose. Not me, obviously.

Trial and error is really a variation on play, but where there is a real objective in mind. Let's say, for example, that you buy a new DVD player, but on setting it up you discover that the instruction manual is missing. Rather than going back to the store, or looking it up online, you start pressing buttons on the remote control to see what happens. Note that a very old person might be reluctant to do this for fear of 'blowing up the TV', but we are from a generation that knows that with technology the consequences are never so severe that they can't be remedied by turning it off and on again.

Feedback

This is probably a good point to talk about the last of the 'push' approaches that I wanted to cover: feedback. In this context, 'feedback' means having someone (or a system) describe to you some of the consequences of your behaviour that you might not be aware of.

Picture the following: we set up a flight simulator for pilot training. One young pilot learns that he can successfully execute a barrel-roll in a 737. On his first real transatlantic flight he celebrates by performing a barrel-roll mid-way between London and New York. There is a tapping on the cabin door. One of the cabin crew, looking uncharacteristically unkempt, says: 'Um – little bit of feedback: some of the passengers were a tad perturbed by that manoeuvre'. 'Thanks,' he says, 'that's useful feedback'.

Oftentimes we go through life with only a partial awareness of the consequences of our actions – we have our own metaphorical 'cabin doors'. Because the affective consequences of our behaviours shape our later behaviour, not being aware of these may bring our development to a halt. A leader who doesn't realize that they are perceived as insensitive and abrasive may not progress to more senior positions if they are never made aware of this.

We all have limits on our ability to sense the consequences of our actions; for this reason, if you wish to continue to develop and learn throughout your lifetime, it is vital that you have as many sources of feedback as possible, otherwise you will simply rise to the limit of your self-awareness and stay there.

It's also true that with young children, adults sometimes struggle to give feedback in a way that is meaningful for them. Two-year-old Bobby whacks his sister Sarah with a rubber mallet. She starts crying. His mum takes him aside and says: 'How would you feel if Sarah hit you with a hammer?' and Bobby has a glazed expression because he literally can't imagine that, and the actual affective outcome is a parent talking to him. This is why parents sometimes say things like: 'Do that again and I will take away your sweets' instead.

Something similar happens in big organizations where the management team are worried about surviving in an increasingly volatile market, and say: 'We need to learn to be more innovative', but the glazed expressions on the faces of employees suggest that they don't feel very strongly about it. Honestly, if you wanted to do anything remotely transformative in your organization, the starting point would be a map of the things that your employees are currently concerned about – either that, or just hire people with different concerns.

In corporate settings (as well as in parent–child relationships), this 'affective misalignment' can present problems. The things that the management team worry about are very different from the things their front-line employees worry about. They wonder why their 'town hall' addresses fail to have the desired impact or their change programmes fail.

As I hope you can now see, a big part of it relates to this affective disconnect; people who are worried about getting home in time to collect their children from school are not inspired by the CEO's speech about the need for everyone to be innovative. In order to make these connections, we would have to use the same techniques described here: taking time to understand what it is that our audience care about, telling powerful stories, building powerful experiences – or just ensuring that the right incentives are in place.

On the subject of feedback, people vary tremendously in their ability to receive and accept it. Some will become immediately defensive at the hint of negative feedback, for example. Our sensitivities will tend to vary according to our cares – the more someone cares about a characteristic, the more sensitively the feedback must be handled. For example, if someone values interpersonal sensitivity and believes themselves to be sensitive, they may react strongly to the suggestion that they have behaved insensitively.

A final word on 'push' approaches to learning: this is sometimes interpreted as a request to make learning more 'engaging', and the criticism is then raised that not everything that is engaging necessarily leads to deep learning; for example, one might go to see a film about a mountaineering disaster and not recall very much detail, despite the film being awash with dramatic tension.

By way of response to this: first, we should not equate affective significance with engagement. Engagement is a term that is typically used to mean attention-grabbing content. It is the kind of thing one might come across in traditional marketing, that is, marketing that is designed to have the greatest impact on the greatest number of people, simply by virtue of appealing to our shared nature.

But, as I have pointed out, this is not really a very effective approach, as it doesn't directly address the things that *I* care about in *this specific context.* So, all things being equal, a dramatic fall from a great height is likely to be one of the more memorable and engaging scenes in a mountaineering movie – but what really matters is whether I am about to climb a mountain myself. It is *my* affective context that determines what is stored, after all.

So long as we neglect the personal significance of experiences and simply strive to produce 'engaging' content, we will achieve only a tiny fraction of the learning that we might otherwise accomplish.

'Pull' approaches to learning (elimination)

So far, I have been talking about 'push' approaches – ways that you can transfer affective significance to people, so that they care about something, which in turn drives their learning. But what will they learn from?

Resources

Once someone cares about something, they will be quite happy to draw on resources that are available to them. They will 'pull' from the sources of support to hand. It's quite easy to get 'push' and 'pull' situations mixed up. Let me tell a story about a time I did exactly that.

Around 20 years ago I was working for a global telecoms company that sells the kinds of phones that you have on your desk, if you still have one (either a desk or a desk phone). They were massively functional and blindingly complex to use. So we were tasked with building e-learning for customers wanting to get value from their complicated phones (basically we were patching a poorly designed system with training).

As mentioned previously, we built an e-learning programme, featuring a computer-based simulation of the phone in which artificial characters would call you and ask you to perform a range of tasks, which gradually increased in complexity. The characters had an element of artificial intelligence, their expressions and tone changed in response to their degree of satisfaction, the storyline was branching and randomized – the whole experience built into a complex gamified environment.

I was an idiot. The point when someone learns how to set up a conference call is the point where they are on the phone to someone important who says: 'Can you add Bob to this call?' – and at that point they do not need a

40-minute gamified simulation. They need a one-page guide beside the phone that says 'Press X, Y and Z to set up a conference call.' We built a course. We should have built a resource.

Note that if we had built a handy resource it would probably have remained, dog-eared, by the phone for months. It's unlikely that people would memorize it; at best they would become so familiar with the more frequent functions that they no longer needed to refer to them.

So when you know that people care about something, it is best to build a resource. But what is a resource?

Resources are sometimes called 'performance support' because in general they are anything that is effective in helping you to tackle the task at hand. You probably create resources yourself without realizing it – for example, have you ever taken a picture of something important that you think you will later forget, so that you can view it on your phone? WiFi codes, for example? Congratulations. You created a resource – you thought: 'I probably won't remember this, so I will take a picture that I can refer back to later'.

A resource can be a person, or a map, or a checklist, or any number of handy things – there are some more suggestions for experiences and resources in Figure 5.1 at the end of this chapter.

These days, people often use Google as a resource – they hit a problem and they Google the answer. My favourite example of a resource is the map of the London Underground. Many years ago, I had a folding paper version that I would carry around. These days I have it as an app. Either way, there is absolutely no doubt that it helps me to get from one place in London to another place in London, on a daily basis.

Note that there is something really important about this definition: sometimes you will find yourself looking at a piece of content that someone has called a 'resource' – but if you can't actually think of a situation where this would be the best thing to have to hand, then it probably isn't a resource at all. It's just 'content'.

Before I talk about different types of resource, it's worth explaining what makes them distinctive.

First, as explained above, a resource is not what you get when you chop learning content into smaller pieces. It is not 'micro-learning'. I see this mistake a great deal. It happens because people still have a model of learning in which learning is all about getting content into people's heads. These are the people who tried 'dumping content' into two-hour lectures, and very little of it stuck. So they broke the same content into smaller 20-minute 'e-learning modules', and people hated that and it wasn't any better. Now they are breaking it into 5-minute videos and calling them 'resources', but the underlying approach is still the same – it's still content dumping.

A resource is task-centric, not topic-centric. When you look at a resource, you should be able to think of the task that it would help you to do. When I look at the Underground map, I can immediately see that it would help me get around London. On the other hand, when I look at a five-minute video where someone pontificates about 'leadership styles', I have no idea what that would help me to do. Except, perhaps, pontificate about leadership styles.

Of course, this implies something about how you create resources – you can only really create effective resources by talking to people and understanding the things that concern them, and what they are trying to do. If, on the other hand, all you have done is gather up some stuff that you think might help people and shove it in a course – then probably you are content dumping.

This distinction gets easier to spot with practice. If you are asked to look at some 'learning content' that is being presented as a resource, ask yourself: 'What would this help someone to do?' If there is no specific task for which it would be really useful, then it is almost certainly content dumping.

CASE STUDY   A Sherlock Holmes mystery: A story
about resources and courses

At the start of my career I worked for an organization that had a great many field-based engineers. They were typically men, with a background in telecommunications, and they would drive around the country in vans, fixing the kind of complicated telecommunications equipment that big organizations procure – such as a PABX (Private Area Branch Exchange). No – don't nod off – still with me? Good.

My team, the e-learning team, were, essentially, corporate vampires. People would point us at some bloated beast of a training course and we would descend on it from a great height, suck the life out of it and leave them with the bare bones. Regular training professionals would shudder when we entered the room.

In this particular story, we had been asked to take a look at a five-day training course that the entire population of field-based engineers were currently going through. The backstory is that the company was introducing a new product – a hulking new kind of PABX the size of a small wardrobe – that was difficult to install and they needed to get everyone trained before they started selling it in six months' time. The expectation was that we would take the five-day format, strip out some of the content, stuff it into an e-learning course and save everyone time and money.

I was curious about this course. I was pretty sure that if I sat through five days of dense technical instructions, I wouldn't remember much of it six months later – but maybe the engineers were just a different kind of creature. So before we did anything, I exercised my management prerogative and sent one of my team on the course to find out what was going on.

He returned a week later, looking a little worse for wear, and we talked about the course (I've decided to render our conversation in the style of Sherlock Holmes/Dr Watson):

'So, Watson – tell me about the course. Don't leave out any detail,' I commanded.

'Well, Holmes, it was unbelievably boring. Crushingly so. At times I felt as though I could feel my soul leaving my body.'

'Details, Watson, details!' I urged, tapping my pipe on the mantelpiece impatiently.

'Just countless hours of software configuration, installation, technical parameters – I confess it is all much of a blur,' Watson replied rather apologetically.

'Ah ha!' I expostulated. 'Just as I suspected! And surely our hapless engineers are not up to the task of committing that claptrap to memory?'

'Precisely, Holmes. As ever, your presentiments proved correct. They dull their period of incarceration to the extent that they are able, spending their evenings in merriment and drink, then descend into a catatonic state during the day, suitably anaesthetized.'

'Pray tell – is there an examination of some manner at the end?' I mused.

'There is not – they are sent on their way clutching an enormous, cumbersome, training manual.'

'Great Scott! And to what use do they put this instructional behemoth?' I exclaimed.

'None whatsoever. They heave it to the luggage compartment of their motor car and put it out of mind.'

I pondered the mystery for a while, the wheels of my mind turning like cogs in some great steam engine as I pressed the fingers of my right hand to my forehead.

'And in the likely eventuality that they should, in time, encounter a situation in which they are compelled to complete the installation procedure – what then?'

'Oh – the canny chaps have come up with a capital scheme,' Watson replied. 'They've fashioned a manner of "checklist" in Microsoft Excel – which document contains step-by-step instructions on what to do. Should they find themselves in the unfortunate position of having to install the confounded thing – they simply telephone a fellow engineer, and request that they email the checklist.'

It was an instructive mystery for me to unravel, for two reasons: first, it illustrated how much more powerful resources could be than a course. Courses suck. The whole premise is that you will carry all this stuff around in your head and people almost never do. A map is *so* much better than having to remember directions.

Second, it illustrated the power of being audience-centric in your design approach. Had we not taken the time to understand the context in which our audience were operating, we could quite easily have cooked up an e-learning course based on the very same instruction manual that was being handed to engineers. It would have been equally useless.

Since that time, it has often been my experience that when we talk to people doing a job, they have figured out a more effective way to get it done than training – often creating resources of their own. Usually, these informal resources bear little or no relation to the standard operating procedures that we have been given to work on.

As a result, we decided not to build an e-learning course. Instead we built a sort of video companion where you could watch someone do something instead of being told about it. I imagine it was all the same to our sponsors ('e-learning – video-guide – whatever'), but the engineering team made much better use of it.

The next interesting thing to note is whether or not people *use* the resources that we create for them. Have you ever had that experience where you need the answer to a question – such as how to cook something – and when you Google it you have a choice between a page of text and a video – and you choose the page of text? Why is that? Don't people prefer video?

As a rule of thumb, people will use whatever is easiest in a given situation, and so unless your resource is the route of least resistance, people will choose the alternative. This is probably why you choose text over video on many occasions – video is a richer format, but when it comes to resources, simplicity is king. It is quicker to scan a page of instructions than to listen to a video (pausing and replaying, skipping the annoying intro).

This problem sometimes emerges where organizations create really useful resources for people, then bury them in some horrible IT system where they are impossible to find. Instead of tracking down the resources, people simply turn to the person next to them and 'ask a friend'. It's just easier.

This consideration becomes really important when engineering environments to optimize performance – not only do the right resources need to be designed, they need to be accessible at precisely the points when people need them. A neat example of this is the washing instructions in clothes. Clothes don't come with an instruction manual, which inevitably makes its way to the bottom of a kitchen drawer – instead you pick them up as you are about to throw them into the washing machine, and the instructions are right there.

Finally, let's revisit a deep, philosophical point: good resources often *eliminate* learning. In fact the better a resource is, the more it reduces the need to learn. As humans, we are cognitive misers. This means that if it is easier to avoid storing information in our heads, we will. These days, we seem to be referencing more and more – Googling our way through life rather than memorizing information. And why not? Learning is cognitively costly, so it makes sense to look things up whenever possible.

Some of you may have noticed that my Underground map is not (strictly speaking) a learning tool. In fact, quite the opposite. I have been using the same map daily for many years, which suggests that it has actively *suppressed* my learning. What I mean is that if I were forced to find my way around London without a map, I am pretty sure I would have picked up much of the layout in a matter of weeks. But *with* the map, I barely know a single route.

Here's another example: a shopping list. Imagining sending two groups of people to the supermarket: one group has to memorize 50 items, the other has them on a list. Who do you imagine will remember more of the items a day later? The list works to remove the need to learn. There is nothing stopping a person memorizing the items on the list, should they wish to do so – but under what conditions would they do that? Perhaps if the writing were illegible, or the list written on a giant cumbersome cardboard box. You get my point: the better a resource works as a resource, the less likely we will learn.

This is another reason why we cannot equate resources with 'microlearning'. Oftentimes resources *eliminate* the need to learn – so we can't really call them micro-learning. But I imagine some of you are not entirely happy with this. Quite right. There are times when we Google something – or YouTube it – and we *do* learn; we do store the information in our heads.

For example, I might look up how to cook pancakes, watch a short video, then know how to do it next time without looking it up. So when does learning happen from a resource and when not?

Consider this: how long would it take me to memorize a map of the Underground? And how long to remember how to cook pancakes?

The key to understanding whether or not a resource aids or suppresses learning is the relative costs in a specific context: it's easy for me to reference the Underground map (since it is on my phone) and would take months to memorize. On the other hand, if I am cooking pancakes more than a couple of times, it's easier for me to remember a couple of steps than it is to listen to that annoying TV chef all over again while trying not to get batter on my phone screen.

This point is worth considering, because there is no absolute answer – it will vary from individual to individual and from context to context. It might be easier to use an iPad app to identify stellar constellations, but if your objective is to impress a date on a hot summer's night, you might commit them to memory. We will invest the effort, given sufficient affective returns.

This final aspect of resources makes some educators quite uneasy, I suspect; educators are used to thinking in terms of learning objectives and the information that people 'must remember'. Our new model shifts the locus of control to the learner: our job is to create effective resources, but whether or not they choose to learn from them or just use them is entirely up to the individual.

The implication for learning measurement is also important: it becomes irrelevant to measure what knowledge someone has been able to memorize; instead we focus on what someone is able to do and leave the decisions around what to learn and what not to learn to them.

From a training perspective, it is important that the assessment conditions resemble the operating conditions; for example, if I am unlikely to have access to a laptop computer in the operating environment, I should not have access to it during the assessment.

I will return to this topic – learning elimination – in the next chapter, since it is especially important from the perspective of the future of learning. But for now let's consider some possible resource types.

Video

When education people get their hands on video, bad things happen. Once again, these things tend to happen because people still have this corrupt notion of learning as knowledge transfer, and they see new technologies and media as a way of doing precisely the same awful things they did before – only more efficiently.

Imagine, for example, that you were a university with lots of teaching staff busily giving lectures, and students who pay to attend the university but frequently don't attend the lectures. You are under pressure to reduce costs and modernize, but you don't really know what that means except that it should involve doing something online.

One really awful thing that you could do would be to film those lectures, put them online together with some documents and a chat box and call it a MOOC (massive open online course), and charge people in far-off places a small amount to watch them. Why would this be a bad idea?

First, it's a bad idea because students are there for the certificates, not the lectures. Since generally they get the certificates for passing the exams and not for turning up to the lectures, they will figure out the most efficient way to achieve that result – which is not attending the lectures. If you attend the lectures it is typically not to learn, it is to take notes. A person takes notes so that they don't have to remember what was said, but instead can refer back to the notes. Students then use the notes to revise for the exam at the shortest possible distance from the actual exam that they deem feasible, which is sometimes the night before.

Of course, knowing that this is how it works, the smart student won't go to the lectures but either make use of the textbooks or just borrow the notes of a student who is so terribly anxious about their future job prospects and afraid of their parents that they actually go to lectures.

It might sound a bit sweeping to say: 'People don't attend lectures to learn'. Theoretically you could learn from a lecture – if it was largely based around conversations, stories and practical activities. But of course they are not; in part because universities bump up the student/teacher ratios in the interests of saving money, but largely because teachers believe that getting information into people's heads is what they are there to do and they have a huge amount of information to get through. Ironically, they literally don't have time for learning.

When you put videos of lectures online, people will sometimes go and take a look – often just because of an institution's reputation – and quickly figure out that 1) you don't get a certificate, and 2) the lectures don't actually help them to do any of the things they are trying to do (so aren't useful resources).

So respected Ivy League institutions share their teaching materials with the world, only to find that hardly anyone does more than glance at them, for the simple reason that education is not really about learning but about granting certificates (which grant access to jobs), and if there are no certificates on offer, there are better ways to learn. You would have thought that if these courses really *were* about learning, the world would be awash with highly educated people by now, but it is not.

Even if there *were* certificates on offer, people would quickly figure out (as students have been doing for decades) more efficient ways of obtaining them – through forgery, subcontracting or just good old last-minute revision. This all sounds crazy, but is actually fine, since if you actually ever get a job it is likely to bear scant relation to your area of study and in any case you will learn how to do it on the job.

The upshot is: don't use video for content dumping.

So what are good uses of video? Video works well in two specific contexts, one 'push', one 'pull'.

In the 'push' context, video can be good for telling a story or communicating an emotion. We know this; we go to the movies. But a good story is rich in emotion, so if your speaker is as dull as ditchwater, don't put them in front of a camera, and for heaven's sake *get people to tell stories* (rather than trying to tell people what they know).

Also – never script video. Having spent many years filming people trying to communicate something, I have noticed that use of an autocue has two highly damaging effects: first, unless you are a professional it is immediately obvious to everyone watching that you are reading a script – and so any value in using video is lost (since you might as well have sent them the script); second, if *you* can't remember the points you want to make, what are the chances that someone watching will?

In the 'pull' context, video is useful for showing people how to do something that would be tough to describe in words. If I am trying to learn to dance, for example, it's much easier to watch someone do it than it is to translate a description into words. A good example of this is game walkthroughs, where people stuck at a point in their video game will watch to see how someone else has mastered the challenge.

Mostly, though, when we are looking for a resource, for example when Googling, we avoid video and click instead on links to text formats. This is because we intuitively know that videos are often used for content dumping: the laborious extended introduction where the presenter blathers on and on.

With a document, we can quickly scan and find the bit we need – so we choose these. There are a number of resource formats: infographics, guides, tips, flow-charts and so on. The important thing is not the format itself, but the extent to which it directly addresses a person's concerns.

For example, 'top 10 mistakes' is usually a popular resource in any field, since most people are implicitly concerned about not looking stupid. Despite this, it is very rare to see 'top 10 mistakes' feature in an educational programme, for the reason that education is typically content-centric rather than context-centric.

Tips for creating resources

When creating resources it is important to keep things as simple as possible and resist the temptation to slip into 'what people need to know' mode. Here are a couple of bits of general advice in simple text format:

Make it practical: talk to the context, not the content. It goes without saying that you need to understand the concerns and tasks people have if you are going to stand any chance at all of designing useful resources. Organize your resources by task, not topic: if I am trying to put up shelves, I just need 'How to put up shelves', not something that begins with 'Chapter One: The history of home maintenance'.

Keep it short: if your resource is not absolutely the easiest thing to find and use, people will use something else. In practice, this generally means nothing is more than one page. If it's longer than that, break it down.

Be visual: use diagrams and graphics where these will be easier to understand than words, but not just for the sake of it.

Design for use: good design isn't about making things look elegant, but about making them fit snugly into the context where they will be used. For example, you might design a screen of guidance for people driving subway trains – and then realize that black text on a white screen is very distracting when driving through tunnels.

Talk like a friend: something horrible happens to us at school, with the result that whenever people are asked to write something to do with learning, they slip into a 'teacherly' tone and attempt to sound vaguely academic.

Curate if you can: people will often create resources that already exist, and are better. Have a look at what is out there already before creating a resource.

Make it accessible: good resources will fail if you can't find them when you need them. Education still suffers from its authoritarian past, expecting people to learn *our* content from *our* systems – which of course is why students will skip lectures if they can get the information on the internet. Find out what your audience prefer, and use *their* approaches.

In summary, there are three key ingredients for effective resources:

1 **Utility:** they have to be genuinely useful (and not just some stuff that you threw together because you thought it looked useful).

2 **Accessibility:** they have to be the easiest thing to access and use when and where people need to access them (or they will use something else).

3 **Awareness:** people need to know where the resources are (so you may need to do some marketing or awareness-raising).

I hope that the examples in this chapter give you a good sense of what I mean when I describe the two classes of learning activity along the push–pull spectrum: experiences add to our concerns, while resources respond to them. The list above is just scratching the surface. Figure 5.1 might give you a better sense of some of the other things that you might consider when designing experiences or performance support (as well as some capabilities you might wish to develop) – but I am sure you can probably think of many more.

Some of the things I have listed above may sit on either – or both – sides of the diagram at times. For example, both 'mentoring' and 'coaching' I have listed as experiences, since they are generally scheduled sessions. But one can imagine situations in which coaches or mentors are available on demand – in which case their role is more akin to that of a resource. It is possible that they may play different roles at different times. As we have seen above, a video might be a simple 'how to' or a more extended narrative.

In order to support these two types of creative activity – the creation of resources and the creation of experiences – learning professionals will need a core set of techniques related to human-centred design. Many of these techniques already exist and are in use in other areas of design, such as product development. Learning professionals will have to extend this toolset, especially in the area of experience design, which is still largely unexplored territory.

Figure 5.1 Experience, resources and capabilities

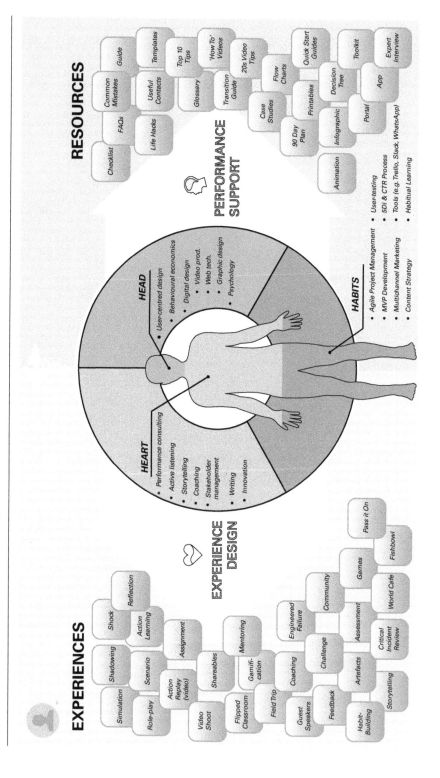

Allied with these techniques, learning professionals will need a wide range of creative capabilities in order to create the kinds of resources or experiences that will be most useful or impactful respectively.

Key points

- In any learning context we are either responding to the concerns that a person already has, or we are trying to create new concerns.
- These correspond to two types of learning intervention: 'pull' and 'push'.
- Pull: Build resources, not courses. These may well improve performance by reducing learning.
- Push: If you wish to build capability, design experiences. The defining characteristic of an experience is that it is emotionally impactful.
- You cannot design effective resources or experiences without understanding the people for whom you are designing them. Learning design must start with an analysis of what people care about.

As organizations anticipate the future, it seems that resources and guidance are set to play an ever-greater role in delivering employee performance improvements and competitive advantage as we inch our way towards automation.

The next chapter considers the shift from courses to resources in more detail.

Endnotes

1 J S Bruner (1966) *Toward a Theory of Instruction*, Belkapp Press, Cambridge, Mass.
2 Of course, if you want people to care about something that currently they don't, then getting them involved in meaningful interaction is a good place to start. In our experiment participants knew that they would be tested at the end – we had set them a familiar little challenge – so they were all equally engaged.

3 I have no idea if Ali actually said this, so please don't put it in an inspirational meme alongside a black and white photo of Ali and circulate it on the internet.

4 N Noddings (1992) *The Challenge to Care in Schools: An alternative approach to education*, Teachers College Press, New York

5 JaneElliott.com, janeelliott.com (archived at https://perma.cc/HS2T-XT8F)

6 Office for National Statistics. Graduates in the UK Labour Market: 2017, 24 November 2017, www.ons.gov.uk/employmentandlabourmarket/peopleinwork/employmentandemployeetypes/articles/graduatesintheuklabourmarket/2017 (archived at https://perma.cc/MAG8-JM95)

7 Although, as Jaak Panksepp notes, conditioning works best when pre-existing behavioural responses are being moulded: 'In the early years of my career I made an open challenge to my department's graduate students in psychobiology to train a hungry rat to run backward down an alleyway to obtain food... Many tried, but none succeeded.' (J Panksepp (1998) *Affective Neuroscience: The foundations of human and animal emotions*, Oxford University Press)

8 This sense of 'gamification', in which learning is made into a game, is much closer to what is later described as simulation. Describing it as simulation serves to differentiate this approach from the element of positive reinforcement, but also to focus attention on what will make it effective: namely whether or not the simulation actually resembles reality in a manner which allows for the transfer of learning.

9 A Bandura (1962) Social Learning through Imitation. In M R Jones (Ed), *Nebraska Symposium on Motivation* (pp 211–74), University of Nebraska Press

10 James Rilling et al found that areas of the brain that activated pro-social behaviour behaved differently depending on whether a participant believed they were playing against a human opponent or a machine (J Rilling et al. A neural basis for social co-operation, *Neuron*, 2002, **35** (2), 395–405).

11 S Choudhury, S Blakemore, S and T Charman. Social cognitive development during adolescence, *Social Cognitive and Affective Neuroscience*, 2006, **1** (3), 165–74

12 J Panksepp (1998) *Affective Neuroscience: The foundations of human and animal emotions*, Oxford University Press

13 G Anderson. Video games: Attitudes and habits of adults age 50-plus, *AARP Research*, June 2016 Washington, DC

14 Even here we can see how individual differences might come into play; conceivably someone who is very rich might play a game where they stand to lose a significant sum of money, having developed an immunity to consequences of a lesser nature.

15 And also because what educators might guess would be useful stuff to know in a situation often turns out to be wrong, so we end up teaching vastly more information than people actually need to know.

Learning elimination (performance consulting)

06

Resources, not courses

Have a look at Figure 6.1. It's a visual illustration of something that I have come to call the learning elimination curve.

The premise is simple: the further away from the point at which people need information ('point of need') you are, the more time and money you are going to waste trying to get people to memorize the information.

If, for example, you spend two days in a classroom learning about performance management six months before you are due to apply it, you might only recall three things. If you could deliver those three things to someone immediately before they need them, you would achieve the same outcome at a fraction of the time and cost. In other words, this curve represents the shift from courses (top right) to resources (bottom left).

You may have experienced this effect in your personal life where, for example, you use Google or YouTube to look things up as an alternative to having to memorize them.

If you are wondering where the curve comes from, it is Ebbinghaus upside-down; and while we have established that Ebbinghaus was a bit of an idiot, his research does hold true for mental flotsam – which is precisely the kind of information that people tend to push in educational programmes.

Further support for this phenomenon comes from a surgeon called Dr Atul Gawande, author of an excellent book called *The Checklist Manifesto*.[1] Atul was interested in how one might improve outcomes in life-and-death situations in his own professional field. He looked at how high-risk procedures are

Figure 6.1   The learning elimination curve

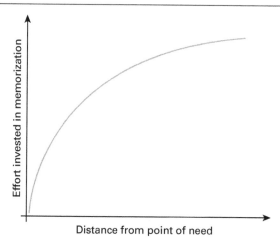

The amount of effort required to achieve a given performance outcome

successfully handled in other industries, spending time with Boeing, and began to appreciate the critical role played by one particular kind of resource – the checklist.

He subsequently designed and implemented a checklist to be used by surgical teams, and was able to cut deaths by half and reduce complications by 36 per cent – an extraordinary outcome, and considerably more successful that that achieved by lengthy training sessions. In essence, he had demonstrated that point-of-need performance support can be much more effective than conventional training at changing behaviour. The checklist had removed the need to learn, by externalizing the information.

Interestingly, some of the people who attempted to reproduce Atul's impressive results were unable to do so – the checklists didn't seem to make much of a difference. When they explored why, the most likely explanation seemed to be that they just didn't care enough to use them. Note that this is *precisely* what the affective context model would predict: resources are an effective approach for people who care about something, but for people who don't they will just be more noise.

That resources work extraordinarily well in some circumstances but not at all in others is a reminder of how important it is to understand the concerns of your audience: without knowing what is driving their behaviour, you can't confidently predict which approach – resources or experiences – will achieve the desired outcome.

But perhaps this is the right point to return to a question that may have continued to trouble you: when we produce resources, are these really 'learning resources'? Are we, in other words, just breaking the big chunks of learning that people encounter in courses into smaller pieces so as to deliver 'micro-learning'? The answer is: probably not.

As we saw previously, a resource is usually something that *reduces* your need to learn, so it cannot really be called 'learning' or 'micro-learning' – or any other kind of learning. Think back to my map of the London Underground example. I use this resource on a daily basis to help me get from one place to another around London – but at no point do I attempt to memorize it.

In fact (rather sadly) I have been using the same map for several years, but still have to consult it for familiar routes, which suggests the opposite: it is actually a *substitute* for learning. If someone had deprived me of my map, I suspect I would have learned a lot faster.

You may have experienced the same when using GPS in your car; you use it to drive a particular route frequently, but one day it doesn't work and you realize that you can't find the route on your own.

This is ominous news for note-taking in class. Why do you think students are taking notes in class? So that they can better remember the material? No! So that they *don't* have to remember the material! So they can *reduce* the learning that they do in class, and instead use the time to construct a useful *resource* that they can use to cram for the exam. That's a pitiful picture, isn't it? Lecturers reading from notes so that they don't have to remember the lecture, to students writing notes so that they don't have to remember it either, in order to create a resource they can use when the need arises.

You have probably observed a modern variation of this at conferences: people who see something useful being projected up on the screen take a snapshot of it with their mobile phones. They do this in order to create a resource – so that they don't have to commit it to memory. I sometimes do this with WiFi codes in public places on the assumption that in the 10 paces it takes to go from where the code is printed to the place where I am sitting, I will have forgotten it.

The bad news is that we are living through an era where the need to learn is being systematically eliminated. The good news is that if you're a learning professional, that's now your job (or maybe it's the other way around).

To understand why learning is being erased, imagine that you are running a London taxi company in the 1980s. Every single one of your cabbies needs to have The Knowledge – a gruelling accreditation, certifying that they are intimately familiar with over 60,000 streets and more than 100,000 places of note. Of course, someone with that kind of capability has a pretty scarce skill. They can command a certain salary.

And then someone invents GPS and at a stroke everything changes: now anyone can be a taxi driver. With real-time traffic data they can even outperform experienced London cabbies. Your entire business model changes, and then a new business model springs up – Uber.

Now imagine GPS for every job: GPS for every job means resources and guidance that allow people with little or no capability to get up to speed very quickly, and then outperform employees with years of experience. At the same time, our technology is being designed in such a way that it ships with no manuals. Nothing to learn.

All this should remind us of the Great Horse Manure Crisis of 1894. At around this time there were in excess of 11,000 horse-drawn cabs transporting people around the streets of London. In addition, there were several thousand horse-drawn buses and an estimated 50,000 horses. Each of these horses produced anything up to 16 kilos of manure a day and around 2 litres of urine. The crisis had reached such proportions that in 1894 *The Times* confidently predicted: 'In 50 years, every street in London will be buried under nine feet of manure'. But this nightmarish scenario never materialized – instead we discovered the motor car.

The modern equivalent of the Great Horse Manure Crisis is the Future Skills Crisis. In 2015, the UK Commission on Employment and Skills catalogued a chronic shortage of skilled workers. Other reports suggest that by 2024 there will be four million too few skilled workers to meet demand.[2]

But there is no future skills crisis. Not if we make (almost) every job doable by someone with next to no capability (unless automation is a better option, or as a stepping-stone on the way to automation).

It is a mistake to see this process – the process of learning elimination – as incidental rather than thematic – as merely a side effect of technology rather than a fundamental trend. Human beings are systematically externalizing knowledge, so that their need to learn is reduced. This activity takes a variety of forms – for example the provision of context-sensitive guidance, improved user-experience design, hybrid human/AI working and, ultimately, automation.

We do this because of homeostasis. As described at the outset, homeostasis describes an organism's efforts to create optimal living conditions. For example, simple multicellular organisms may move from environments that are too cold to ones that are warmer. As they grow in complexity, organisms are able to moderate, to some extent, their internal environment independently of what is happening around them.

Learning represents a sophisticated homeostatic mechanism – our attempts to adapt to our environment in complex ways – for example to anticipate danger or find food. But with technology we have unprecedented latitude to *externalize* homeostasis; to create an environment that responds to our every desire – in other words, one that requires no learning.

As an example, when I was younger you needed to learn complicated commands and programming languages in order to communicate with computers, so as children we learned programming skills in anticipation of a world where we would need to communicate with computers. But then people invented touch-screen devices that were so simple that even a three-year-old child could use them. The need to learn complex commands was eliminated.

In terms of human–computer interaction, the next frontier is voice: the ability to talk to machines using the same language that we develop as infants.

When we imagine the future, it's easy to picture sophisticated voice-controlled devices like Amazon's Echo in the workplace, providing expert step-by-step advice. But actually, guidance and resources can be much simpler: a first step on the road to automation involves codifying what makes for good performance in a given role – for example in the form of simple tips, checklists or easy-to-follow guidance.

In other words, we could largely erase the future skills crisis by building simple, easy-to-use resources such as checklists. Equally, despite all the dire predictions about robots taking your job, you don't have to worry about automation if nobody has actually taken the time to transcribe how you do it today.

As I say, the good news is that, at least for the foreseeable future, learning professionals are well positioned to undertake this learning elimination work. We possess the capabilities to design and create resources and guidance that accelerate performance in a wide variety of roles, paving the way for a business model that can deliver greater performance with a fluid workforce and lower levels of capability – and at lower operating costs. If you are a business and you aren't already doing this, your competitors soon will be.

Performance consulting

In recent years, businesses have developed a name for the approach in which the need to learn is reduced: performance consulting. In essence performance consulting is an extension of the same trick used by the Egyptians – we have evidence that they, too, externalized knowledge in the form of checklists to avoid people having to learn information.

Performance consulting works by systematically identifying the critical stages involved in optimum performance and changing the performance context to make getting the job done as easy as possible. Since learning is inherently effortful, we remove this where we can.

Here's an everyday example: you have to buy 50 items at the supermarket. Are you going to memorize them or write a list? Memorizing them is the educational approach. It's arduous, time-consuming, unreliable and often pointless. Making a list is the performance consulting approach – it's quick, reliable and saves you time. It eliminates the need to learn.

Note that performance consulting is not limited to creating checklists and guides ('performance support'), we may also want to change other aspects of the performance context. To see how this works, consider once again the challenge of having to go to the supermarket to buy 50 items. Memorizing them all would be time-consuming and effortful (but you would be learning in the educational sense).

At the start of a project, we have to make a decision as to whether learning will pay off. If you were going to be buying the same items every week for ten years, it might – but chances are your shopping list is going to change, so learning may not be the best approach.

A performance consulting approach would suggest a checklist. Not only is this quicker and easier than learning, it reduces the chance of error. This is why aircraft pilots use checklists every time they fly. So resources *eliminate* learning.

But note that performance consulting need not stop with resources: we might design a fridge that creates the shopping list for you. We might then wonder why you were shopping at all, and instead have the fridge send your list to your supermarket for them to deliver the items when you are in. Now, not only do you not have to memorize the list, you don't have to learn how to shop at a supermarket or drive a car.

This broader scope is common when we do performance consulting – we end up with a range of recommendations starting with performance support, and extending to larger changes to process or operating environment. Oftentimes the latter are more costly to change, so it is only the former that are implemented.

One point I need to reiterate, though: performance consulting owes its effectiveness at improving performance to externalizing capability and knowledge; changing things around us so that we don't need to learn, rather than changing us. This means that performance consulting tells us nothing about learning, includes no techniques for learning, and is not based on any approaches to learning whatsoever. It's a wonderful technique for side-stepping all that.

Of course it's not impossible that someone might memorize a checklist, just as it is not impossible for someone to memorize a map of the underground – but these resources are designed to encourage the opposite. You will learn things more slowly if you are using a resource than if you had to commit things to memory. So at the beginning of every project aimed at improving performance we have to figure out if we want to do that by creating learning experiences (and changing people), or eliminating learning (and changing the context).

It would be mischievous of me to suggest that 'learning professionals' using this approach should be renamed 'unlearning professionals', but the serious point is that our focus as a profession shouldn't be learning, but performance and experience and the various techniques for changing them.

I have found that many people struggle with this idea – that information might discourage learning rather than encourage it; intuitively they feel that if we provide performance support this will inevitably aid learning somehow. Let's consider the following hypothetical situation so that we can bring the mechanism into focus.

Imagine the task of learning the irrational number Pi (3.141592... etc) to one thousand places. This is the kind of thing that very few people would do. Why is that? The answer is that the cost is high – it's a very laborious and difficult thing to do – and the benefit low – it's not the kind of thing we need to do often, and if we do there is rarely a big benefit in having memorized it.

So imagine you are performance consulting on a type of job where people occasionally need to know what, say, the 337th digit of Pi is. A sensible thing to do would be to produce a one-page document that people could easily access when they need it, enabling them to look up Pi whenever they need to.

Now, it would be very odd to go back to people, a few weeks after providing this document and say: 'Well – have you learned it yet!?' Your audience would look at you oddly: 'Of course we haven't learned it! What was the point of providing the quick reference if you expect us to learn it!? In fact, now we can easily look it up there is less need than ever to learn it!'

So you see, you have actually *reduced* the likelihood that people will learn by providing the resource. In essence this is because people are cognitive misers, and if there is an easier alternative to memorizing something, they will take it.

But some people still come back to me and say: 'But surely there are some circumstances in which providing resources encourages learning?'

The answer is that learners can always choose to memorize something if the benefit outweighs the cost – but the whole point of good resources is to discourage this by reducing the cost of *not* memorizing something. This is why the London Underground map prevents me from learning routes – it's so accessible (on the wall, on my device) and so easy to use that there really is very little cost to me referring.

Paradoxically, the worse a resource is – if it's hard to understand or find – the more likely it is to encourage learning (because you have raised the cost of referring and made memorizing relatively attractive).

To see how this works, let's consider a context in which someone *would* use our Pi resource to learn: imagine someone who is a maths nerd – someone who obsesses over mathematics, cares deeply about it and is part of a club of like-minded individuals. They pride themselves on their prowess – but like almost all humans they instinctively care what their peers think of them too.

They realize that memorizing Pi to a thousand places would be a great way to show off and win respect and admiration from their fellows. Despite the significant cost of – night after night – committing the numbers to memory, they put in the hours because the benefits are so great.

Do you see how this works? It is the challenge, and the things that people care about that drive learning. So whilst performance consulting aims always at externalizing knowledge and capability, there is nothing to stop people learning if they care sufficiently. If you wanted someone to learn, you'd need to make them care.

This is where performance consulting, in isolation, is limited. You are tacitly assuming that what people care about is fixed – but if one person cares about patient outcomes they may use the checklist, whilst another who does not, will not. Changing what people care about *is* learning design, the rest is up to them.

The dangers of focusing on tasks alone

Whilst performance consulting is a quick way to improve performance, the focus on performance and tasks means that it will always miss the complete set of things that affect how a person behaves, and so will always be limited in its potential for impact.

To see this, consider a small child on their first day of school. A performance consulting approach would identify one by one the tasks on the 'critical path' to achieving their goals, then analyse the changes that would make achieving these easier.

For example, new students might need to identify their teachers – a gallery of staff with pictures and names posted in communal areas might help. They need to get to classes on time, so a printed personalized timetable would be handy. They may be unfamiliar with the layout, so a school map – perhaps even lines painted on the floor – would help a new student get to classes on time.

All these things are good to do and will measurably improve performance against a number of key metrics.

But what performance consulting *doesn't do* is analyse and address concerns – and these are what are ultimately driving learning. If you talk to new students, you will learn that what they are really worried about is fitting in, making friends, not embarrassing themselves, looking cool, dressing in a way that impresses people, saying the right things, not having their parents be mad at them and so on (interestingly these are almost identical to the concerns adults have when joining a new organization).

If you understand these concerns, there are a whole host of additional experiences and resources that you can design to address them. Performance consulting is not an approach designed to surface or address concerns, so it will always miss a big piece of the picture. Sure, kids want to get to class on time, but if you don't understand *why* then you can easily design the wrong solution.

Conversely you might struggle to understand why kids with all the right performance support are nevertheless turning up late. It might be that this is deliberate – that they want to look cool, and being regularly late to class is part of their 'rebel' image.

Despite its shortcomings, performance consulting is a huge step forward from conventional education. So what stops learning professionals embracing this approach? It's an approach that dramatically improves performance, time to competence, productivity and employee experience – all top concerns for business leaders. So why not?

In short, it's tough for people with an emotional attachment to learning to switch to learning elimination. To let go of the (educational) idea that somehow our job is about getting knowledge into people's heads. It's tough for us to switch from building individual capability to building organizational capability.

But if we *can* let go, we can become the future architects that our organizations need, and for the first time have a genuinely positive effect on performance and employee experience. If we don't, there is every likelihood that companies offering 'performance guidance systems' will rapidly replace the role of learning and development in delivering improved performance.

CASE STUDY   Tie off: A story about the importance of learner-centricity

I joined an organization that had about 80,000 employees based around the world, and a similar number of contract staff.

The induction programme included eight hours of e-learning modules, which were classed as mandatory. Since these modules were now my responsibility, I had a look at the usage data. In the four years that the modules had been live, only 300 people had successfully completed them. We had around 6,000 people joining each year.

We decided that fixing this problem should be a priority, since when people join an organization this is both a time when learning is likely to occur and when things may go badly wrong. Changing jobs is a kind of transition and transitions are interesting because the word 'transition' describes a collection of interrelated challenges. Transitions are typically intensely emotional phases in a person's life.

As explained above, challenges drive learning, so if we are to make the best use of resources, we should look to support people as they make these transitions, since this is where they are learning the most and where their future behaviour will be defined.

The conventional way to design a learning programme (of almost any kind) is as follows: scoot around the organization and ask important people or experts for a list of things that people need to know. This is true whether we are talking about university or corporate education. While this may sound like a reasonable approach, it is terrible in practice, since learning is actually driven by the concerns of the people learning – and these are invariably very different from those of experts and senior people.

That is not to say you shouldn't talk to these people – just that their concerns can only be addressed in the context of the learner's concerns. An organization may want people to be more inclusive, but just dumping content related to 'inclusivity' into an induction programme will not achieve that outcome.

Instead, we talked to people who had recently joined the organization – 13 focus groups in all – using the techniques described above. We discovered that their concerns and tasks varied across a spectrum: at one end a general anxiety about fitting in and not making a fool of themselves, at the other end more specific tasks, for example figuring out how to access work emails on their personal mobile device.

In discussing these areas with new starters, it becomes clear that seemingly trivial resources can have a big impact on confidence, engagement and performance.

One of the most popular resources we produced was a simple checklist with step-by-step guidance for the first few days, weeks and months. While this might seem like a fairly uninspiring item, it is actually very demoralizing for people to join on an emotional high, then rapidly deteriorate as a sense of uncertainty and confusion about what they are doing sets in. In practice, organizations that worry about 'building engagement' might start by cataloguing the ways in which they are systematically destroying it in the first place.

Overall, we discovered a complex matrix of interrelated concerns and tasks. We itemized each, and during the design process we involved a diverse group of people in thinking through what kind of resource or experience might help people address each of the things on the list. Some things were clearly suited to video treatments: for example, we helped people get a sense of the culture by interviewing people in informal settings, without a script.

We included the executive management team. It was the first time they had been filmed without a script. At one point the CEO asked: 'Tie on or tie off?', and in retrospect I realized the answer to that question probably changed the culture of the organization. We created simple checklists and guides.

Of course, nobody worried much about what we were doing – as far as they were concerned we were creating some grubby e-learning content that hardly anyone would use, so there was no real risk of us having much impact.

But what we created was not e-learning modules. We avoided working with companies that produced learning content and instead worked with agencies more used to producing games, marketing or apps. We fretted over the 'user experience'. We created a rich mix of video, animation, guides and so on that people could access easily on their mobile devices and which answered their questions.

Some of these questions had been, essentially, unanswered for decades – questions such as: 'How do I fit in to the bigger picture?' and 'What do we stand for?', or 'What is our culture?', or 'What do the different parts of this organization do?'

The results were literally unprecedented. In the four years that the site was live, it enjoyed more than a million visits. Most people in the organization had used the site multiple times. All of the activity was by choice, and it was the most popular content site anywhere in the company. Interestingly, it wasn't perceived as a 'learning' site, due to the fact that it actually contained helpful stuff presented in an easy-to-use format. Different parts of the organization began to approach us to ask how they might do something similar, and the communications team began to take a keen interest in our activity.

The most negative consequence was a proliferation of people attempting to use technology in a superficially similar way, without understanding that the 'secret sauce' was user-centricity.

These days, creating a short film, an app or a website is not terribly difficult – but if you skip the step where you analyse what people care about and what they are trying to do, then once again you are content dumping. I saw a lot of this, and still do today: misguided attempts to imitate this approach, by mimicking the application of technology. Invariably they fail.

Another negative consequence was that different parts of the organization would approach us with content they expected us to dump on people:

> 'We'd like you to put this on the induction site.'
>
> 'What is it?'
>
> 'A 40-slide update on our project management philosophy.'
>
> And we would say: 'What, exactly, would this help someone to do?'

The thought had never occurred to people that learning content should help someone to do a specific task – they had just assumed that our job was to transfer information into people's heads.

So we rejected the 40-page document, but if they liked we would help them to think through questions about their audience, the process for discovering their audience's tasks and concerns, and then the options for designing useful stuff or challenging experiences.

People struggled with the conceptual shift: they would ask odd questions such as: 'How long does it take to *do*?' and we would reply: 'How long does it take to Google?' They would ask about 'completion rates', and we would point out that there were no completion rates (since it makes no sense to track completion of a one-page guide that in any case we were expecting people to use rather than memorize), but that instead we used Google Analytics to track activity and develop our content strategy.

We also did away with instructional designers: our team had a mix of media production, digital marketing and user-experience design capability.

> ## Key points
>
> - Providing resources at the point of need will often be a far more efficient and effective way to shift performance than training.
> - Resources won't work if people don't care enough to use them, or if they are inaccessible.
> - Resources often eliminate the need to learn. Whether or not they increase or reduce learning will depend on the individual and the context.

You may be a bit worried about some of what I have said – and rightly so. Whilst eliminating the need to learn is a fast track to performance in the majority of cases, there may be times when we want to transform people – for example to prepare them for organization change, to change the way they feel about something important, or simply because we care about their growth.

To change people, we need to design an experience that matters to them. In the next chapter we will look at how to do this.

Endnotes

1 A Gawande (2011) *The Checklist Manifesto: How to get things right*, Profile Books
2 UK Department for Education. UKCES Employer Skills Survey 2015: UK report, 28 January 2016, www.gov.uk/government/publications/ukces-employer-skills-survey-2015-uk-report (archived at https://perma.cc/D5QR-8FXT)

Defining experiences

07

How one becomes who one is

'Find what you love and let it kill you.'

CHARLES BUKOWSKI

As someone who has never been terribly troubled by social life, I confess I struggle to understand why people devote so much time to it, I mean – parties, socializing, meetings – honestly, there is only so much superficial chit-chat I can stomach before I feel like slapping someone with a large fish.

Certainly I can envisage situations in which people might be useful, but by and large I try and keep my interactions to a minimum so that I can focus on the things that matter: like for example learning, cognition, philosophy, neuro-science and the future. So far this has worked out fairly well for everyone concerned – I think about stuff like that, and people don't invite me to parties.

In the previous chapter we talked about individual differences: but how do those differences come about? What made you the person you are today – and if I wanted to change you, how would I do that?

Imagine, for the sake of argument, that people start out in life with a 'pool' of 'care points' that they can choose to spend on a number of classes of experience that they may encounter – things like 'people' or 'routines' or 'numbers' or 'theories' or 'visual experience' or 'music' and so on. If, for example, you spend all your care points on the 'people' category, then you become a tremendously social person – the life and soul of the party – constantly craving social interaction and sensitive to the moods of people around you, but useless with a spreadsheet and with very little to say about postmodern philosophy.

I use the expression 'for the sake of argument' because although I am not aware of any research that suggests we have something like a pool of care points, I would like to suggest that this is a useful analogy.

What we *do* know to be well supported by research is the finding that the brain has a number of areas of functional specialization,[1] which to some extent encroach on each other – so for example having a large area of your brain dedicated to social interaction may mean that you are not quite as good at something else, depending in part on which areas of the brain tend to sit next to each other. This is why there is nothing worse than a disco for neuroscientists.

As a result, if we are happy to think of affective significance as being a more or less global way of functioning – in other words various stimuli whether social or visual for example – are processed in terms of their affective significance, then you arrive at something like my proposed points system.

If you have ever played role-based games (whether dice-based games like Dungeons & Dragons or computer-based games) you will recognize this approach to character creation: you have, say, 20 points that you can allocate to characteristics such as strength, agility, charisma and so on. But more of one means less of the others.

As I type this, I realize that if you *are* the kind of person who has purchased this book, then this system may well be familiar to you, whereas if instead you are the kind of person with great social skills then you were probably not sitting in a basement playing Dungeons & Dragons during your youth and are – right now – not reading this book, but instead out making friends. So far, so good.

The point of all this is that thinking about affective significance in this way may well help us to understand neurodiversity. What would happen, say, if someone put *all* of their affective significance points into 'routine' (let's assume there is a part of the brain specialized for handling routine). These would then be people who are tremendously sensitive to routine and small variations in them, become very upset at disruption to routines, and hardly seem to notice people and social situations.

Do we know people like this? Yes, we do – at the extreme end of the spectrum we are describing some autistic characteristics.

Likewise, we also know people who spend all their 'affective context' points on social skills. These are people who thrive on social stimuli and are quite happy to use social interaction as a means to navigate the world rather than, say, routine.

Individual differences

We sometimes fall into the trap of thinking of individual differences in terms of 'types' or diagnostic categories: autism and attention deficit hyperactivity disorder (ADHD) being two topical examples. In recent years, advances in genome analysis have made it possible to understand the contributing genetic factors underlying these superficial categorizations.

No psychological type is the product of a single gene. Although there is a strong genetic component to psychological variation, this is the product of the interactions between thousands of genes. In other words there is no single gene for 'autism', any more than there is a single gene for 'healthy' – there are just lots of genes that make a bit of difference.

This means that a categorization like 'autistic' or 'manic-depressive' is exactly like saying that everyone over 6 foot 2 inches in height is 'tall', and everyone beneath that 'short'. It's an arbitrary distinction.

Although the things we are genetically inclined to care about vary, they often do so according to a normal distribution. At the extremes of this distribution are the 'superpowers'. In a gaming context, spending all your points on one characteristic – such as 'stealth' or 'strength' results in a character who is rubbish in a whole host of situations but seems almost superhuman in a narrow range.

Imagine someone who said 'to hell with it – I'm going to spend all my affective context points on numbers, or on music!' what would happen then?

Our model would suggest that by virtue of attaching inordinate affective significance to stimuli that are only moderately significant to most people, such people would demonstrate extraordinary abilities – for example something that appears to average people to be 'photographic memory' or 'musical genius' or the ability to be a human calculator. Autistic savants, in other words.

These individuals have these abilities because they literally *feel* differences that you and I don't. To you, the numbers 3765342 and 3864521 may not feel very different. But to someone you has spent all their affective significance points on numbers, they feel as different as – say – goats and dogs do to you. This enables them to store and process them in ways that are astonishing to you and me.

It is probably also true that as a pushy parent, one might *drive* affective significance for something like numbers or music, so that a person developed an unusual level of ability in that area. In my own case, not worrying too much about people has probably freed up some bandwidth for learning theory and philosophy. Little wonder that philosophers so commonly seek to rise above the apparent silliness that pervades everyday interaction.

In summary, our individual differences depend in large part on the things we care about. I don't mean this just in the obvious sense, but in the more specific technical sense in which the tendency of our brains (whether through nature or nurture) to attach affective significance to different classes of stimuli determines the kind of person that we become. You are, quite literally, defined by the things you care about. The high degree of neuroplasticity that humans exhibit enables each of us to develop a unique portfolio of stuff that matters, which in turn defines our personality, and governs our cognition.

It is difficult to grasp a new conception of learning in a world where so much emotion is invested in the old. Picture if you will, Charles Darwin standing before an audience of people, all of whom had spent their entire lives believing themselves to be God's creation – suggesting that their ancestors were apes. There were, of course, no end of counter-arguments; but only now can we see them for what they really were. But while we scoff at their attachment to religious doctrine, we entirely overlook our own.

What is missing here is 'play': when we cease to be playful, we begin to attach tremendous personal significance to things, and then the cost of changing our opinion becomes too great. Education, in robbing us of playfulness, simultaneously strips us of the ability to develop and learn. We become people offended and threatened by challenges to our views. Fossils.

Applications of the affective context model

When we start to apply the affective context model to our own lives, it quickly becomes apparent that some things are more significant than others. Some years ago, I decided to take my nine-year-old daughter for a walk in the nearby forest. 'It will be lovely,' I thought. 'It's important for her to spend some time in nature,' I reasoned.

So I persuaded her to put down her iPad and come with me on the walk. Twenty minutes in, she began complaining that she was physically exhausted and close to collapse. Shortly thereafter she began to worry that we were hopelessly lost in the wilderness and would never again find our way back to civilization.

After what I felt was an instructive but ultimately non-reassuring chat about how we might conceivably live on pine cones, berries and squirrel-on-a-stick, I abandoned the walk which she later described as The Worst Experience, Ever.

The return journey gave me time to reflect on why, exactly, I had felt it important to take her for a walk in the woods. Expertly tuning out the sounds of misery and distress, I was able to come up with any number of reasons: 'The fresh air will do her good', 'Exercise is beneficial', 'Everyone should learn to appreciate nature' and so on – but the truth is these were all rationalizations, at heart I just felt that it was the right thing to do. So why did I *feel* that it was the right thing to do?

Many people take their kids to football matches. I can't imagine why. I mean who would willingly battle through extreme traffic, extending their repertoire of curse-words as they struggle to find a place to park, parting with their hard-earned cash to pay extortionate ticket prices for the chance to be herded like cattle into a mass of people who are forced to watch a pointless sport at a great distance (which in any case they could watch from the comfort of the sofa)? But then, that's just me.

If you reflect on your own life you will realize that certain experiences – what I will call *cornerstone experiences* – have a kind of deep and absolute significance. It is not that they are really important (though doubtless you can come up with reasons why they are important) – rather they are the kinds of experiences that you feel obliged to share with significant others or pass on to your children. They may be fishing, or family traditions, or sporting events, or religious observances.

Quite often – though not necessarily – these cornerstone experiences will have been laid down in childhood. It is hard to say what exactly character-izes them – except that they are emotionally self-sustaining, and driven to reproduce. What I mean by that is that we are drawn to act them out again, and to pass them on to others. My parents took me for walks in the woods – and now I feel that that is something I should do with my daughter.

It is worth noting that this is not about habit; I am not in the habit of going for walks in the woods on my own. Neither is it rational behaviour – of course I can come up with reasons why walking in the woods is good, but I would be lying if I implied that these are truly my motivations.

This affective mechanism sometimes lies at the heart of relationship difficulties: a young couple meet, date, and after a suitable amount of time get married. Things are fine for a while, then cracks begin to emerge. Jane has asked Dave on several occasions to sort out some additional shelving for the kitchen, but he just hasn't got round to it.

In fact there are a whole list of things that Dave hasn't done that cause Jane to feel frustrated – for example, he often forgets to take out the bins. So Jane nags him. For his part, Dave has started to feel that *all* Jane does is nag. He doesn't see why if the bins are such a big deal, Jane doesn't take them out herself. And although he did say he would put up the shelves, he's never really been into DIY, and his anxiety about the whole thing ('Do I need to buy power tools?') is holding him back.

In addition to that, there are a few things that have begun to bug him about Jane – her cooking leaves much to be desired (though when he last hinted at this, it ended with Jane suggesting that he do the cooking himself).

One day, when they are both feeling a little stressed, they have a big row and all these things come out. But what lies at the heart of their dispute is probably a set of cornerstone experiences. Jane's dad, for example, was handy around the house and always took out the bins. Dave's mum took pride in her cooking. Without even realizing it, these sentiments about how a partner should be have caused frustration to build up.

Note that Jane and Dave aren't consciously aware of this comparison that they are drawing; in all likelihood they haven't both drawn up a list of shortcomings (let's hope not!) – rather it is just a feeling of annoyance and dissatisfaction that builds up, a kind of affective dissonance.

They might subsequently go into couples' therapy, and the therapist might have the sense to bring all this to the surface – but the key thing is that rather like our judges' verdicts example, the mechanics are *emotional*; the thoughts just make the unconscious, conscious.

Notice that to make progress the couple have to do a sort of 'affective mapping' exercise – through talking through their feelings and telling stories about their past they surface the things that matter to them. Obviously it would be a good idea if they did that before getting married – but I would suggest that there might be a more systematic, more scientific way of doing it. Just imagine if we did this with people as they entered an education system.

These cornerstone experiences may be laid down at recognizable points in a person's development – for example their first day at school, or their first experience of leading a team. When we share powerful experiences with our children, we may be laying the foundations for the way they behave and teach others to behave. It's a woefully inexact science: we cannot be sure of how they will react, and it is their reaction – not the experience itself that is transformative.

This may be especially true when they are doing something for the first time. In these uncertain situations they may be in a fluid state, and quite malleable.

Putting people into this fluid state – or spotting when they are in it – is critical in shaping an individual's personality. For most of our lives we will find ourselves running on rails, conforming to norms, and doing what is expected of us. It is at times when we do not know what to expect that we define ourselves.

Whilst cornerstone experiences may be some of the recognizable land-marks in our mental real estate, there are many smaller less permanent occupants.

Memes or femes? From big experiences to small nudges

The author Richard Dawkins coined the term 'memes' to describe ideas that survive and reproduce in a way that is similar to genes. An example might be the idea that the human mind works a bit like a computer. The point is that the meme has an existence that is independent of its host – and rather like genes, memes survive by being passed from one person to another.

But if it is true that our ideas are built from our affective responses, we can see that the real nature of memes extends far beyond ideas; in fact, any set of affective responses that can successfully travel from one host to another and survive can be a meme.

Although this may sound odd, consider for a second that the expression 'meme' has recently taken on a popular usage and is used to apply to hu-morously captioned pictures. These circulate in social media groups, and typically achieve success by being voted 'up' or 'down', with the more popu-lar ones quickly spreading via platforms like Facebook or Instagram. A popular meme might be an image of a cute dog, wearing a bow-tie, performing a high five with the caption 'good doggo'.

My point is that these are not memes in the sense of coherent ideas – gen-erally they are just put together to make us laugh, or feel shocked or surprised. A good meme is relatable – meaning that it accurately captures a feeling or situation that you recognize. In short – they have nothing to do with what we think and everything to do with what we feel.

You would be hard pressed to explain the idea communicated by the 'good doggo' meme. The same is true of emojis – the icons we use most com-monly to reflect our sentiments – which have recently experienced an explosive rise in popularity.

The affective context model can help us to understand what is going on, whether it is our desire to subject our offspring to the same experiences that mattered to us as kids, to tell a story about a fight on a train, or to share an amusing picture we received via social media. At their core, memes are not ideas – memes are feelings ('femes'?). They are reactions that are strong enough to persist, and to be passed on – for example as a story, as a song lyric, or as a picture.

The curious popularity of social media platforms such as Snapchat or TikTok, which overwhelmingly centre on people's facial expressions and reactions to events, is now explicable. Our faces are one of the best ways to convey an emotion, and combining them with music and cartoon effects deepens the impact.

Sentimental expression and marketing

The viral nature of sentimental expression is not a new phenomenon. When Thich Quang Duc, a Vietnamese Buddhist monk, sat down at a busy road intersection in Saigon in 1963 and proceeded to set fire to himself, the pictures and descriptions of that act travelled around the world.

President John F Kennedy learned of the incident whilst talking to his brother on the phone, reportedly interrupting the conversation to exclaim: 'Jesus Christ!', and later remarking: 'No news picture in history has generated so much emotion around the world as that one.'

It goes without saying that intention behind the act – raising awareness of the persecution of Buddhist monks by the government – was Thich's ultimate aim. But this purpose rode the coat tails of the emotional force, and whilst the images are still familiar to many, the political agenda has largely been forgotten. Compare this with our old friend Heraclitus: ironically we might only learn about his metaphysical philosophy by virtue of the story of his demise in a pile of dung.

In thinking through these ways in which emotion occupies the cognitive 'real estate' of our minds, it is worth noting a theme which will come up time and time again: there is one end of the spectrum where we are looking at mass appeal and the generally powerful – and another end where it is humble and about what matters to a specific person in a specific context.

If you are showing me a photograph of a monk setting himself on fire, that is the sort of thing anyone would be expected to remember. If, on the other hand, you are showing me a picture of your favourite bar at your favourite holiday destination, that is a specific feeling powerful to you, but one which I will likely forget.

Our concerns are organized rather like a tree: a trunk made up of the core concerns we share with other humans and animals, and branches which reflect our individual differences and development.

Take marketing, which is more obviously all about emotion. Arguably there are two kinds of marketing: the first is the kind of 'wow' ads that we were used to seeing on TV or billboards. These are the kinds of ads that are just sprayed out to a mass market, and need to have maximum impact for the largest number of people. For that reason they have tended to use emotional reactions that are common denominators – sexual arousal, shock, status and so on – emotions that are nearer our homeostatic roots. This is the conventional world of marketing.

But there is a problem with it: marketing isn't terribly effective. Only a small percentage of people change their behaviour as a result of marketing. If this sounds counter-intuitive, remember that for a large company to achieve even a 0.5 per cent shift in sales can amount to a lot of money – so that's roughly how it works.

But at the other end of the spectrum, in a world of social media and Big Data, we can operate in a very different way: you can send me a very dull, cheap, advert and it has a much higher chance of altering my behaviour. Why? Because it is precisely the kind of thing that concerns the kind of person I am, in the situation I am in right now.

Picture this: I have arrived at London Waterloo train station, but have a little time before my first meeting of the day.

The data that is held online about me reflects that I like to drink coffee in the mornings, that there is a coffee shop at Waterloo station, and that my favourite beverage at this time of day is a caramel latte. It also knows that I am currently at Waterloo station (via geo-location) and have a little time before my next meeting (since I use Google calendar).

As I arrive at Waterloo, a notification pops up on my phone for a 20 per cent discount on a caramel latte. I think 'Why not?', and head to the coffee store a few paces away.

This is the reason why some people are concerned about the data that social media companies are collecting, and selling. In sufficient quantities they allow a person not merely to predict, but to control our behaviour. They reveal the points at which you can be swayed one way or the other, and what it will take to do that. Over time, such systems can drip-feed enough nudges to take me to almost any point in political or behavioural space.

Experiences and resources

In the context of human development (and education) this typology corresponds to two classes of activity: 'experiences' (which create new concerns), and 'resources' (which respond to your concerns).

For example, let's say you discover that your partner (Jane) has booked you on a trip to climb Everest. Just knowing that you will be doing it fills you with excitement and anticipation. The anticipation of the experience causes you to search the web for advice and useful information – drawing on the resources that Google has catalogued. Some of these you will take the decision to commit to memory – because you don't want to be Googling stuff half way up the mountain, with an ice-axe in one hand and your glove gripped between your clenched teeth.

An 'experience' is an event that you remember, and your memories (among other things) shape your behaviour. In designing experiences, we look to have a lasting emotional impact – it's a 'push' intervention, in that it pushes you in a new direction developmentally.

By contrast, a resource is a 'pull' intervention – usually something quite simple and humble that helps you tackle the task at hand, for example some advice discovered using Google.

Whilst an experience, if successful, may change the way you behave, the best chance of altering your behaviour will probably come from understanding what you already care about and providing resources at the points when you need them. If you wanted to dramatically alter performance in an organization, you would do it with resources, not experiences.

Think about GPS. If I could hack into the GPS route-finding algorithm I could change the driving habits of millions of people at a single keystroke. This would be much more effective than an expensive TV ad persuading people to 'try a new route to work'.

Now of course organizations have lots of standard operating procedures, but here's the thing – *no one is following them!* Standard operating procedures are not the resources that organizations might imagine them to be – guiding workplace behaviour. People's behaviour is largely determined by how they think the people around them will react in a given situation. So if you take the time to talk to people in organizations, you will learn that what really governs their behaviour is culture.

And what is culture made up of? Stories and feelings – about what is normal, what is bad, what is good – all of which embody people's desire to do what is expected of them in a given situation. To not embarrass themselves.

So unlike driving a car, in a social context, your GPS is the faces and reactions of the people around you.

The sorts of feelings that stick in my head, and which make me the person I am, the person who does the things that I do – these feelings may range from the big dramatic ones that impact many people in a generation (like being at war) to the small very personal ones that impact me personally (like the 'gherkin' comment). Sometimes they are just the things that come up time and time again (like Coca-Cola).

Learning design as designed experience

At the outset of any project we need to be clear on what we are trying to accomplish. At a bare minimum we shouldn't fall into the trap of attempting to get people to memorize information simply because 'that's what education does'. Instead, we should look at the outcomes we are trying to achieve and define these in measurable terms.

It's really important to remember that an outcome might not simply be a shift in performance; it might be a shift in someone's experience. For example, we might want people to feel more engaged, innovative or included. We might want them to enjoy their work more or to identify more closely with the company's mission. We might want them to feel that the organization values them.

In case these sound a bit woolly, they can have a very real impact on things like performance, morale and retention.

Once more: if we are trying to make a measurable difference to performance, we can do it one of two ways (setting aside hiring different people): we can reduce the need to learn (through performance consulting), or we can create environments that promote learning (experience design). There really are only two options.

Learning design *is* experience design. In designing an experience we can go big or we can go small: for example, we can design an induction event where people are flown to Florida and get to meet the CEO (or put in place a new incentive scheme) or we can focus on the little things that matter to that particular person – for example, ensuring there is a hand-written, personalized note on their desk, and someone who knows about them ready to greet them.

You might wonder why organizations spend money on big, impactful events when they might achieve similar results by focusing on the little, smaller, experiences – but the answer is twofold: the big, impactful events can (if carefully designed) be cornerstone experiences for many people, and second it's really difficult to gather enough information and use it correctly to achieve the same result on a personal level.

The best experience designs probably sit somewhere in the middle: that is to say, amazing experiences that resonate with participants because we've taken the time to segment and understand that audience.

Nobody yet knows how to do experience design scientifically. There are plenty of experience designers – even schools of experience design – but without an underlying theory from which to generate testable predictions, the field remains intuitive and trial and error in nature. A good analogy would be bridge building: you don't need physics to build bridges – but some will fall down for reasons you don't understand, and you will struggle to move beyond the tried and tested patterns if you don't really know why things work and why they don't.

The affective context model provides a start; the next step will be to develop techniques for mapping concerns in detail, and understanding how one influences another. I thought it might be helpful to summarize some things I have found to date.

Consider milestones or transitions

One of the best candidates for experience design are transitions – for example when a person joins an organization, when they become a leader for the first time, or when they arrive at a new location. Transitions are good candidates because a change in context marks an opportunity to redefine expectations. In other words, you have an opportunity to create new rules, new ways of feeling.

Consider – for example – what happens when a person first arrives at Disneyland. Do they queue for hours to pass through a turnstile, or are they greeted by a wizard who welcomes them by name? When someone joins an organization, will they be expected to complete hours of compliance training, or will the CEO shake them by the hand, answer their questions and offer advice? When a person becomes a leader, will we celebrate this achievement? If we do celebrate it, how should we celebrate it?

In a new situation, people are in a 'fluid' state, by which I mean they are alert to the norms and expectations that exist in this context. Because of the way these are laid down (the 'anchoring effect'), they can be very hard to change later – which is why it's so important to carefully craft an experience from the outset: the first day at school, the first day on the job, the first communication someone receives, the first experience on arriving at the venue.

Sometimes it can help to create a clear transition where none currently exists – by creating milestones. Milestones are experience designs, such as graduation ceremonies or pledges, that create a greater sense of significance.

Ask the question 'What story will people tell?'

Here's a story: I was working on the design of a new leadership programme for a big pharmaceutical company. During the early stages, people kept comparing it to a programme that they had run before and suggesting: 'It needs to be as good as that'.

I wondered what it was about the previous programme that made it great. It turned out to be an egg. The programme focused on many familiar aspects of leadership, there was plenty of good practice around feedback and reflection, setting expectations, etc – but this was not what people remembered.

When I asked them about the thing that made the programme iconic, it was the point where, stripped to their undies, they were invited to sit inside a giant plastic egg that measured their body mass index (BMI). This is what they remembered.

It's worth thinking about how weird that is. You would be hard-pressed to argue that this is the part of the programme that had the greatest impact on their performance – other contextual elements may have done the heavy lifting – but this is the story that they told, and without it there is a good chance the whole event would have vanished from memory.

As you have probably guessed, we want to avoid our stories being 'gratuitous' – once we understand that it is the story that sticks, we want to link it to critical behaviour change in a deliberate fashion. (In the case in question, the measuring of BMI was situated within a portion of the programme that talked about leader resilience, energy and health. It wasn't perceived as gratuitous, therefore.)

That said, this is the easiest way to challenge a great deal of conventional learning design: 'What's the story people will tell?' If you can't agree what it is, chances are you are wasting your time. Put the story at the heart of your experience design.

It should feel on the edge of acceptability

The 'define' stage had surfaced a desire for leaders to be better at handling conflict, but the 'discover' stage had revealed that leaders tended to be engineers and typically introverts who were poor at spotting conflict and uncomfortable with confrontation. So we started a fight.

Participants showed up for the leadership training session, and right from the outset something wasn't right: the two facilitators didn't get on, pretty soon they were bickering over who was responsible for getting the slides mixed up. A few minutes in, things escalated to the point where one pushed the other over.

Then we stopped the action. We introduced our two actors, then invited people to talk about what they had seen, when they should have intervened, why they were uncomfortable doing so, etc. Then we ran the whole thing again – forum theatre style – and gave people a shot at intervening.

A good experience design needs to be out of the ordinary. It needs to break the pattern; it needs to surprise us and defy expectations. We have to do this if we want learning to take place, because our memories selectively attend to those things that don't fit with our mental model (our 'schema').

Imagine you go to a restaurant and – for no particular reason – the waiter does an odd dance. How many waiters can you remember? You would remember that one! (I actually do remember a Mexican restaurant in Warsaw where when it was someone's birthday a figure dressed as Zorro delivered a birthday cake with candles).

But there is a problem – departing from the script it precisely the sort of thing that makes us anxious. You probably cringed inwardly even at the thought of having a waiter do a dance at your table. This creates a very real challenge for effective experience design.

Many of your stakeholders will feel uneasy about doing anything that departs from the standard educational schema. Many will assume that a learning programme should entail people sitting quietly listening to an instructor talk. Paradoxically, doing something that departs from the script will make stakeholders uneasy for precisely the same reason that it will make it effective.

So experience design is always a battle – a battle to win the trust of your stakeholders, and fight for the space to do something that breaks with tradition. One of the most effective ways to do this is to pilot and experiment. Stakeholders will be horrified at your suggestions, but if you can reassure them that you are going to try things on a small scale and test first, they might let you do something a little different.

From experience, the sweet spot is the edge of acceptability; throwing marshmallows at people is a little weird, but were I (like the DJ Steve Aoki) to fling a large iced cake into the shocked faces of my front row business audience, this would probably be taking it too far.

In one experience design we talked (boringly) about the importance of getting to know your customers to an executive audience, introducing some customer personas along the way, based on social media profiles. We then (unexpectedly) marched the real customers into the room and had small groups of executives sit with them and talk about their lives. (The 'real' customers were actually actors briefed against the company's market data, and for whom we created fictitious social media accounts.)

They said it was incredibly memorable. They also discovered that they didn't know how to sell their new products to real customers.

It should feel real

Years ago I worked at improving safety training at BP. I had the privilege of working with a chap called Jim Wetherbee – the only American to have commanded five spaceflight missions. Look him up, his Wikipedia entry is staggering.

Under the leadership of a friend called Urbain Bruyere, he and I flew out to meet with another impressive chap – Jonah Lehrer (author of *How We Decide*) – to talk about the latest thinking on brains and how that knowledge might help make BP a safer place. One thing I remember Jim saying is: 'You know a simulator is working when it makes you sweat'. It's such an interesting remark: the learning effect of an experience is felt, first and foremost. It means that when we design an experience, if you want the learning to be transferrable, it needs to feel like the real thing in significant respects.

How do you make an experience feel like the real thing? Well, for one thing you need to be able to map how something makes people feel. This is what verisimilitude in this context means – a simulation is a good simulation if it feels the same as the real thing.

This is one of the reasons why I have consistently been sceptical of 'leadership simulators' in which people click through screens displaying a series of branching scenarios relating to team members. Real leadership doesn't feel like that. Real warfare doesn't feel like chess. Leadership is sitting across a desk from someone in tears as you try to react appropriately to their feelings of being bullied.

You might think that it's very hard to recreate this experience, but because a lot of leadership is primarily visceral (in the same way that parenting is), it's not as hard as you think. A person might know that they are role-playing with an actor, but have the actor break down into tears, or stand toe to toe with them yelling abuse and you will see them physically react as they would for real; their pulse races, their thinking is muddled by adrenaline, they mirror emotions and respond as they would were this not a simulation.

In creating experiences, we should consider putting people in environments that don't resemble conventional educational ones – either by taking people out of them, or using them differently. This is not so people can have a 'fun time', it's either so we can create learning experiences that are more memorable, or those that transfer better to the performance context. It is also true that when you place people in an unfamiliar context (for the reasons above), they are more likely to try something they haven't tried before. A new environment is liberating.

Create uncharted territory

Have you ever been in a fight? Not an online argument but a real, spaghetti-Western fist fight? If you haven't then would you turn and run or would you stand your ground? Are you a coward or a scrapper?

If you have been in a fight, then you know which of these you are. If you haven't, you don't. You know which one you would *like* to be, but you are as yet undefined. Were you to find yourself in this situation, you would exit it knowing definitively what kind of person you are, and it would likely change the way you see yourself forever.

The point I am making is this: people are defined to a large extent by the decisions they take in certain situations where they cannot simply 'follow the crowd' – for example, new situations where they cannot copy past experience or use social referencing as a guide. In those moments they make a decision and reveal themselves as they are.

We can (carefully) create these kinds of uncharted situations, allow people to experience them safely, to review the decisions they took and – if necessary – redefine themselves by running them again.

A classic example of this might be Stanley Milgram's obedience experiments. He created a situation in which an experimenter convinced people to administer fatal electric shocks to another person (mirroring the behaviour of Nazi officers during the Second World War). At least, people *thought* they had killed another person – in fact the individual was a stooge, the whole set-up designed to test how obedient people would be under pressure.

Many of you will be familiar with his work, but the point I want to make here is different. People watching themselves back would (rightly) conclude that they were far more obedient than they had previously believed. Our uncharted territory would have redefined them.

But what if we allowed them to re-run the experiment (or a similar situation)? In fact, this was done and the experience effectively *inoculated* people against the dangers of behaving similarly in comparable situations – they were more likely to object.

In designing experiences, we look to create situations where people are challenged and cannot simply do what everyone else would do, but have to decide for themselves. But – as the saying goes – with great power comes great responsibility: we have to be very careful in the way we define these experiences so as not to damage people.

Imagine creating an experience (perhaps like Zimbardo's Stanford Prison simulation) in which a person can decide to be a sadist, or a racist (some diversity training approaches this, and can leave people feeling bruised or 'labelled'). If a person has been revealed as such, what impact might that have? How would you handle that carefully?

In the learning industry there is justified anxiety regarding creating powerful experiences that damage people rather than helping them grow. This is why it's important to understand one's audience, and to carefully test experience designs. But we must accept this challenge. Theme parks would be nothing without rollercoasters, but every rollercoaster is carefully calibrated to provide high levels of excitement without damaging its passengers.

Understand what matters to people

Whether you are designing a big experience (such as an event) or a small one (such as a piece of feedback), the key to understanding the impact it will have is the extent to which it moves people.

But how do you know that? You can go one of two ways – you can do something that by its very nature moves the vast majority of people, or you can do something that resonates with a particular individual. Both approaches depend on addressing someone's core concerns – in the former case you are aiming at some of the core concerns that human beings naturally share, in the latter you are aiming at a core concern specific to the individual.

Let me give you an example: imagine that you gather your leadership team together and, instead of the usual battery of PowerPoint presentations, former president Barack Obama takes the stage. Everybody will remember this, everybody will talk about this. How do I know that? Well – whether you are a fan of the president or not, celebrity is a deeply human concern. Celebrities are high-status individuals and humans are hierarchical creatures.

A cheaper stunt might be the one I routinely pull at my own talks: I unexpectedly throw giant marshmallows at people. Everybody remembers that – and I encourage them to think about why that is. The answer is that human memory selectively encodes stuff we react to – and we react to surprising or peculiar behaviour.

But there may be times when this brute force approach is not going to achieve the result we are looking for; for example where we want a parent or a leader to realize that they could do better – to achieve a moment of insight. Here, it might be a single comment that acts as a transformative experience.

These moments are harder to design, because we need to know a lot about the individual. We need to understand their core concerns in order to bring about change. For example, let's say someone cares deeply about fairness – but some of their behaviours are giving rise to accusations of favouritism. You might think that this critical feedback would strike them to the core – but unless it comes from someone they deeply respect, there is every chance they will dismiss it.

Heider's balance theory can help here: if we want to change an attitude towards oneself we need both the compelling evidence *and* someone that we are so deeply attached to that we can't simply dismiss either the feedback or the person.

Another way to think about the power of personalized experience design is the concept of 'skin in the game', an expression used to describe the extent to which an individual in personally invested in something. For example, at one point in history Roman bridge builders were required to live beneath the structures they built for a period of time – that's skin in the game!

In an everyday setting we encounter this, for example when someone gets up in front of their classmates or colleagues to speak, or when they engage in some kind of competitive activity in front of an audience. It is not their life that is at stake here, but something pretty close: their pride. People have powerful memories for their successes, defeats and humiliations in these kinds of situations.

A common way to design an experience is to use an audience that we know people care about – their senior leaders, their peers, their parents – to create a high-stakes situation. People will work really hard to achieve peak performance in these contexts, and the outcome can have lasting impact.

Create challenges

As a rule of thumb, challenges drive learning. If I am looking through a learning programme design and there are no obvious challenges – then the chances are no learning is going on. Why?

The simplest way to answer this question is by reference to Jean Piaget, the learning theorist. Jean noticed that people tend to a point of 'equilibrium' in their learning – a point where their internal mental model of the world matches the outside world, and at that point things go as expected (and we tend to stop learning).

This makes a lot of sense: learning is a homeostatic mechanism designed to help us survive. Once we have figured out how the world works – how to achieve optimum conditions – we stop learning, since learning is costly.

What re-ignites our learning is 'dis-equilibrium': moments when the world surprises us, when things don't meet our expectations, when reality emerges shockingly into our carefully arranged mental living room like a small child covered in paint.

There are infinite ways to be surprising, but if we want people to develop new capabilities and not merely *remember* something, then we will need to put them in challenging situations where the learning transfers to other contexts.

It's my experience that doing one thing when we should be doing the other has often given experience design a bad name: at some level people realize that 'zany antics' (e.g. drumming, raft-building, horse-whispering, primal screaming) make for memorable experiences, but businesses became rightly sceptical about the impact on performance.

In the movie *Dead Poets Society*, maverick English teacher John Keating – played by Robin Williams – introduces his bewildered students to a succession of life-changing experiences, to the horror of his traditionalist educational colleagues, who eventually manage to get him fired. It's a tale about experience design versus education, progress versus tradition, and difference versus conformity.

Until we have proven techniques for mapping concerns, our safest territory is challenges that bear some obvious relation to real ones.

Note that 'challenging' has a specific technical sense here: an experience is only challenging if your mental model doesn't currently incorporate it. I guess to many people this idea – that learning experiences should be challenging in some way – might seem obvious.

Isn't it odd, then, how little of education is challenging? How readily we accept that it's OK to design a 'learning' programme where the vast majority of time is spent sitting, listening?

I do see programmes with tokenistic challenges – for example a discussion about what people have just heard. Oftentimes these comprise less than 20 per cent of the time, with 80 per cent of the programme given over to instruction. Learning designers are addicted to content.

Flip the model! How would you design a programme where 80 per cent of the time is challenges? Better still – where it is entirely challenge-based? This is, in practice, a great starting point for the design of a learning programme: 'How do we make this programme entirely challenge-based?'

This was how we designed the award-winning induction programme for Deloitte – a five-day, challenge-based learning programme. And because this was 2021, the whole thing had to be digital! In short: turn the content into resources, make the experience challenging.

I've made the process of designing challenging experiences simpler than it actually is. Did you notice the hidden question: how do we figure out what is challenging for a given individual?

The problem is that people react differently to the same challenge (consistent with our affective context model). Some people – for example – might be utterly crushed by failing at a challenge and resolve never to try again, whilst others might be itching to give it another shot. At the other extreme, some people might not take it seriously at all, and consequently learn nothing from it.

A simple example is public speaking: a pretty standard experience design for a learning programme has participants giving a speech in front of their peers at the end. This challenge can really drive learning, since people generally care what their peers think. We can ramp it up with parents and superiors – make it more intense with *Dragons' Den* or courtroom theatrics.

But hold on a second: some people are terrified of public speaking, whilst others relish the opportunity. We have to be careful to take care of people. We have to consider, for example, ways to support people and flex the format to enable people to calibrate the intensity of the challenge appropriately. For example, perhaps a person is part of a group giving the presentation and can control their level of participation.

One last but very important thing to say about creating challenges: you probably don't want to use 'happy sheets' (the standard Likert 1–5 level 1 and 2 evaluation for training programmes) to evaluate your experiences.

Put bluntly, if something is an effective learning experience, people may not be having a lot of fun; instead they should feel challenged. So a better way to evaluate the success of your programme (aside from the actual behaviour change) would be the question: 'How challenging did you find the experience?'

It is a source of immense shame that the learning industry descended into using happy sheets – essentially a measure of how much people enjoyed a training experience – as a measure of our work. Level 1 evaluation has relegated us to the role of second-rate entertainment, whilst level 2 has lumbered us with the additional pressure to behave like schoolteachers at the same time. In moving from education to learning, we need to let go of all this.

Test and iterate

Experience design is not yet a science; we don't yet have a science of cognition or learning, just a theory. Experience design to a large extent is still a combination of intuition and trial and error.

This means that – like our bridge builders – the best way to proceed is to dream big, experiment on a small scale, and try a variety of approaches. I don't think I have come across a single experience design that has worked quite as we imagined it would. I have also run experiences that worked quite differently with different audiences – both across cultures, and within a culture.

The best way to address a desired learning outcome is to come up with a handful (say, three) candidate experience designs, get approval to test them, and scale up the most successful one to a pilot, redesigning as you go. This 'test and iterate' approach is your best chance of arriving at a powerful experience. It will work best if you involve your audience in co-designing it, since it is their reactions that are central to success.

Another approach that I have found useful is to look at experiences in other environments that have a big impact, and try to figure out what it is that makes them so memorable: for example, an especially memorable dinner party or a wedding.

The process of experience design

In summary, there is a sequence I would recommend you follow in designing an experience, which goes something like this:

Define the outcomes you are looking for using the 'think/feel/do' model. We may want people to be better at a specific task, or we may want people to feel that they made the right decision in joining an organization. Both deliver measurable business benefit.

Discover what matters to your audience. You'll need to know what they really care about as a basis for your design. Who are their heroes? Why do they come to work? What are they most proud of? What are the experiences that shaped them in the past?

Design a number of experiments that push the limits of acceptability and depart from the norm. These will typically be challenges of the kind that people haven't experienced before. Ask yourself: 'What story will people tell?' and actively design opportunities to share the experience (e.g. using social media) into the format.

Develop these ideas iteratively, running experiments with small groups from your target audience to understand the impact they have. Don't be afraid to dump stuff that isn't working.

Pilot the best idea(s) in the form of an MVE (minimum viable experience). Continue to develop your design based on feedback and observation of the pilot.

Deploy the experience at scale in a way that allows for some flexibility – for example for different cultures, or different individuals. The 'experience in a box' is one way of doing this: an experience toolkit that local regions can adapt to fit their culture.

Iterate in line with your evaluation: consider using questions such as: 'How challenging was this experience?' instead of the conventional ones, and look for measures of business impact. Amplify the effect of your experiences by encouraging people to share them.

You might be wondering why I have not mentioned instructional design in my discussion of learning design. That's because, in the words of *The Hitchhiker's Guide to the Galaxy*, instructional design is at best 'Mostly Harmless'.

The vast majority of instructional design – for example cognitive load theory[2] – relates to a narrow range of educational applications, typically recall of factual information, and won't help you significantly with learning design.

In other words, if what you are trying to do is get someone to briefly memorize some facts so that they can pass a recall test (education), then by all means take a look at instructional design. It will tell you how to hammer a square peg into a round hole, i.e. completely disregard the concerns that shape the learner and learning process and instead focus on techniques to force-feed content regardless.

But if you are interested in learning you should set it aside. It will only mislead you. A learning professional taking an interest in instructional design is like a doctor taking an interest in homeopathy; it won't help, but it may distract and even undermine you.

If we move beyond thinking about experience design in the deliberate sense, to the kind of unintentional experiences we inadvertently design in everyday life, there are some important considerations – considerations that might cause you to stop and reflect on your life.

There are many things that can shorten your life: drink, drugs, obesity and cigarettes. But the one which will do the most damage by far is – routine. I don't mean that routine will damage your body (although it probably does); imagine that your life was so terribly routine that every single day was pretty much the same. As a result, at the end of your life, you would only have lived just one day.

This is because, as the Czech writer Milan Kundera wrote, 'Memory retains no more than a millionth, a hundred-millionth, in short an utterly infinitesimal bit of the lived life'.[3] It is as if, during our lives, we only retain a handful of snapshots of what we have lived. The highlights. We live only to the extent of our feelings; we live only so far as our stories.

In fact, research shows that people tend to recall more events from their teenage years, tailing off into their late 20s. This is probably because you are encountering more experiences for the first time during that period, but also because your emotional systems are at their most intense and unconstrained (since your higher-order emotional regulation is still developing). Novelty and emotional intensity work hand in hand to create lasting memories.

What I am saying here is more than a poetic hunch. The psychologist David Eagleman had participants experience a frightening free-fall of 31 metres, then measured their estimates of the time it took to fall.[4] Their estimates were out by 36 per cent (as compared to observations of others' falls).

His conclusion was that this 'time dilation' effect was a consequence of recollection, not perception – emotionally charged experiences lead to richer encoding, which in turn distorts our memory of them. Live a dull life, your life shrinks. Our lives are measured in adventures, not years.

So now we come to you: would you live your life differently if you knew that all the non-extraordinary bits are erased? That everything 'routine' is lost?

More importantly: are you extraordinary for other people? In what way do you enter into other people's stories? Do you think of your own personal presence as a piece of experience design? When the people you encounter look back at the scattered fragments that make up their lives, will you be among those fragments, or will you share the fate of Ebbinghaus' trigrams – shed from memory at the first opportunity? Are you inadvertently shortening the lives of those around you?

If you wish to vanish from living memory, I can tell you the secret: dress as you are expected to dress, say what you are expected to say, do what you are expected to do. That way it will be almost as if you never existed.

These days I get to travel to the offices of a wide variety of organizations in which people sit in small cubicles carrying out routine work. Occasionally there are cards pinned to the walls of these cubicles. They are usually handwritten. They are from people who wanted to thank that person for their work, or difference they made to their lives. Have you ever written such a card? These small cards may stay pinned to a cubicle for a decade. They are extraordinary.

The extraordinary can be quite small. As organizations or individuals, do we create opportunities for the extraordinary experience, and do we celebrate the extraordinary?

This question matters to us both in our personal relationships and in the context of education. It is our responsibility to craft the extraordinary. The extraordinary is what shapes people, and it is only the extraordinary that they will remember.

Transformative experiences

If we are trying to change people, we must endeavour to take them away from the routine and to design an experience that will become a part of who they are, and a story that they will tell. Perhaps a behaviour or concern that they will pass on to others. You might take your date to their first opera, and in so doing create an extraordinary experience that is later to become a part of who they are, and a passion they will pass on to future generations.

Such experiences must connect to an individual on a profound, emotional level if they are to be transformative. This, in essence, is where education fails: it is not designed to transform people, it is not intent on deep connections.

Doubtless transformative experiences do occur during a person's time in education: bullying, success at sports, the teacher who thought you would never amount to anything, the mentor who told you that you could achieve anything that you put your mind to. None of these are the *intent* of education, they are learning accidents of the happy and tragic kind.

There is something else you will find pinned to those cubicles, next to the thank you cards and family pictures: pictures of a beach far away. Have you ever had that experience where someone shows you their holiday pictures and you feel you should feign excitement as the other person animatedly explains: 'And this is the bar where we had the most amazing cocktail! And this is the spot we went to every day on the beach – just look at that sea! And this is me swimming with dolphins! And this is our hotel room!'

Isn't that odd? Probably both of you sense that something is slightly amiss – they took the pictures to try and capture an intensity of *feeling*. The pictures are actually quite dull, but looking at them brings back the feeling *for them* whilst it does nothing for you. The other person senses this and strains to close the gap with over-the-top descriptions: 'This barman was *amazing* – I know it looks like an average bar, but the atmosphere was just *incredible*'.

This phenomenon – the frequent inability of mere photographs to convey an experience – should be familiar. Imagine you are taking an early morning stroll through the woods. From the corner of your eye you glimpse movement and turn your head to see the most magical thing: a stag has emerged from between the firs and is silently grazing a little distance away. You are transfixed by the presence of this majestic creature. You reach for your camera, hoping not to cause it to take flight. As you raise the lens, the stag raises its head. You take the shot – the deer bolts into the depths of the forest. You are thrilled that you got the photograph.

On showing the photograph to your friends, you realize that they are a little less 'whelmed' than you would have hoped them to be. To be fair, the photo merely looks like a rather poorly composed picture of some trees, with some kind of animal in the distance. The disconnect happens because the sheer emotional impact of the encounter is not easily captured visually.

Our lives are spent like this: trying to share what we feel through story, song and image. When two people care about the same thing, a connection is made. A father takes his son fishing, and in doing so forms a bond that will last a lifetime. Over coffee one woman tells a story about something that happened to her; her companion explains how a similar thing happened to her, and now they are friends. Over the radio we hear a song about a person that we loved but never loved us back, a song full of hope and pain, reflecting our sentiments so well that we can't wait to play it for our friends. A person asks us about our favourite movie, and we quietly hope it will be one of theirs too, since then we will form a connection.

When people transition into a new culture, what makes the most difference to their experience is someone who is there to help. If we really wish to change behaviours, we must start by understanding the concerns that govern the way someone behaves today – perhaps through listening to the story they tell about themselves.

Often, changing the way people act will necessitate changing the way people around them react. When we endeavour to form a connection with someone, our starting point must be those things that matter most to them. Something that matters deeply to people is fitting in – so you can effect change on a massive scale simply by shifting a convention. Two conventions that have changed dramatically in my lifetime are church-going and family dinners.

Recent years have also seen an exponential increase in the affective impact of the digital media surrounding us – almost an 'emotional arms race'. It troubles me that in our pursuit of the emotionally stimulating, we are systematically desensitizing ourselves to life.

Scientific research for affective context

To conclude this chapter: the picture that I have presented here is of a human mind where the things that we say are really just a manifestation of a complex world of affective reactions, largely hidden from sight. There are many areas of scientific support for this model, but one that might interest you is a piece of research carried out by Michael Gazzaniga in which he questioned split-brain patients.[5]

Split-brain patients are people for whom the corpus callosum – the fibres that connect the two halves of the brain – are deliberately severed. Horrifying as this sounds, it is a treatment that can be effective for certain kinds of chronic disorder, such as severe epilepsy, preventing the spread of seizures across the brain. It does, however, have the side effect that the two sides of the brain subsequently operate independently. Since each side controls a separate hand, this can lead to interesting results.

In one experiment, one side of the brain (the side without language ability) was asked to choose something to go with a picture – which was a picture of a snow drift. The hand chose a shovel. The other side of the brain only saw a picture of a chicken. So imagine you are the language half of your brain: you see a chicken, and you see your other hand pick up a shovel and you think: 'Why the blazes did I pick up a shovel!?' Participants asked why they had chosen a shovel (given that the part of the brain with language ability could only see a chicken) would quickly give rationalizations such as: 'Well, you need a shovel to clean up the chicken shed'.

It's a nice illustration of how easily we come up with rational explanations for our actions, and of how our own mind hides its inner workings from us. No doubt each of the judges we encountered in the judicial bias research would, if asked, come up with elaborate justifications of their 'guilty' or 'not guilty' verdicts. But you and I know it's really all about the lunch.

Key points

- People's growth is shaped by the things that matter to them, and these may be determined by nature as well as nurture.
- Cornerstone experiences are those that are central to determining attitudes and behaviours thereafter and are frequently revisited in some way.
- Implicit differences in the things that matter to people can lead to conflict if not surfaced and discussed.
- We can impact people by addressing common human concerns, or ones specific to a given individual's identity.
- Learning design is experience design.
- Experience design changes an individual by linking new concerns to existing ones.
- Experience design is often about creating meaningful challenges.
- People are most susceptible to change at transitions, milestones or when in a novel situation.
- We need to design experiences carefully, using a human-centred approach, experimentation and iteration.

Now that we have covered both experiences and resources and the role that they play, you may be wondering in which circumstances you should build resources and in which you should design experiences. What resources will help people most, and which experiences will transform people? Once you have understood learning, you will understand the need to design learning around the things that matter to your audience.

Fortunately, there is a process for doing this - human-centred learning design – and in the next chapter we are going to explore how it works.

Endnotes

1 A Damasio (1994) *Descartes' Error: Emotion, reason, and the human brain*, Putnam Publishing

2 aconventional. A few words on Cognitive Load Theory, 27 July 2019, www.aconventional.com/2019/07/a-few-words-on-cognitive-load-theory.html (archived at https://perma.cc/LTZ9-AADL)

3 M Kundera (2003) *Ignorance*, Faber & Faber

4 C Stetson, M Fiesta and D Eagleman. Does time really slow down during a frightening event? *PloS One*, 2007, 2 (12), e1,295

5 M S Gazzaniga. The split brain in man, *Scientific American*, 1967, **217** (2), 24–29

Human-centred learning design

08

Introducing 5Di

'There is no single right answer or path forward, but there is one right way to frame the problem.'

CLAYTON CHRISTENSEN

Day to day, we prefer not to think too deeply about what we are doing; we rely on routines, conventions and pocket-sized rationalizations to keep the cognitive load to a minimum so that we can worry about other things – like what we should wear, or have for tea. So telling people that they should rethink what they are doing from the ground up can be disconcerting to say the least.

And people aren't much influenced by thinking, to be honest – really they *feel* their way through life, doing what they are excited about, or is expected of them (i.e. not going to embarrass them), or just whatever feels right. I hope I can excite you about a different way of working, but unless there are ways I can make the affective context model feel normal and right, it will probably end there.

The good news is that over the past couple of decades, working with the affective context model has resulted in some techniques for applying it in practice, and I wanted to share those here.

The first thing to say is that putting the affective context model into action very quickly starts to look like human-centred learning design. There is a simple reason for this: if our concerns drive our learning, then we can't design 'learning stuff' without first understanding the concerns that a person has. This immediately leads to two options: either someone *does* care about something (in which case we should be thinking about resources), or they don't and *should* (in which case we should be thinking about experiences).

The idea of human-centred design is not new, but without a model that underpins it, it is still possible to go wrong. Let me return to an example I used earlier: it is a child's first day at school; here are three types of learning design approach:

1 Here is a list of the things *you need to know* (as decided by the authorities) and documents you should read. This is the conventional approach to learning, which I have called 'content dumping' above.

2 Based on the things *you need to be able to do* (get to class, identify teachers, avoid detention), here is a collection of helpful material. This is a lot better, and reflects the conventional performance-support approach, where we take time to find out what people are trying to achieve.

3 Based on the things *you are concerned about* (fitting in, making friends, not making a fool of yourself), *together* with the things you need to be able to do in the pursuit of these concerns, here is a collection of useful resources. This is an even better approach, since what is really driving a person's learning is a person's concerns. Just focusing on the things they are doing will only take you so far.

This idea, of first understanding people's tasks and concerns, and second designing either resources or experiences as part of a learning solution, is the central idea I want to explain. If you are able to apply it to your learning programmes, it will likely bring about a dramatic shift in three things:

1 how successful those programmes are (for example, whether learners choose to use them or not)

2 the impact on behaviour

3 the experience of the programme[1]

It goes without saying that if you want to achieve different outcomes, you will need to change the way that you are doing learning design – so… how *should* it be done?

The 5Di learning design model

Over the past decade or so, I've been using a design process that I have called the 5Di (because – let's face it – if you don't have a catchy acronym you won't make much progress). Here it is, summarized.

Figure 8.1   The 5Di model of learning design

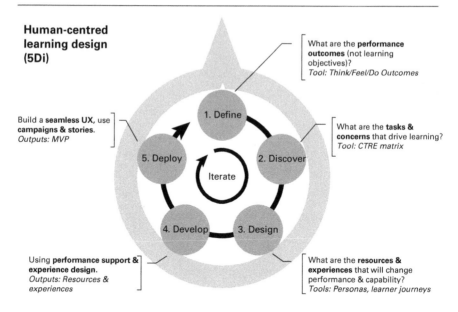

I'd like to explain each of the steps in turn, but before I do perhaps I should point out that any process where you really take time to understand the tasks and concerns that together make up the current picture of performance, before engaging in design, will deliver better outcomes than conventional training design approaches.

1 Define

We have to rescue learning. We have to rescue learning because these days almost everybody has this horrible idea that learning is somehow about stuffing information into people's heads by any means necessary. Even people who don't realize that they believe that, really do.

If you work in learning or education, you will have encountered this in the following way: in essence, someone approaches you with some stuff that they want people to know and they say: 'We've decided that everyone needs to know this information. Please use your instructional design wizardry to create a course.'

What I mean is that the basic set of assumptions is that learning is knowledge transfer (moving information from one location, into a person's head) and that your job is to make this happen.

As an example, people are very fond of the idea of 'learning objectives', which usually end up being a list of the things people should 'know' or 'be aware of' at the end of the learning. Learning objectives are often the pointy end of a bizarre ritual that begins with something called a 'training needs analysis', which endeavours to decide how much training people need.

The problem is in the name, of course: the process assumes that training is the answer, whatever the problem (it is a bit like a 'Marshmallow Needs Analysis' – i.e. a process to determine how many marshmallows everybody needs). And as it turns out, training is *never* the answer – if by 'training' we mean 'content dumping'.

Quite often a training needs analysis is conducted by wandering around asking important people what they think less important people need to know. They usually have no shortage of ideas.

A course is then constructed which reflects the opinions of key stakeholders (so keeps them happy) and is subsequently inflicted on bemused employees who play along for the sake of lunch and a chat and don't really want to put us out of a job.

All that remains is for us to hide the lack of any discernible impact – a process facilitated by a fancy-sounding evaluation model that allows us to imply some kind of business benefit if people liked the experience.

Overall, the model assumes that productivity relates to something called 'capability', and that this is improved by training. However, real people are never 'improving their capability' (you can ask them if you like) – instead, they are trying to do something or other, and unless you are actually helping them with the things they are trying to do, it is unlikely your efforts will have much effect. Did anyone talk to them about what they are trying to do? Probably not.

My point is that if you want to stop something terrible happening, this is where you need to take a stand. You need to say something like: 'Wonderful! But can we just set the learning objectives aside for a minute and talk about what it is that people will be able to *do* if this programme is a success? How, for example, would we see them behaving differently?' Of course, this also makes it very much easier to assess whether or not the programme has been a success at the end.

In other words, at the beginning of a learning design process there is a critical opportunity to divert the conversation from being one about what information people should hold in their heads to one about what people should *do* differently.

As you saw above, we have redefined learning as 'a change in behaviour or capability as a result of memory' – so there is a very real risk that, even if we are successful at getting people to remember stuff, learning will not have taken place in anything but a very trivial sense (and this is often what we see on training courses).

During the define stage, we define the outcome in terms of results, not learning objectives. By 'results' I mean the measurable change that we are trying to bring about.

A technique that I sometimes find useful for these conversations is to draw up three columns titled 'Think', 'Feel', 'Do' and to ask people how these will change as a result of the learning programme. For example, will people *feel* that diversity is genuinely important? Will they speak up if they see something unsafe? Will they spend more on coaching their teams?

While this might seem like a small step, it can be tremendously helpful: without it, something like this tends to happen: 'OK, we've agreed the learning objectives, let's start listing all the topics we should cover!' Let's be clear: *there are no learning objectives, there are no topics.* If you find yourself in a conversation about learning objectives and topics, you have almost certainly already lost your way and are one step away from falling into the uncovered manhole signposted 'education'.

Instead, there are only *behaviours* and *concerns* that will change, and the methods which we can employ to bring about these changes – which, as we will see, are either resources or experiences. In the case of experiences there is very little 'content' as such.

In the case of resources, there is lots of content but we make no assumption about whether or not someone chooses to store it in their heads. They can if they like, but that is entirely up to them.

In a sense, we stop worrying about learning entirely. Instead, we worry about helping people to do things they care about, or creating opportunities to care about something new.

2 Discover

This is the most important step, the step that makes this approach different from any other learning design approach you have used. Here you do something really radical: you actually *talk* to the people you are designing a learning programme for.

Imagine a vast, multinational organization that produces products that it sells to its customers. It has a complex value chain – which in normal-person language means that there are lots of parts of the business that all work together to produce the products: procurement, logistics, operations, manufacturing, retail, strategy, marketing, HR and so on.

Like most companies, they are regularly coming up with new products in an effort to grow the size of their business and their profits. But they have recently noticed a disturbing trend in their product sales data: their success is a bit hit-and-miss. Some of the products sell well, others bomb. They have tried to tackle this by throwing more marketing budget at their failing products, and coming up with weird and wonderful incentive schemes to encourage people to buy them. But it's not working.

And then someone points out something they haven't tried: they haven't tried involving their customers in the design of their products. Someone immediately objects, quoting Henry Ford: 'If I had asked what my customers wanted, they would have said "faster horses"!' But the proposal is not really to ask people what products they *want*, but to understand what *drives* them – I mean, if by talking to people we discover that they want to get from A to B faster, there might be a few ways we could help them achieve that.

Strange as this story sounds, it is precisely what companies have done for decades – and are still doing today. General Electric, currently ranked as the 13th-largest company in the United States by revenue, recently introduced a new product development approach called FastWorks,[2] which is – in essence – about involving their customers in the product design process.

It may seem hard to understand why companies don't think to do this, but when you have lots of departments and processes the customers – well – just get in the way. They represent a risk – a risk that you might have to change things, or admit that you are wrong.

Talking to learners

This is an excellent analogy for what we do in learning and education: it's a complex system, with lots of conventions and processes, and if we talked to our customers about our products and services there is a risk they might tell us things we don't want to hear. Like, for example, how school is boring, or training a waste of time.

In point of fact, they do tell us these things. My daughter tells me this at the end of almost every single day. But education doesn't ask people what they care about, so neither does L&D.

Jane Hart has been surveying thousands of learners in organizations for decades now, and publishing the results on her website.[3] People consistently report that they dislike e-learning and find it next to useless. Despite this, an entire industry has grown up around e-learning production, and universities are hungrily eyeing this as a potential next step in their evolution.

No one is suggesting a 'jelly and cake' option in which we give learners whatever they enjoy; but if, for example, we ask learners what they are trying to accomplish and all they have to say is 'Pass the tests that you set', this should give us pause for thought. Perhaps they might say: 'Get a good job' – in which case we might need to discover what, exactly, would count as 'good' for this person, and what employers with those jobs are looking for. They might say: 'Keep my parents happy'. At what point in life should people stop doing things just to please their parents? At 30? At 45? Never?

But by putting the individual at the heart of the design process, we can bring about a radical shift in the appeal and effectiveness of the things that we design – not because we let them do the design, but because our design is a response to what matters to them, which in turn drives behaviour (such as purchasing or learning). So how do we do this?

During the discover stage, we talk to people about their concerns and tasks. This is not at all like the traditional 'training needs analysis'. An audience's 'concerns' are the things they care about – the things they worry about, which perhaps keep them awake at night. Their 'tasks' are the things that they are spending most time doing – the activities that occupy their time.

These two things may well overlap – for example, a person may spend a lot of time in meetings, and worry about how they come across in meetings.

The emotional curve

There are a number of tools one can use to get at concerns and tasks. One of the simplest is to get people to list their 'top 10 tasks' and 'top 10 concerns'. In some cases, you may be able to anticipate the majority of these and give people cards that they can put in order – which makes it easier to do some statistical analysis.

But this technique can fail to get to the heart of the matter, because people aren't used to thinking about their 'concerns' – frankly, no one has ever bothered to ask them – so an alternative, the 'emotional curve', can be helpful.

An emotional curve is drawn by an individual and represents their feelings over a period of time. The period can range from a week to months. Often, the curve is drawn for a transition period – for example, joining a company, the first day at school, moving to a new country. Each individual is asked to draw a curve that represents their journey over a period of time and how their feelings ranged from high to low, including along the way any milestones of significance.

Figure 8.2   The emotional curve

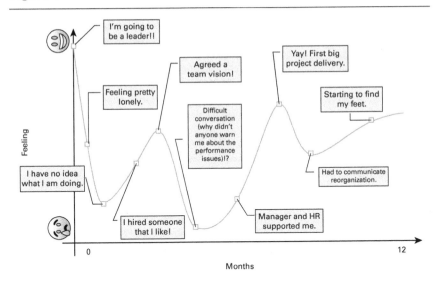

Once people have drawn their curve, they are asked to share it with the group and tell the story. And when people start to tell a story, you can see what they really care about.

It sounds a bit touchy-feely, I know, but besides being therapeutic it is also remarkably revealing regarding the concerns and feelings that are really driving the learning process. If you listen to people's stories you can very quickly get a good idea of what might help them, and what things they are keen to learn. In fact, the 'emotional curve' is a type of user journey.

The power of this approach is that the design process takes as its starting point the customer experience and considers how to improve it, rather than simply ignoring it altogether.

Consider the example in Figure 8.2. This is not an actual curve, but a composite based on hundreds of new leaders' stories that I have heard over the years. But let's imagine that it is Bob's story.

Bob is a process engineer in a big company and is good at his job. When Bob hears that he has been promoted to team leader he is excited and proud. He feels that his expertise and dedication have been recognized, and that his status is elevated.

But Bob's transition into his new role turns out to be a bumpy ride. They haven't been able to find someone to take his old position, so he is still struggling to do his previous job even as he takes on the new one. The promotion process wasn't nearly as structured as Bob was expecting. There was very little in the way of handover: his own boss didn't seem to have much time and, frankly, he was afraid to ask questions for fear of looking stupid.

Bob's impression of leaders was that they have confidence and a vision. He didn't want to admit to having neither. It felt like he was very much in at the deep end.

All of a sudden Bob started to feel quite alone, and to lose confidence. He had suddenly gone from knowing exactly what he was doing to having no clue at all. As a result, Bob reverted to type: as an expert at process engineering, he threw himself into picking holes in the team's work, telling them what to do, and generally micro-managing. His rationale was that he was raising standards, but his team complained of feeling demotivated – and some of them left.

As a result, Bob was now not only lonely and uncertain – but overwhelmed. He decided to flex his new powers of recruitment, but having never done it before he made some errors which could have exposed the organization to reputational damage, and he recruited in his own image. Basically, he recruited his buddies. While this made Bob feel better, it didn't necessarily create a high-performing team, with the added complication that the organization was now lumbered with people who might not be the best fit.

Regardless, Bob ploughed on. Feeling happy about setting out a team vision (although most of the team didn't really feel that they had been involved in coming up with it), Bob set about improving things – even things that seemed to be working quite well. It didn't leave him much time for the 'people stuff', such as one-to-one or team development, but now he was busy with management meetings and considered the 'HR crap' to be of secondary importance.

When he finally found time to have those performance conversations that HR had been pestering him about for weeks, he thought it was a good opportunity to get some things off his chest about some of those he considered underperformers.

Well – it didn't go to plan. He lost his temper with one of the team and said a few things that he wasn't proud of (but felt they deserved), and anyway now he was subject to a formal complaint. The formal complaints process dragged on for months. He lost sleep over it. The team seemed very demoralized. On the positive side, he felt he was getting some support from his own manager for the first time.

Some months later, the team completed a big project and Bob felt pretty good about that. And just when he felt they were starting to turn the corner came the reorganization announcements.

When you listen to people tell their stories, you will be struck by a number of things: first, how great it feels for people to be given the opportunity to talk about what they have experienced and how it felt. It is remarkable how little opportunity some people have to share what they are going through – and probably accounts in part for the popularity of corporate training events and coaching.

Second, how much of a person's activity is driven by the things that they care about. Finally, how many missed opportunities there are to support people in how they feel and how they perform, whether the person is starting school or a new job.

Let's take Bob's example. If Bob is delighted at being a leader, why don't we make the most of that enthusiasm? Perhaps publicize it within the company. If he is unsure of what to do in his new role, why not provide him with a checklist?

Bob feels isolated and uncertain – but worried about giving the wrong impression to his manager, so why not find him a mentor from another part of the organization and – while we are at it – capture some advice from senior leaders on creating a good impression? He doesn't really know what is expected of a leader.

It might help him to watch some videos of people in his company talking about what they expect, and value, from leaders – or maybe have a one-page handout on the dos and don'ts of leadership.

If the handover process seems poor, how about a shopping list of documents and systems to review? If Bob has a tendency to micro-manage rather than delegate and coach, maybe some guidance on both areas would be helpful, together with an opportunity to practise. Recruiting people for the first time can be confusing, so a step-by-step guide, a list of good interview questions and an HR partner in the interview process would probably help.

Having never created a 'team vision', Bob would probably also appreciate some guidance around the right way to run this kind of session – but when it comes to having difficult conversations, it may be that a simple resource might not be enough. It seemed clear that Bob didn't care much about the impact his criticism might have, or didn't understand. Maybe this is an area where Bob would benefit from an experience – a chance to practise giving feedback – and for that matter, a system that ensures that Bob regularly receives feedback.

Reading this, you may have thought: 'Some of that isn't strictly *learning*'. I would like to challenge you on that: what you really mean is: 'Some of that isn't strictly education'. In other words, you too may hold this deeply held belief that learning is about getting people to memorize stuff, and that this is what 'learning' should look like – a list of things to remember.

CASE STUDY   Big shoes: A story about leadership

What were your parents like? Were they strict? Did they have high expectations? How often did they express their emotions?

Over the years I have had the privilege of interviewing several hundred leaders about their transition into a leadership role, and the vast majority handle it in the same way: they act like their parents.

There's a peculiar thing about leadership: despite the remarkable investment organizations make in hiring, developing and employing leaders, and despite the central role leaders have to play in areas such as productivity, culture and engagement, most organizations have no idea whatsoever regarding who are their good leaders and who are their bad leaders. Often, their only measure of success is an annual performance review process, which frankly says more about the relationship between the leader and the person they report to than anything else.

Generally, people becoming leaders have a very unclear sense of what is expected. In many cases, people are promoted on the basis that they are good at their jobs, which, paradoxically, may make them poor leaders. The one thing they know for sure is that they are 'in charge'. While they have seen other people 'in charge', their cornerstone model for what being in charge looks like is something they get from their parents.

In a conventional, hierarchical, organizational model, this tendency of leaders to default to 'parenting' can actually be an advantage – such organizations tend to attract obedient employees with good test scores, who worry about meeting deadlines and are happy to do as they are told. But it seems that many more organizations are looking for creativity and innovation – or just more autonomy and collaboration from their people – and as a result they look to leaders to focus more on development, innovation and creating the right culture.

If you want to change an organization – whether to transform it or to change the culture – your leaders will play a pivotal role.

One of the organizations that I worked for had around 25,000 first-level leaders (people supervising teams), around 5,000 senior leaders (people supervising people supervising teams) and 500 group leaders (people leading a division or function).

Superficially, leadership development was working well: there existed a Leadership Academy with a permanent staff of around 50 people, and a faculty (comprised of independent leadership experts and coaches) of around 100, based around the world. The team were tremendously busy, delivering programmes around the globe to the organization's leaders. Roughly half of these programmes were tailored to a specific need, the other half were part of a suite of 'management essentials' courses – delivered face to face and on topics such as 'difficult conversations' and 'personal impact'.

But a closer look at the usage data revealed a different story: only about 14 per cent of the total leadership population had ever actually been on a leadership course. For those that had, the average time in role before attending a course was around 4–5 years, suggesting that in fact the training was remedial training – for example, where the individual hadn't advanced or some issues had arisen and training had been suggested. Realistically, it seems unlikely that someone who has been a leader for four years will change their training as a result of a two-day course.

Finally, the training was costly and exclusive. The business estimated that it cost around $1,000 per delegate, per day – meaning that an average two-day course might cost between $40,000 and $60,000 once travel and accommodation were included. Most of the people trained were from major hub locations in the UK and United States, suggesting that only certain privileged populations were well supported.

We recommended a shift to a transitional model. In their book *The Leadership Pipeline*, Ram Charan and Stephen Drotter identify the major shifts required of leaders as they transition into roles of successive seniority.

It seemed clear that the most effective and efficient use of the training budget would be to systematically target leaders as they transitioned into these roles, ensuring that they were guided in the right direction at precisely the points when they were most hungry for advice. We wanted to shape their behaviours using performance support and establish 'cornerstone' experiences of leadership while they were still in a fluid state.

Practically speaking, the only way to implement a transitional model of this kind is to do so digitally (or to create 'pools' of pre-fabricated leaders in the way that, for example, the military does). Coaching can be very important, but the logistical challenges in reaching people with experiences at precisely the point at which they take on a leadership role make this near-impossible.

In our case, it was possible to use the organization's people data system to identify when people moved into a leadership role, but it might be some months until the next programme in their region became available. This meant placing an emphasis on digital performance support.

In order to explain what we aimed to do, I would go to meetings with a survival kit – the kind that used to come in a tobacco tin and which contains everything you need to survive in an emergency. I would place it in the centre of the table and explain: 'We are not building training. We are building a survival kit for leaders – everything they need to survive in their first few months as a leader.' It amused some people – but importantly it helped to shift people to a performance-support frame of mind regarding our project.

We began construction on a digital solution which we envisaged as 'everything you needed to know, on a single web page, accessible on your mobile device'. We created a 'destination postcard', mocking up the planned solution in Photoshop as an alternative to lengthy explanations and business case presentations.

We used the 5Di process and we talked to leaders in groups. As usual, we discovered that their tasks and concerns ranged from soft focus (being taken seriously by my peers) to sharp focus (what to do in my first 90 days).

Many of the things that we constructed, based on what we heard, would not have featured in a conventional learning solution: for example, leaders complained about the use of jargon – 'It was like learning another language,' they reported. So we built a jargon dictionary for management-speak, explaining expressions such as 'ballpark' and 'across the piece'. While this might seem trivial, misunderstandings can lead to mistakes, and the overall effect can be to exclude people unfamiliar with American-British management jargon.

We listed the top 10 mistakes that new leaders make, since new leaders are concerned about screwing up in their first few months. There was a 90-day checklist, and other one-page guides.

We used videos to capture views from team members regarding what they wanted in a leader; often this is at odds with what leaders feel they are there to do. Leaders expect to provide direction, vision and take key decisions. Team members look for someone who cares, can be trusted, and communicates regularly.

We also used video to tell stories, fictionalized accounts that summarized the four central narratives that we had encountered in our focus groups, so that new leaders would know what to expect.

As with any resource, people needed to know where to find it. Our marketing strategy was sensitive to the fact that in many operational sites leaders may carry their own smartphone, but are not regularly sitting in front of a company computer. We created posters with the strapline 'useful stuff, on your device', setting the tone for what they could expect. We deliberately avoided the use of the word 'learning', which for all the reasons above had become associated with HR initiatives masquerading as support, but in fact force-feeding content for regulatory purposes.

In the first six months after launch, we had around 20,000 unique visitors to the site. None of this activity was driven by mandate; all visitors elected to use the content. The Net Promoter Score for the digital solution was higher than that for the live event.

In follow-up interviews with a sample of new leaders, they reported that they felt more confident, better supported and that it had shortened their 'time to autonomy' (the time it takes for a new leader to perform to expectations in their new role).

The introduction to an organization (often called onboarding) and the transition of people into leadership roles are, I believe, two of the most significant ways in which an organization can transform its culture. Leadership is especially important, since leaders can have such a big impact on the lives of the people who work for them. If you work for a leader who you feel is a bully, this can make your life miserable on a daily basis for many years.

The human cost of poor leadership is enormous; we quantify it partially though 'employee engagement' measures and through a record of the people leaving an organization ('employee retention'). Leaders are one of the biggest influences on whether a person looks forward to going to work or dreads going to work, on individual growth within the workplace, and on creativity and the quality of decision making.

Almost without exception, the process of becoming a leader is so utterly broken that it is hard to know where to start: organizations choose the wrong people to be leaders, then throw them in at the deep end. Not only do they suffer, everybody in their team suffers. The kind of leader they turn into is hit and miss – usually they end up resembling something like their parents.

In summary, it's childishly simple to dramatically improve your organizational culture via your leadership approach: just give new leaders what they need, when they need it – and point them in the right direction.

In conclusion, my point about the 'discovery' phase is this: if you take the time to design *with* people when you design *for* people, it really pays off. Almost immediately you will see how resources might help them, or experiences might push them.

If you have followed my example above, you may have begun to wonder if this is really what we think of as 'learning' at all – and this is precisely what I am getting at. The learning is not in your control: it is not a matter of shovelling information into people's heads. You can create the right conditions for learning via experience design, or provide the right materials when those conditions are met – but the learning itself is out of your hands.

There are other kinds of questions that you may find useful to ask in such groups – for example, where people go when they need help today, what technologies they use, what they find most helpful today – and which things are the most frustrating.

3 Design

Design ideas tend to present themselves quite naturally when you spend time finding out what people care about, and what they are trying to do.

Once again – we have to put a stop to the conspiracy of convenience in which we draw up a list of things we want people to know, shove them into a course, and force people to consume it somehow. The words 'learning objectives', 'topics' and 'content' should all be considered warning signs – they strongly suggest that somebody has content dumping in mind. Instead, we should substitute 'tasks' and 'concerns', 'resources' and 'experiences'.

In designing an environment where people can learn, we are only ever doing one of two possible things: either we are designing experiences designed to make people care about something they didn't before, or we understand what they care about and we are designing resources that will support them in doing what they are trying to do. All learning activities fall into one of these two categories, sometimes (for example, with mentoring) both.

Now that we know what people care about and what they are trying to do, things get a lot easier. One technique that I have used a lot is the CTRE matrix (Concern–Task–Resource-Experience matrix). It sounds more sophisticated than it is. In essence, we list the tasks and concerns that people have along the left-hand side of a grid, and some of the formats that we are considering along the top – formats such as video, guide, checklist, infographic and so on (there's a longer list of formats below).

At this point, we may notice that something we want someone to be concerned about – say, data protection – isn't actually on their list, so we add it on the left-hand side. We also add a column for 'experience' in the event that we decide something really requires an experience. Table 8.1 shows a simplified version of a CTRE matrix template for a new starter.

The next step is to populate this grid, working line by line, and deciding on the format(s) which will work best. So, for example, if someone is feeling pretty lonely we might set them up with a buddy (experience) and a one-page guide to networks that they can join (resource).

As you can immediately see, this is much more about 'performance support' than it is 'content dumping'. We are not expecting them to memorize all the networks on the list, then pass a test to show that they can recall them.

When it comes to getting emails on a device, it may be that a one-page guide works best, and perhaps if the procedure is complex a short demonstration video. Here, again, people may only need to set up their emails once – so one would not anticipate that the resource would result in learning since the individual is unlikely to use it over and over again (unless, say, they are joining the IT department and will be setting up email access on behalf of multiple users).

There is no definitive answer as to which format will work best; it depends largely on the specific use case and also on the individual. There are three things to consider, however: first, it's a good idea to have a diverse group of people (including people from the audience) help make these design decisions. Whether or not a piece of paper or a mobile app format works best may depend entirely on precisely when someone is likely to use them.

Second, it's not a bad idea to have more than one resource format, to cover individual preferences and different situations.

Table 8.1 The Concern–Task–Resource–Experience (CTRE) matrix

Concern/Task	Res 1	Res 2	Res 3	Exp 1	Exp 2	Exp 3	Comments
Feeling unconfident *(concern)*	First 90 days checklist	Building my Confidence - peer videos		Meet & greet evening with peers	Buddy matching for all new starts		• There are multiple checklists. Harmonize • Sales already have a buddy system – check with Sue
Getting emails on my mobile device *(task)*	Step-by-step guide			Live IT drop-in sessions			• We need to simplify the existing guidance • Joe is happy to run the drop-in sessions

Finally, this whole design process is iterative – which means we don't assume we get the answer 100 per cent right at the outset, but that getting things right can never be achieved except by a series of successive approximations. This is something of a mindset shift from the fantasy of a world in which we just get the experts together and they figure it out, but it is this fantasy that has resulted in an educational curriculum that doesn't work for students. It's not iterative, and they weren't involved.

In practice, our intuitive judgements about which formats work best are a pretty good starting point, especially if we have a diverse design group with audience representation: if someone is learning dance moves, a video may work best. If a pilot needs to know what to do before aircraft take-off, a checklist is ideal – while passengers may need a format that actually makes them care about safety procedures. Performance conversations might benefit from dos and don'ts, but because of the tacit nature of the capability it's the kind of thing you might want to practise in an experience.

From content to context

The good thing about designing a learning programme in this way is that it 'degrades gracefully' (or comes together gracefully, depending on which you prefer). Once you have decided on formats, you can assign different people the task of creating each element. This means that development runs in parallel, with some parts of the programme coming together quicker than others.

This is quite different to the conventional 'course design' process where everything needs to be scripted, storyboarded, signed and sealed before it can be delivered. In this process, we start to get useful resources to people very quickly, adding more elements as we go.

It's also worth comparing this approach to the school or university education system, where currently the curricula have to be agreed by a governing body. In this model we shift the emphasis from content to context; to demonstrable skills, regardless of where the learning comes from. Imagine instead a model where there is no curriculum, just an array of clearly defined accomplishments across a number of different domains.

In a typical business context the design process is predominantly about identifying the right resources. This is because you have been given a problem to solve, and solving it consists largely of helping people with the challenges they face. However, in an educational context, much more time would be spent considering the challenges that a learner should tackle.

Each of these challenges should be accompanied by resources matched to the task. Quite often, people interpret this to mean 'every document that might conceivably be considered relevant dumped in a single place'. Sometimes organizations mistakenly create what they believe to be a catalogue of resources, but which are actually just all the related documents and materials gathered in one place.

Equally, some people see this as curation – but this is not curation, neither is it providing resources. A resource is the best thing to help you get the job done in a specific situation – it might be a person, a video or a document, but it is not a library.

If we produce something that we call a 'resource' and subsequently find that people are turning elsewhere for help, then there is a good chance we didn't produce a resource at all – we just created more content, and heaped it into a pile in the name of curation.

Imagine that you want to create an experience that brings home to people the importance of inclusivity, in particular the importance of micro-inequities in making people feel either included in or excluded from a group. You review the literature and discover that, in general, conventional diversity and inclusion training not only makes no difference to people's behaviour but in some cases has actually been shown to worsen it. You decide to try something different.

People arrive at a training venue and are told that they are to take part in an exercise in collaboration. Each individual is handed a set of instructions which they are told to keep to themselves. The facilitator explains that they will be collaborating on a project to design a fictional startup company. 'Ho-hum,' they think, 'another training workshop. When's coffee?'

What participants don't realize is that some colleagues have been given instructions to exclude them in quite specific ways: talking over them, avoiding eye contact, asking them to do menial tasks such as note taking, excluding them from decision making, ignoring their suggestions.

As the exercise progresses, some people begin to experience a burning sense of frustration at the way they are being treated, which in turn causes their behaviour and feelings to change.

After a few hours the facilitator pauses the exercise and asks participants to describe how they are feeling, what they have noticed about how they are being treated, and how this has impacted their behaviour. In this way, participants experience micro-inequities first hand and learn to appreciate the way they affect a team dynamic.

This example once more illustrates a central point: experience design is nothing like instructional design. It is not content dumping; instead, the focus is on creating affectively significant situations that resemble those in the real world.

With this lens it isn't hard to imagine experiences for other areas; senior executives might meet dissatisfied customers, for example, to understand how it feels to be on the receiving end of poor customer service.

4 Develop

Once you have a shopping list of resources and experiences, these can be assigned to individuals or teams to develop. The greatest risk at this stage is that instructional design thinking will influence the output negatively; for example, producing lengthy lecture-style films or pages of operating procedures disguised as guides.

There are a couple of things you can do to mitigate this risk. The first is to look to people who have a background in other disciplines to produce your content. Marketing professionals, for example, often have a better grasp of content production. People who have worked in experience design will understand the importance of user testing. Actors will usually have a good feel for what makes for a powerful experience. Involving members of the audience will help avoid straying too far from producing useful resources and impactful experiences.

It is not a question of giving an audience what they want; rather, that we can only really design solutions that work if we take the time to understand what people need.

For example, a person starting a new job might say they want someone to stand next to them to advise during the entirety of their first few weeks. While this might be impractical, you may be able to satisfy the need to have advice and encouragement on hand in other ways.

This shift in the nature of the things that we develop has significant implications for school and university education, where the 'sage on the stage' model – while not exclusive – has been the norm, especially at university level. It is hard to see what future role there might be for professionals who are, at worst, little more than walking encyclopedias.

By implication, if you are a learning and development (L&D) professional (or a professional interested in supporting learning as part of your portfolio of activities), you might want to think about developing capabilities that will prepare you for the future – skills you might need to develop a range of resource and experience types. Capabilities might include: acting, storytelling, coaching, performance consulting, human-centred design, digital design, psychology, marketing, graphic design, film, content strategy and prototyping. Since this is quite a diverse range of skills, you might choose to specialize in either resource creation or experience design.

The second way to mitigate risk is to use templates or exemplars of content. If, for example, someone knows that they are expected to produce a checklist that fits on a single page, this reduces the risk that they will return a 40-page standard operating procedure formatted as if it were a checklist.

To avoid the 'gravitational pull' of conventional educational formats, such as classroom and e-learning modules, Figure 8.3 shows a list of other formats to consider. It's not exhaustive, but might provide some prompts.

5 Deploy

Deploy describes the point at which you begin to make resources or experiences available to people. It is often best to aim for a minimum viable product (MVP). MVP describes the bare essentials of a product – the minimum that are required to work.

This approach to solution/product development is much better in many cases; it's a humble approach to development. What I mean by that is that we don't assume that the output of our design is necessarily the right solution, in fact the opposite – we assume that there will be errors and things that we didn't anticipate.

By deploying a pilot or MVP, we can quickly gauge which parts of our solution work and which don't and integrate those findings into the next version of the product.

This approach avoids the more arrogant, top-down development process that you may be familiar with. This kind of conventional process begins with 'experts' who design a solution which then goes through a series of reviews by Important People until, eventually (and it does take a long time), everyone is either agreed that the solution is perfect or they are fed up with reviewing it, at which point it is launched.

In almost every case it immediately becomes apparent that the solution is not perfect, and that certain things were overlooked, but it is now impossible to do anything about it since 1) the project plan specified a final version, and 2) revising it would imply that the experts and Important People got it wrong.

Figure 8.3 Formats to consider

Checklists, guides, videos and infographics are common formats, but there are variations of these and complex formats that are worth considerations. This is not an all inclusive or prescriptive list of design types – just some creative stimulus.

Formats (simple)

Mind-set guide
One-page Guide
FAQs
Task-specific checklist
'When things go wrong' guide
Life hacks
Templates
Useful contacts
Glossary/Dictionary
Day-in-the-life videos ·
Top 10 tips
'How to' videos ·
Things you should do
Common mistakes
People to talk to
Role transition/handover plan
20s video tips ·
Case studies·
21 challenges for your team
Flow-charts
Visual role map
Process graphic
90 day plan
Story video ·
Curated resources
Fishbowl (pick a question) expert video ·
Expert advice
'Dummies Guide'
Printables
Screen captures ·
Quick-start guide
Animations ·
Infographics
Self-check
Common mistakes
Decision-tree
Perspectives from those you impact·
Unwritten rules
Cultural Variation Guide
Exercises 'in a box' (anyone can run)
Reading lists
Thought-leadership/TED talks
Tangibles/artifacts
Email subscription
Blogs
First-person video ·
Reminder stickers/physical reminders
Local/site factbook
Episodic newsletters
Coaching and mentoring
MindMap
Role expectations
Roadmap/planner
Expert interviews ·
Content rating

Formats (complex/functional)

Automation performance guidance
Native apps
Web apps
Buddy-matching system
Badging systems/badges
Search/predictive search
Mobile integration
Digital behavioural guidance
Instant message an expert
Net promoter score
Masterclasses ·
Tinder for learning
Learning playlists
Personalised recommendations
User-generated content
Simulators
Messages to your future self
Pintrest for learning
Remote control
Drones
'Better you' event
Awards & ceremonies
Google for work
Application-technique-exercise
AI (Siri-like) performance support
Wikis
Live links to alternate locations ·
Personalised push notifications
WhatsApp broadcast
Shazam for work contexts
iBeacons
eBooks
Branching storytelling
Personal brand-adapted learning
'One thing I've learned' app
MOOCzs
Digital Mystery Tour
Wearable learning (e.g. Apple watch)
Immersive theatre
Toolkits by post
Consumer-app integration (e.g. TikTok)
Pacer for work (digital trainer)
Outlook push integration
Simple reaction tracking (smiley face)
General purpose challenge engine
Immersive experiences
Feedback loops
YamJams
Voice control
Printed learning diary
Timetable-based content (push)
Learning fitness programme
100 days of...
Printed postcards
360 VR 'go see'/customer visits·
Printed AR documents

Themes

UX (User eXperience)
Design Thinking
Performance Support
Gamification
Challenge-based
Content strategy
Product management
Mobile
Just in time
Flow of work integration
Consumer-grade
Generational shifts
Data-driven
Internet of things
Social media integration
Virtual/augmented reality
Tangential reality
Biometrics

So an MVP approach to deployment is generally much better, since people see results much quicker, you're less likely to waste money and you can continue to revise the product in line with the reaction to it. This approach also avoids much of the stress that people experience when working to a 'final version' deadline: invariably some of the elements of a solution won't be delivered quite as quickly as you hoped, but you can still deploy what you have.

Deploying a solution also involves making people aware that it is there. It's no good designing something wonderful, then burying it in a filing cabinet in a basement lavatory bearing the sign 'Beware of the leopard'.

Like many things these days, you need to market them – and to market them in a way that is designed with the audience in mind. For example, Head Office may communicate everything via email updates, but your audience may keep track of what is happening via a noticeboard in a shared kitchen. Again, finding out about your audience will help you succeed in raising awareness. A resource cannot simply be 'useful stuff' – it has to be 'useful stuff immediately to hand' (in the way that Google is, for example).

Overall, you should look to deploy a solution in a way that is sensitive to the context in which it will be used. To be successful, your solution has to be the easiest thing to do in a given context. This often means understanding how people get stuff done today, and integrating with their expectations rather than expecting them to meet yours.

Use of technology

This last point is yet another example of conventional 'top-down' thinking and it crops up time and time again. In essence, the educational organization makes the assumption that you will use whatever technologies you are told to use, in the way that you are told to use them.

There was an era where they were able to enforce behaviour to some extent; a time when the only technology that people used was the technology they were required to use at work. But organizations don't seem to understand that times have changed, and that now the technology that people own and bring to work or education (such as smartphones) is often superior to that which they are presented with by their organization.

As a result, they do what any sensible person would do and figure out the most efficient way to get the job done. This means, for example, that people will use systems such as Dropbox and Google Drive in preference to clunky and poorly designed systems such as SharePoint. They will ignore Yammer in preference for WhatsApp, and find the idea that they should learn via the learning management system's 'social learning community' laughable.

Put simply, your approach to deployment should not presume that your users have to adopt a new way of working, or install some new technology on their own device. Today, around 80 per cent of people who work in big organizations have only visited their learning management system in order to complete compliance training.

As a learning professional, you can kid yourself that you are contributing to organizational learning by creating courseware and putting it on the learning management system – but I can assure you, you are not. You can keep quiet and pretend that you are doing something to do with learning – you won't be alone – or you can assume that the learning technology that people will use is the technology they choose to use in their personal lives, and start there.[4]

Finally, a reminder that the best resource is not necessarily a digital one nor the best experience a physical one. Digital environments can provide opportunities for exploration that would not be possible to create physically, and sometimes the best resource is something printed on a piece of paper – or a person to talk to. Your goal is to be part of the everyday, not the once-a-year.

6 Iterate

Once you have deployed an MVP, you track usage, seek feedback from your audience and continue to improve the product. Typically, feedback can be grouped into minor and major changes, which you may choose to implement on a periodical basis – for example, making minor changes on a monthly basis and major changes every six months.

By now the conventional role of an instructional designer is barely recognizable and has become something more like a product manager. Traditional instructional design starts with a body of knowledge (for example, a new policy) which is converted by the instructional designer into a final course format (via a series of reviews) which is then deployed, leaving the instructional designer free to move on to the next project.

The deployed course often has shortcomings at the outset, but will remain in place until everyone agrees that it is hopelessly out of date and needs to be revised – whereupon a different instructional designer will be tasked with the redesign.

In the new world, a learning professional is typically concerned with a challenge or set of challenges and with the people tackling it – for example, new joiners or new leaders. As product managers they remain accountable for all aspects of a solution as it evolves over a period of time – for example maintaining the content strategy, the marketing strategy and the functional improvements. They may also be responsible for both the experiential and performance-support dimensions of a solution, ensuring that the two things play complementary roles.

The product manager guides a process of continual course correction through consumer feedback. For this reason, learning professionals will need a broader set of skills if they are to be able to play a useful role in improving performance and employee experience within organizations.

Experience design

Now that you understand the 5Di process, something may have become apparent to you: it works well where everyone knows what they want to do, not so well where they don't.

If, for example, you know that people are going to be leaders, or salespeople, or health advisers – this process works fine. You can develop experiences and resources which together link the things that people are worried about with the outcome everyone is hoping for.

The 5Di is a good way to identify resources that will support learning, and areas where an experience might be needed (though it won't tell you exactly how to design that experience). In other words, it works best at the 'pull' end of the spectrum.

But in some situations you don't have this kind of clarity: two obvious examples being in early years education (where most children don't yet know what they want to be) and situations where nobody yet knows how to do something well. An example of the latter might be the introduction of a new set of technologies to an organization – since we don't yet know the best ways to work with the new technology, it's very hard to build the resources that people will need in advance. Another example might be an organizational transformation, where the future state is not yet well defined.

In these cases, the focus shifts to experience design.

A good experience design should affectively resemble the real-life context. This is true whether we are talking about a simulation or a story. In undertaking experience design, the goal is to identify the key challenges and affective shifts that people are required to make. In the case of a pilot, for example, these might be: take-off, landing and critical problems such as engine failure or heavy cross-winds.

If we think of this as an analogy for other types of challenges or roles it is helpful: what are the critical challenges for a business shifting to a lean approach, and a digital product range? These might be: understanding a new type of consumer, organizational redesign, recruiting the right employee, deciding on the best go-to-market approach, public relations and customer care. By re-creating each of these as simulations that resemble real life *affectively* (rather than at an informational level), we can create the conditions for learning to occur.

Another good example might be training soldiers due to deploy to a Middle-East conflict zone. A critical challenge they might face is de-escalation of confrontations with local civilians, given complex cultural sensitivities. One could easily imagine a digital solution – for example a cartoon-style scenario, with multiple-choice conversational options.

The problem with this conventional approach is that while it may convey the agreed 'learning objectives', it doesn't affectively resemble real life: sitting in an air-conditioned office leisurely clicking your way through a series of computer screens is dramatically different at an affective level from standing in full body armour in 120-degree heat in a hostile environment as someone inches from your face hurls abuse in a foreign language.

If you are currently working in school or university education, this chapter has probably struck you as quite odd and alien: your world is more likely about curricula, lesson plans and textbooks. But pause to imagine for a minute a future world, a world in which learning and the real world are blended so that, for example, a person who wants to become an astronaut gets to experience a little of what that might be like, and is presented with some of the challenges that astronauts face. How would you design for that kind of world?

You could do something terrible, namely, develop an entire curriculum containing topics you think it might be handy for an astronaut to know – or, you could talk to people who have become astronauts and get them to catalogue their concerns, tasks and challenges in the ways described above.

In talking to them, you'd want to avoid the trap of defining topics and capabilities. Instead you'd want stories – stories about the challenges people faced and how they felt. You would want the affective context for each significant task to be mapped in as much detail as possible, since it would be your job to recreate it.

How do you evaluate learning?

If you start with incorrect assumptions, you will never reach correct conclusions. Because for many years people have thought of education as a process by which people store knowledge in their heads, and because corporate learning and development have mimicked school in their approach, learning evaluation has centred on tests of what people know.

But if we accept our new definition of learning, in which learning is a change in behaviour or capability as a result of memory, then it looks obvious that what we should do is measure the things people can *do,* and their attitudes towards doing them.

This seems simple, but there are several complications. Organizations, by and large, are not interested in learning per se. They are interested in business results, and have broadly accepted the premise that learning can contribute to performance, but are growing increasingly sceptical about the value that learning activity can bring to the organization.

This is a consequence of a number of contributing factors – in particular, research that suggests that the vast majority of employee learning does not take place during the organized activities that L&D departments run (whether classroom-based or digital), and the difficulty which those same teams have had in coming up with much compelling evidence that their activities are making a difference.

The continued existence of L&D departments against this backdrop is remarkable, but can often be attributed to two things. First, many regulated industries are required by law to demonstrate that they have provided training in accordance with legal requirements. This means that training serves the purpose of shifting accountability for policy breaches from the management team to the employee. In other words, compliance training shields the executive (and the learning team).

Second, those people who attend training events generally enjoy them. Usually a training event held in a physical location involves a break from work, an opportunity to meet and chat with other people, meals, and an element of fun or self-reflection. While it is unlikely that any of these aspects will directly impact performance, they are enjoyable and give a person the sense that they are valued by the organization.

Managers generally understand this, and when, once or twice a year, they are obliged to sit down with their team members to discuss their development, they see 'training' as an opportunity to give individuals a bit of a boost. In this context, training is a lever to pull, along the lines of discretionary bonuses.

It may strike you as strange that organizations do not take the simple step of measuring the impact of training on performance, by measuring performance. There are three things worth bearing in mind here.

First, today many organizations do not have the ability to measure performance nor even to define what it is. There are notable exceptions to this – for example in sales environments and call centres, but unless you have detailed measures of behaviour, assessing impact is very difficult. Instead, they will look at whether the business is making money and infer the rest. Most organizations run an annual performance review, which tells you more about the quality of the relationship between line manager and team than it does anything else.

Second, organizations are not controlled environments in the scientific sense. A simple experimental design, in which one group receives training and the other does not, rarely happens, since training delivery is driven by other priorities and a whole host of other variables are affecting performance.

Finally, and most importantly, if everyone believes that learning is largely about retaining knowledge, and that knowledge affects performance, then the general expectation is that the L&D team will use a quiz to assess the effectiveness of the training. Though many L&D teams do exactly this, it doesn't address the problem that memorizing information is unlikely to influence behaviour.

Many models for learning evaluation essentially whitewash this problem. The Kirkpatrick four-level model conveniently provides measures of learning evaluation that do not relate to behavioural change, allowing L&Ds to continue to obscure the lack of any performance improvement while simultaneously justifying further content dumping. Of the four levels presented (reaction, learning, behaviour, results), only levels 3 and 4 are meaningful measures of learning, and level 2 'learning' is not learning but memorization.

To put it another way, I can memorize a great deal of information without it affecting my behaviour or capability in any meaningful way (which, you may recall, is our definition of learning). Picture a model of learning evaluation with only 'behaviour' and 'results', and your framework is starting to look pretty thin.

If the organization in question does not have accurate measures of behaviour and results, one option would be for the L&D team to tackle this – but this generally gets mired in problems since actually measuring behaviour is often a more significant and costly challenge than delivering the training itself. As a result, there is a token attempt to do this with self-report questions: 'Did the training alter your behaviour?'

The consequence of this is a sort of tacit deal in which employees give the training team positive evaluations depending on how much they enjoyed themselves at the event.

Four approaches to learning evaluation

I have come across four better ways to tackle the problem of evaluating learning. The first thing to say, in any case, is that in the 'define' stage of a project, it is important to define measurable, observable behaviours at the outset.

If someone tasks you with developing an 'innovation' training course or an 'excellent leadership' training course, it is perfectly possible to pull something together based on content you can find on the internet and deliver it in a lively way that gets good 'level 1 and 2' evaluations. But you will be left entirely in the dark as to the likely impact this course will have.

Unless you have actually agreed a list of things that you would expect to see happening differently, you shouldn't start work. In environments where behaviour is closely monitored, specific behaviours might be: a significant reduction in average call times, an increase in customer satisfaction scores, a 15 per cent increase in sales.

The second general point to make is that most often achieving these outcomes will not involve learning, but rather developing the resources and guidance that will enable people to perform to a higher standard. Again, the Underground map analogy is useful here: if you want to reduce my average travel time across London, you could spend time and money forcing me to memorize the London subway system – or you could just give me a handy map that *reduces* my need to learn these things.

This last point is important, since if you are sold on the idea of 'level 2' outcomes, then, paradoxically, this may actually *prevent* you from creating anything that makes an actual difference to behaviour.

Actually measure performance

The first approach to evaluation involves tackling the problem head-on. Some years ago, impressed by the popularity of FitBit and similar wearable devices that track your activity on a daily basis, my team wondered if we could do the same for leadership. So we did.

In the end it turned out to be an app rather than a bracelet, but one which gave you a regular update on your overall score and a detailed breakdown of what had contributed to that.

The first thing we had to figure out was: what is the product of good leadership? Our conclusion was that the best bet would be team engagement. Effective leaders drive team engagement, which in turn influences discretionary effort and productivity. There is also a well-established set of behaviours that contribute to engagement, and these are measured using the Gallup Q12 index – 12 questions that are reliable indicators.

Leaders signing up to use the app could set a time period (say, a week) for the app to auto-poll their team on these questions, which in turn returned an overall score, detailed trend data and a comparison with the average. Finally, we were able to use this data to make personalized recommendations for resources.

My point is that, while the idea of being really clear about the outcomes you expect to achieve as a result of your programme will probably not come as news to you, technology can provide us with new opportunities to measure (and drive) behavioural change. We don't need to be standing over learners with a clipboard. Many of our audience are already generating significant amounts of digital data as they go about their business. Working within data security and privacy constraints, this can give us a new window into their behaviour.

Talk to your learners

The second approach to learning evaluation is the one we most commonly use. I describe it as the Brinkerhoff Approach, but mainly only because I know that within L&D there is an instinctive preference for anything that sounds academic. Brinkerhoff's case study approach involves looking at the most and least successful cases within your programme and studying them in detail.[5]

In fact, what we tend to do is a variation on this that is more consistent with the human-centred design approach outlined above: we talk to people. When we are developing a programme we get a representative group of our target audience (the people we are aiming to support) together and, in essence, we ask: 'What are you struggling with?'

We then go away and come up with resources – and experiences – that we believe will make a difference (and often involve them in this process), and then we launch a pilot and see what happens.

I have never followed this approach and not had our pilots massively oversubscribed (in some cases by as much as 4,000 per cent), which in turn results in healthy activity data. Using this data you are able to return to your audience group and, in essence, say: 'We can see that you are using these things – how are they impacting your day-to-day work?' as well as 'Which things are not so useful, or missing?' This generates a really rich list of specific benefits and quotes.

It's true that this approach does not establish a causal relationship in the way that, say, running an experiment might. You might also wonder how this is better than Kirkpatrick level 1 and 2 data, since the information is based on self-reports.

To that I would respond that the information you get is of a different order; since performance support is designed to address specific challenges that people face, you get very precise descriptions of how resources are being used to shift performance, backed up with activity data. Where people overwhelmingly subscribe to a system, we rarely question its usefulness – I see no reports on the return on investment (ROI) of email, for example.

Equally, if I am standing in front of a group of people who want me to explain the ROI for a programme, a combination of healthy (and elective) usage data, combined with verbatim reports from employees themselves on how the programme is helping them to do their job better, is a far better position than some course evaluation data, quiz scores and vague insinuations towards performance.

Give learners real work to do

Third, an approach that I have seen work very well is project-based learning. Take, for example, an organization that wishes to drive a culture of innovation. You could put people in a classroom and talk to them about innovation, introduce them to processes, and share a few case studies – but this would likely have no impact. Why not set them a challenge?

In general, learning is driven by challenges – either the ones we have or the ones we are given. In this example, we created a programme that lasted several months, where participants had to use the methodologies that we gave them on an innovation project of their own. They worked with their teams to crowdsource ideas for innovation, they proved these ideas through a peer-review process, they developed those ideas to prototype using some seed funding, then presented to a 'Dragons' Den' of senior executives.

Our role here is less about pushing content, and more about giving people licence to experiment. Teams and individuals who may well have bright ideas do not feel that their organization gives them licence to put them to the test. They are not allowed to play.

By creating a 'safe space' – by which I mean a context in which it is reputationally safe to try something different, and fail – we enable people to learn.

In most cases, these kinds of project-based learning programmes generate ideas that lead to actual improvements, for example in efficiency or sales, that can be assessed using existing business measures. Oftentimes programmes realize returns or savings that greatly outweigh the total cost of the programme.

In these cases, I have found it notable that when people ask about the 'returns' on such programmes, they are not remotely interested in what people were able to memorize – they are quite satisfied to hear that it made a substantial difference to the bottom line. It often seems as if it is just the L&D team who are fretting over 'learning'.

Award badges

The last example of evaluation builds on project-based learning and probably speaks more to the future of learning, as learning and work begin to merge: badges.

If you meet someone who has spent many years in the military, and they are in military dress, you will often notice a ribbon of medals across their chest. So far as I know, there aren't many medals handed out for sitting in classrooms, or for memorizing information. In general, medals reflect accomplishments.

This is a good approach because it means, when you are talking to someone, that you have a fair idea of their capabilities. You know what they have done. I am far more impressed by someone who has their accomplishments pinned to their chest than I am by someone who has their course certificates pinned to their cubicle.

Almost certainly, the future of evaluation will consist of creating an ecosystem of badges that reflect our accomplishments across a wide range of disciplines. As learning professionals, we will be responsible for setting up the challenges via which people can earn these badges, and the resources that people will need in pursuit of them.

If you are familiar with computer games, the system will sound familiar. Each computer game has a large library of possible accomplishments (e.g. completing a mission without getting anyone killed), and as you successfully complete the missions you accumulate trophies. These are added to your gamer profile.

This means that when you are looking at a gamer profile you can instantly see what sorts of games they have mastered, and where they are still novices, and precisely how accomplished they are in each. If you were choosing team members for an online team, these would give you an excellent idea of whom to pick. Now imagine something like this for learning/work.

Organizations will choose to pay people for work, based on the badges they possess, using automatic selection processes to identify a suitable badge profile. Equally, an individual's choice to work on a challenge will be based on the badges that they may earn. If you are an organization that doesn't offer sufficient badges ('learning opportunities' in conventional terms), you will be dead in the water.

A good design model should work in every context. Recent years have seen some dramatic shifts in the nature of work, the workforce and the workplace.

In the next chapter we will take a look at what that means for learning and development.

Key points

- The 5Di model for learning design puts the individual at the heart of the learning design process by discovering the concerns that are driving learning.

- It is essential to discover what concerns and challenges people face, since these will determine whether to create resources (that learners will 'pull') or experiences (that will 'push' new concerns).

- Define: in the first stage we ensure that rather than defining learning objectives, we are clear on the performance outcomes – what we are trying to help people to do.

- Discover: in this stage we carefully uncover the tasks and concerns that are driving learning and behaviour in the current state.

- Design: here we identify the resources that we can create to address the existing set of tasks and concerns that our audience have, and the experiences we may need to design to develop new concerns and capabilities.

- Develop: in this stage we split the project into multiple parallel workstreams, and begin developing an MVP.

- Deploy: we ensure that content is easy to access at the point of need, and that our audience are aware of it, so that they can begin to use it.
- Iterate: we assume that we don't get things right the first time round, and instead use feedback from our audience to gradually improve the usefulness of our content and the ease of access.
- Measures of the effectiveness of learning programmes should focus on what people are able to do, rather than what they can recall.
- Business alignment is achieved through learner-centricity in the design of programmes, in order to address the concerns of the audience in such a way as to support the concerns of the organization.

This chapter has considered ways to improve the design and nature of learning programmes through the application of a specific process. Learning programmes are generally organized by learning professionals, and form a small part of the total learning that is taking place informally within an organization.

The totality of learning, and the mechanisms – both formal and informal – that permit it to take place, is what we call an organization's 'learning culture'.

Endnotes

1 There are some examples of these outcomes in the learning stories chapter below.
2 B Power. How GE applies lean startup practices, *Harvard Business Review*, 23 April 2014, hbr.org/2014/04/how-ge-applies-lean-startup-practices (archived at https://perma.cc/XYM9-54AR)
3 J Hart. Learning in the Workplace Survey, Centre for Modern Workplace Learning, undated, www.modernworkplacelearning.com/cild/mwl/learning-value/ (archived at https://perma.cc/P9UH-WFZR)
4 At the time of writing this means systems like Google, Facebook, LinkedIn, WhatsApp, Instagram, Messenger and web pages in general.
5 R Brinkerhoff (2009) *The Success Case Method: Find out quickly what's working and what's not*, Berrett-Koehler

Bringing about change   09

And learning in the new normal

It will be some time before learning and work are truly integrated. Once they are integrated, work will feel very different – since it will be much more about doing the things that you want to do; the things that make sense to you.

Today, the word 'work' owes much of its affective significance to being coerced to do things that you don't find meaningful – a life for which education has prepared you. In the meantime there is the challenge of reorganizing corporate learning activity so that it actually delivers something of value to the business that funds it, and makes life better for the people who use it.

The problem we have to tackle is that corporate learning functions aren't generally designed to help you develop or to do your job. They are designed to push content at you, on the assumption that this will somehow help you develop or do your job. But it doesn't. And employees tell us that, every single time we ask them. And we ignore them.

I suspect that once again the knowledge transfer model is to blame here, together with conventions which broadly reflect the way that school or university education functions. The learning industry has created layers of bureaucracy, ritual and folklore with which to protect its commercial activities. These include concepts such as 'learning maturity' and 'the learning organization'.

Working in learning, as with most jobs, has its hazards. For me, one of the greatest hazards is that I will be minding my business one day when for no particular reason – I may be online, or sitting in a meeting – I come across a 'learning maturity model'.

A learning maturity model is typically some kind of diagram with boxes that purports to show someone how they can get from the dysfunctional state that their learning organization is in today, to some kind of organizational nirvana: 'The Thriving Learning Culture'. I find them depressing since the way to construct them seems typically to be to scoop up whatever fads are currently in vogue and arrange them in some kind of pile, with the more modern ones at the top.

Typically they show you how to progress seamlessly from a simple set of things that (in my opinion) don't work – like classroom training – to more complex sets of things that don't work – like AI and personalized learning pathways – via a whole set of things that no one understands, such as social learning and knowledge management.

The whole picture rests on shaky foundations (a tacit view of learning as content dumping) and the illusion is presented that we will be able to do perfectly pointless things more effectively in future, if only we spend more money.

Two of the most insidious buzz-phrases are 'badges' and 'self-directed learning', which in my experience, may end up being used against learners – they are encouraged to read through vast content libraries created or bought by learning professionals and receive 'badges' in return. Badges are only meaningful where they reflect accomplishments (and clicking 'next' repeatedly doesn't count).

Overall, the purpose of these models seems to be to sell more stuff to people who bought the last stuff that the learning industry sold them – only to find it didn't work, and who are now eyeing salespeople suspiciously as they excitedly explain how a more costly solution will actually do the thing they promised to do before, but didn't. As I write, respectable universities horrified by the prospect of dwindling revenues are shifting uncomfortably in their chairs as someone persuades them that MOOCs are the future.

In case you think I am going too far – think back to e-learning. E-learning arose at the turn of the century and was going to revolutionize learning and education – enabling people to learn 'anytime, anyplace, anywhere' (people ignored the fact that the last two descriptors were the same) and 'at a pace which suited them' while 'dramatically reducing training costs'.

Well, that didn't turn out so well. E-learning is now confined to the naughty-step of learning, together with learning management systems, which around 80 per cent of employees have only ever visited to complete compliance-based e-learning modules. But the learning industry has become adept at failing to learn from past mistakes: what we couldn't accomplish with e-learning modules, websites or video, we are wildly optimistic will be achievable with micro-learning.

Put simply, unless we understand learning, we will not make progress in advancing education – whether school/university or corporate.

A learning design maturity model

In support of that ambition, I have tried to sketch a simple, fad-free model (Figure 9.1) to help organizations understand where they are today, and chart a course to the future.

When you cut through the jargon, many organizations are stuck at level 1 – education. They may have all manner of technology, but they are essentially pushing content at people and struggling to understand why it's not having the desired impact; they bought LinkedIn learning but usage is low. They are busy constructing 'learning pathways' to show how they are 'strengthening their employee value proposition' but no one is using them.

Increasingly I see organizations at level 1.5 – still dumping content, but starting to experiment with performance consulting as a way to help people on the job – for example with checklists and chatbots. Performance consulting works because it focuses on improving the performance environment rather than changing the person.

Some organizations are fully at level 2 – seeing good results from resources and performance support, but scratching their heads about events and experiences? Should we do them? How do we do them well? What is hybrid learning? Surely there is more to life than checklists? What if we actually want people to grow?

Level 3 is a learning organization, not an educational one. At level 3 we are building performance support as well as transformative experiences because we know what people are trying to do and what really matters to them. This is the key to their development – and leaders understand that and provide support and challenge. Learning has always been part of work, but at level 3 we are designing learning experiences in a deliberate way.

What about LXPs, xAPI, micro-learning, social learning platforms, VR, badging…? None of these will matter if you haven't understood where they fit. You'll buy them, then struggle to demonstrate a return on your investment (that's certainly a mistake I have made).

What practical steps can organizations take if they want to improve? There are two.

Step 1: Shift from courses to resources

The simplest and most powerful step organizations can take in shifting away from education is by challenging whether a desired outcome is best

Figure 9.1 Learning design maturity

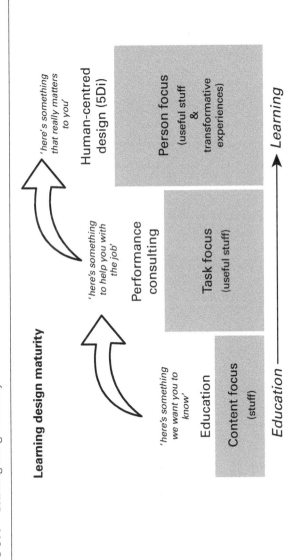

Learning design maturity

'here's something that really matters to you'

Human-centred design (5Di)

Person focus
(useful stuff
&
transformative experiences)

'here's something to help you with the job'

Performance consulting

Task focus
(useful stuff)

'here's something we want you to know'

Education

Content focus
(stuff)

Learning

Education

achieved by building a course, or whether performance support (resources) would be a better option. This challenge needs to take place at the very start of a programme design conversation.

It's harder to do than you might imagine, because often the people asking you – the learning and development team – for a course will assume that what you do is education, and will already have a fixed idea of what they want (a course) and what should go in it (the topics). This is why implementing a user-centred design process (such as the 5Di) can help, because you can say: 'First we need to agree the performance outcomes, then we need to talk to the audience'.

But why bother talking to the audience at all?

Most organizations don't know how their employees do their jobs. I know this, because I have spent a lot of time with organizations trying to build performance support. These organizations have job descriptions, standard operating procedures, and courses to train people in following these procedures – none of which bear much relation to how people actually get the job done, which you only discover when you talk to people doing the jobs in question (although you probably suspected as much).

In one large insurance company, for example, I was told by people who work in the contact centre that the five weeks of new-starter training they received on the fifth floor of the building bore no relation whatsoever to the way they carried out the job on the first floor. The learning team had no idea this was the case.

My point is this, though: if you don't actually know how work is getting done today in your business, you've got little chance of enabling people to do it better tomorrow, or of automating at some point in the future. While producing policies and procedures that hardly anyone reads and next to nobody follows has kept all those folks in Head Office in jobs, organizations will eventually face pressure from competitors who have had the wool lifted from their eyes, and carry a lighter bureaucratic burden.

In the process of building resources, we discover how people are working today; by building performance support we enable inexperienced people (or machines) to do the job by codifying capability.

However, today most of this knowledge is currently tacit and hidden within an organization. This is just one of the things that are implied when people quote Peter Drucker on culture.

The real mechanics of your organization is 'dark matter' – the stories, norms and tacit knowledge hidden in your organizational culture. This is going to be a problem for you with or without robots – for example as people change jobs more rapidly, possess less capability, or as you struggle to maintain competitive advantage.

Many people think that automation starts with a massive data-mining exercise that essentially surfaces implicit algorithms.

While this might work for Google or Amazon, it probably won't work for your company: you don't have enough data, it's too costly, and the interpretation is too complex. You'd be better off just asking people.

Equally, this is a challenge for school and university education: if you wanted to begin the shift towards merging learning and work, you would quickly discover that next to none of the people teaching on business programmes know a great deal about day-to-day business challenges and how to tackle them.

Universities are not well stocked with staff who are experts in cyber-attack and defence, for example, and their experts are topic- and not task-centric.

The first job in making this shift would therefore be a detailed analysis of the critical tasks involved in successfully completing challenges. We can see something like this in the airline industry where a simulator is used to put people through their paces as they tackle critical procedures: take-off, landing, engine failure. They need to work closely with aircraft manufacturers to ensure that the simulation correctly reflects real life, rather than with engineering departments in universities.

The process of creating resources is really about externalizing knowledge, in a usable format. We must be careful to avoid describing resources as 'learning resources', since the objective of resources may be precisely the opposite: to *reduce* the amount of learning someone has to do in pursuit of their goals.

Instead, the focus has to shift to utility. To be an effective resource something has to be the *most* useful asset in a given context. To express this point negatively: if you have created something that you have called a 'resource', but find that people aren't using it, it is likely that it isn't actually a resource at all. This will be because it isn't genuinely useful, or accessible. If you have created what you consider to be an excellent job aid, but people are still phoning their friends, it is time to go back to the drawing board.

There's a flip-side to this too: when we created digital resources for new leaders at BP, I instructed the team to entirely remove any use of the word 'learning' not only from the content, but from the communication and marketing that accompanied it. This is because your audience is likely to assume that by 'learning' you mean 'education' and that anything foisted on them under this banner by HR will be content dumping and a complete waste of their time. If you're doing learning elimination, eliminate the word 'learning'; it will help everyone.

Understanding the role that resources play in people's lives is now simply a matter of observation: people go through life trying to achieve things that follow from their concerns. As they encounter challenges that they are not already capable of tackling, they rely on a handful of strategies. These may include trial and error – or more likely phoning a friend or Googling the answer.

In these latter cases, what they are really looking for is step-by-step advice on what to do next. They are rarely looking for the kind of topic-centric material that we term 'knowledge', and they are not looking to learn (except as a by-product of this process).

A good example might be a map – the kind you might take on a cycling trip. The purpose of the map is not to enable you to memorize the route – quite the opposite: it enables you to refer to it as you go along without having to remember anything.

Step 2: Design experiences

You could take a big step forward as an organization by building resources not courses, effectively eradicating education from your organization. The end result would be cheaper (resources are generally much easier to build and deploy than classroom training), more effective at shifting performance (as Atul Gawande found) and a much better experience for employees (because guidance at points of need makes it easier for people to get stuff done).

This is precisely what the team at Sky did. A reduction in their learning budget provided a catalyst for shifting from the educational model towards performance support.[1]

It's easy to imagine an organization in which education never existed, in which people can easily access useful stuff – resources that actually help them with the job – when they need it, and where learning happens quite naturally as people tackle everyday challenges and watch what's going on around them. There was never any need to lecture people.

But eventually you will realize that something is missing. Human beings are shaped by defining experiences, these are the moments that cause them to develop and grow and change. By contrast a perfectly designed performance support environment is a steady state – everything is easy to do, nobody is learning anything. Performance is optimized but growth is mini-mized because these two things go hand-in-hand.

In reality, in our level 2 organization, development is being driven by the challenges people face on the job. People are getting stuff done, using the resources and guidance we've built for them, and getting better day by day. This is what integrating learning and work looks like.

So what is missing in a level 2 organization? At some point most organizations will be presented with big challenges. An organization may need to transform or develop new organizational capabilities. A checklist doesn't seem to cut it.

Perhaps there is a problem with employee engagement and a root cause analysis implicates leaders and their need to care more about their teams and their development – but leaders don't seem to appreciate how important this is.

Maybe a high-profile incident of discriminatory behaviour damages the company's reputation, and whilst resources on micro-inequities are available few people seem to be taking personal responsibility for change.

Perhaps the organization is diversifying and it quickly becomes clear that performance support doesn't prepare people for challenges they aren't facing right now.

Finally, what if new joiners find the New Start Handbook really helpful in answering their questions, but the organization is still losing staff to a competitor who seem to have created more of a buzz for their graduate population? The CEO wants people to enjoy their work and see a sense of purpose in it, not merely get stuff done.

What's going on in these cases? As a rule of thumb, learning is driven by challenges. The beauty of performance support is that is steps to one side, allows learning to be driven by the challenges people *already face on the job*, and supports them. What's missing is that there are times when we want to *create* a challenge, times when we want to *change and grow* people in ways that aren't present in the existing work.

When people join an organization we don't merely want them to find the job easy to do. We want them to feel excited and engaged – we want them to feel like they *belong*. Whilst less tangible, these outcomes have very real business impact: engagement is directly related to discretionary effort, with a potential performance uplift of around 20 per cent. Belonging impacts retention, and losing staff incurs additional recruitment costs.

Another example: when people transition into a leadership role, they need to change. This change generally needs to be much more than completing a different set of tasks, they need to change their attitude to the people around them. When I was interviewing new leaders for the design of the BP leadership programme, one comment came up several times: leaders would say: 'I think I could do the job if it wasn't for all the people stuff'. Whereupon I would ask: 'What do you mean, "people stuff"?' and they would say something like: 'You know – all the HR crap – performance conversations, development, personal issues...'.

The problem is that 'people stuff' *is* the role of a leader; we found it comprised around 60 per cent of the job. Leaders weren't shifting their focus, and instead holding on to the tasks they were doing before becoming a leader.

In summary, there are times when the people change you want to bring about as an organization isn't sufficiently covered by the jobs they are doing today, where if you want to change people, you need to design an experience.

A good graduate induction programme should be a transformative experience, accompanied by all the stuff you need to perform. A good leadership programme should be an amazing event, and a leadership toolkit. This is the true sense of 'blended' (or 'hybrid') learning.

Performance support versus experience design

The difference between performance support and experience design is that whilst the former addresses existing concerns, the latter builds new ones. Let me give you an example that illustrates this.

When I was at BP, I heard a story about an especially effective safety experience that someone had designed. The fact that it had become a story was a good sign: a well-designed experience should be designed so as to become a story (and part of the culture therefore).

It turned out that some training aimed at encouraging people not to stick their hands in dangerous machinery had been ineffective (presumably because workarounds had become normalized), so instead someone had designed a transformative experience in which participants had to wear a red bag tied over their dominant hand – for a day.

Why? Because people don't work like computers – you can't simply give them instructions and expect their behaviour to change. This is probably the biggest source of failure in training programmes. Wearing a bag on the hand was a powerful experience. It made people aware of just how difficult life would become, of how self-conscious they would feel, how frustrated… how many things they would struggle to do.

They never forgot it, and the story took on a life of its own.

It's a big mistake to think we can show people a PowerPoint presentation and expect them to change. Checklists are great, but people will only use them if they care enough to use them. Change – real change – requires experience design. With performance support we rely on the experiences that working life presents; with experience design we create new ones.

Beyond maturity: the path to automation

GPS is much better than a map. A map is a great resource, but you have to regularly stop and figure out where you are. A GPS tells you what to do next because it knows the map, and it knows where you are.

Once you have created a set of resources that enable someone with little or no experience to do something well, you have already taken a big step forward – but (as we have discovered) you are still dependent on people finding the right resource to use at the right time.

This is how things stand with Google today: it's a great resource, but you still have to look things up – wouldn't it be great if it had enough information about you to know what you need without you having to look it up? (Google have indeed starting experimenting with this approach with Google Now. In all probability they lack sufficient contextual information to make the approach work well.)

The addition of contextual information to resources enables the creation of performance guidance systems, like GPS, which in turn bring about a second dramatic reduction in the level of competence required to do something well. Uber is not disruptive, GPS is disruptive – Uber could not exist without GPS.

Just like GPS, performance guidance systems don't have to be mind-bogglingly sophisticated AI; just a few data points are enough to give leaders guidance on how to improve the performance and engagement of their teams, for example. Once you have the resources that a person needs, that's a good point to start looking for data that might tell you which resource, when. Something simple, like their calendar, might tell you all you need to know.

Hopefully the progression is now pretty clear: by the time you've figured out the rules for what needs to be done, when, in your organization (starting with the realization that these are almost completely different from the rules you have in place today), you are in a good position to consider automation: for example, you know what an HR-bot should say in response to 95 per cent of inbound requests, and you could share these with an app developer.

You know what makes people successful in a technical role, and you could program a machine to work similarly. Instead of saying 'Congratulations, you're a leader, here's some stuff on leadership styles', you know what it is that a leader needs to say and do at various points to improve performance and engagement.

There is, of course, a risk that you are replicating sub-optimal ways of working – but equally there is often a good reason why people do things the way they do today.

In summary, there are things you can do today to prepare for automation in the future, such as the creation of simple one-page guides and checklists. Often, when we do this kind of work, we find that people have already started doing this for themselves, as a symptom of the redundancy of standard operating procedures (SOPs) and training – and these resources are already circulating informally across desks and shared drives.

The vast majority of organizations create something like SOPs as a way of describing how people should do their jobs. The problem is that an idealized description of how a job should be done is typically redundant from the outset, and drifts further and further from reality as time goes on.

So the starting point for this journey is this question: 'How can we capture what people are doing today, as simple instructions?'

CASE STUDY   Albino grave squirrel: Applying new technology to old ways of thinking

Once upon a time I was asked to be a participant in a pilot of a virtual learning environment. I was new to the company, and since my title had something to do with learning innovation, the person running the pilot probably thought it was sensible to include me. Unfortunately for them, this was early on in my career where my grasp of corporate diplomacy was still a work in progress.

The idea was this: in a global organization, it's expensive to get new joiners to a training venue for an induction event. Why not create a 3D virtual environment and have them go there instead – it would be much cheaper and, after all, isn't that what kids today are expecting?

I was moderately excited at the prospect of being a participant in the virtual world. I didn't know quite what to expect – maybe some Wild West setting, or a *Star Wars*-themed simulation. As a keen gamer, I wondered how my colleagues would put a 3D environment to use: would there be weapons, for example? Would flying be enabled? Both contentious design decisions. What fiendish mystery would we have to unravel? I clicked the link and prepared to be amazed.

I materialized in what I can only described as my worst nightmare. The game engine had been used *to recreate a school* – literally everything we were trying to escape from – a boxy dull building, comprised of classrooms.

Immediately I set about trying to change things. I right-clicked on my grotesquely fashioned avatar and selected the 'personalize' option. There was a choice of three t-shirt colours. I was wearing the blue one. Before I had a chance to make up my mind whether I preferred the garish green or sickening yellow t-shirt, an avatar wearing a garish green t-shirt was standing nose-to-nose to me, and I was being instructed to proceed to the 'classroom'.

This would have been a perfect situation for close-range combat, but I was unable to discover the requisite keystrokes. So, reluctantly, my PlayMobil blue avatar scooted along the corridor to where fresh horrors awaited.

Someone had carefully constructed a circle of chairs around what I could only guess was a flipchart. It was like a Stephen King film. Who would take a virtual world, a digital space in which any reality could be explored, a place of infinite recreation and imagination, and create a classroom!?

'Please take your seat!' A message had appeared on my screen. Up until now I had not been aware of the chat box. Other avatars, literally identical to mine, were already seated and it seemed I was to follow suit. Clicking on the chairs revealed a 'sit' option. And now I was seated. Seated in a circle of little blue figures staring at an avatar standing by a virtual flipchart.

What would happen? I wasn't kept in suspense for long. A PowerPoint slide appeared on the flipchart in the virtual world. Through my headphones I could hear the voice of the course instructor monotonously reciting some kind of scripted introductory speech. Since we were all muted, it was true to say that in this virtual space, no one could hear us scream.

I wondered if I could fly. I started pressing keys at random. I couldn't fly but I was able to bob up and down in an impressive fashion. It was short-lived. I was told to desist. I tried cycling through my limited clothing options, which – I learned – was also 'distracting'.

The chat box beckoned. While the instructor droned on, I struck up a lively conversation with the other participants regarding their first impressions of the environment and our collective feelings regarding the unrealized potential for this technology.

'Can I ask you to stop that,' the moderator typed in passive-aggressive text. 'It's distracting for the trainer.' So there we were. A circle of clones, sitting down and shutting up, in a universe of limitless potential.

Looking back, this is probably the point at which I should have conceded defeat and opened Facebook in another window like any normal person. Instead, I began right-clicking on things. Right-clicking often reveals interesting options. The instructor avatar options were locked. Other avatars' options were locked. I right-clicked on the flipchart. I could see options. I was drawn to one titled 'upload media'.

My best explanation as to why I had a picture of an albino grave squirrel on my hard drive was that there had recently been a news story about the threat posed by albino grave squirrels. Certainly it looked menacing close-up: big red eyes, sharp teeth. I am not sure whether I thought hard about whether selecting this particular image as my asset to upload was the judicious choice. Probably it was not.

In an instant the PowerPoint vanished. In its place, the squirrel. Menacing as before, only now loose in a virtual world. I supposed that only I was seeing this. The trainer hesitated, then stopped. Possibly I was not the only person seeing this.

What followed was not especially edifying: it transpired that the trainer had no copy of the original slides and felt uncomfortable continuing the remainder of the script standing beside a huge picture of a threatening squirrel, even though this seemed to me consistent with the overall theme.

The person who was responsible was asked to own up (I would have felt back at school were I not already back at school) and lest we all be made to attend a virtual detention, I confessed and apologetically made what I felt were helpful suggestions – perhaps we could each take turns to share a picture of something of significance to us?

But this was not the plan, and frankly I would have struggled with the squirrel. The pilot had to be postponed; I was not invited to the rematch.

Looking back, there are a couple of things that this story illustrates: often, when something presents itself as 'learning innovation', it is worth taking a look under the bonnet. As is invariably the case, new technology applied to old thinking is not progress. These days, almost everything touted as innovation in the area of learning and education turns out to be content dumping in disguise. Contrariwise, a genuinely new approach can be implemented on any number of technologies – often at minimal cost. The technology will not save you.

I sometimes feel daunted by the sheer magnitude of the task ahead of us in establishing a solid foundation for thinking about learning, and building a lifelong education system like the one described above. And then I remember: if we just stopped doing ridiculous things, that would be a big step forward.

How Covid changed learning and education

I joined Deloitte as the Chief Learning Officer for the UK on 14 March 2020, two days before lockdown.[2] Uncertainty was brewing, I was one of a number of experienced hires split into small groups and ushered into separate rooms where we each received a laptop and a list of instructions. We were to log in, check we had access to the correct systems, and find our way to the compliance learning modules.

Rowena was flitting between rooms, undaunted and brimming with enthusiasm – doing her best in the circumstances to answer our questions. Rowena will always be memorable. There was a kind of bemused acceptance, I suppose. Experienced businesspeople learn to suppress overt displays of emotion, so whatever we were experiencing personally we remained outwardly unflustered and upbeat. After a couple of hours of this we were sent home, and told to return to collect our badges the next day.

As it turned out, the next day was a full-scale test of home-working. I arrived at the impressive London office to find that – barring the security staff and workplace manager – I was the only person there. I picked up my badge and – perhaps from force of habit – found myself a spare desk and sat down to work, alone in that giant building. I needed to feel that I had 'arrived', I suppose.

The next day, like everybody else, I worked from home. It worked out better than expected: we had all held virtual meetings before, we knew how to use the technology and the infrastructure held up. There was even an element of excitement: people ride rollercoasters to experience the thrill of surviving danger. Somehow we were – collectively – riding the wave.

Looking back, it was clear that – in Kübler-Ross change curve terms – we were in 'denial'. We thought we would be working like this for a few weeks, then things would get back to normal.

I could not in my wildest dreams have imagined that 18 months later I would still have not met most of my colleagues face to face. It was inconceivable.

Returning to 'normal'

The 'return to normal' narrative was the prevailing one for many months to come. It was not simply that we were in denial, this denial was driven by a deeper desire for things to 'get back to normal'.

I confidently predicted that things would be back to normal for our September graduate intake, and advised against cancelling our venue bookings. This turned out to be the wrong decision, but the venues (expecting things to get back to normal) were happy to defer our booking until February. I realize in retrospect how powerful this need to adhere to normality is – one might say almost pathological. People went to bizarre lengths to try to recreate normality.

As autumn approached there was flurry of excitement around an app called Houseparty that promised to allow us to mingle digitally. Many of us used it, and ultimately had the same experience: it sucked. It felt as though we had scheduled yet another Zoom meeting at the end of the day. It felt like a chore. It wasn't a good experience, and we all stopped using it without quite understanding why.

Overall, our enforced displacement into the digital world was showing us all how much the physical world mattered and how poorly we understood why.

The same experience was reflected at scale in our organizations: people were suffering from 'Zoom fatigue'. Nobody quite understood what Zoom fatigue was: they didn't have an explanatory framework to account for why doing the same meetings online felt very different from doing them face to face. Rationally speaking it should have been fine. Emotionally speaking, it was horrible.

If it was bad for us; it was worse for our children. There was lots of hand-wringing over the impact on their education, but probably it had a positive impact on their learning: for those who weren't furloughed children were finally able to watch their parents work, listen to how they talked and see what they did for a living.

They also had more time to indulge in real learning tools – such as TikTok – which spoke to the things they really cared about: how to dress, talk, dance – what music was cool, what tribe they belonged to, what social issues they felt strongly about and what was funny.

In the end there wasn't much impact on education – in many cases exam results actually improved – because this mostly comprises cramming for tests in the weeks beforehand. Children were increasingly sceptical about the value of sitting at a screen listening to a teacher lecture them. But they did long to go back to school – desperately. Not because of education, but because they missed their friends. They missed being together and how that feels. And we did too.

Innovating with 'pre-boarding'

From a learning perspective there were some challenges to address early on: in the face of business uncertainty we decided to defer our graduate intake for a period of eight months. Rather than simply sending people a letter saying – effectively – 'Sorry, I know you were expecting to start in September but we will see you in May next year,' I suggested we take the opportunity to experiment with ways to improve the 'pre-boarding' experience.

The truth was that there had always been a missed opportunity to better support our new graduates in the time between signing up to join and the day they joined – often a gap of several months when they might have been motivated to learn more about the organization they were soon to be a part of.

In a remarkable display of determination and adaptability, my team built a multithreaded learning pathway with core and elective elements, based on what previous new starts had said they valued. We organized buddies – typically analysts from previous years' intakes – and set up 'coffee chats' where people were matched with more senior people at random to chat about whatever they liked.

There was a more formal series of sessions covering core capabilities and tasks, such as project management and meeting etiquette, as well as more informal networking sessions. We had internal speakers and external speakers sharing their stories, Julie describing our 'business chemistry' model, and talking about some of the things new starts cared about – like how to make a good first impression.

We had elective modules to cater for the specifics of the business units people would be joining, and core modules relating to firm-wide capabilities.

We organized a Facebook group, pulled together a content strategy, and directed people to digital resources hosted externally on 'Discover Deloitte'.

Did it work? Yes – attendance was high (although we learned not to schedule sessions when people might be at work), feedback relating to specific outcomes such as confidence and engagement was very positive indeed, and most importantly the thing that we most feared – that drop-out rates would increase as a result of the deferral – didn't happen. In fact we had fewer drop-outs than in previous years.

Training sessions

At the same time that this was happening almost all of our internal training switched to digital delivery: predominantly via Zoom. This was something of a double-edged sword: there was a huge reduction in the cost of delivering training, and we were able to return millions of pounds of training budget (predominantly venue spend) to the business.

On the other hand, no-shows and cancellations spiked. Presumably people felt that it was more acceptable to duck out of a Zoom training session than one where they were expected to travel. And to be fair they tended to be dull: a big part of the appeal of training sessions is the opportunity to get together, to step away from the job, and network with colleagues. It's also a way that the organization signals the value it places on employees – everyone understands that face-to-face training is expensive and digital training is cheap.

Of course all of these elements vanished from the Zoom equivalents, which tended to be shorter and predominantly based around PowerPoint presentations.

The deeper point though is this: the pandemic exposed the ridiculousness of educational ritual – in every context. Stripped of all the informal elements that made educational events worthwhile (getting together with friends, going somewhere exciting, being made to feel valued) educational events were little more than somebody reading a script over a video link.

All of which begged the question we should have been asking long ago: if this is all that's going on, why don't we just send people the presentation and ask them to review it? If we needed to know they had reviewed it, why not create a test (which was effectively the role that our compliance learning system was playing)?

This central message turned out to be perhaps the biggest corporate lesson of the pandemic: in-between lockdowns organizations tried to encourage people to go back to the office. As I write they are still doing that. But it was now abundantly clear that there's no point going to the office if you're just going to sit on Zoom calls or answer emails – no point in holding in-person meetings or training events if you're just going to stare at a PowerPoint deck.

Just as education had overlooked all the really important parts of getting together, business had overlooked that presentations were little more than a pretext for people to get together.

For the first time, we were all having to think hard about experience design and consciously consider how to make our time together worthwhile. Leaders were struggling to know what to do with their teams, consultants to know what to do with their clients, and learning professionals were struggling to answer the same question: 'What do we do together, if we're not looking at a PowerPoint presentation?'

Learning beyond PowerPoint

Put yourself in the shoes of your organization's Chief Financial Officer. During the Covid-19 pandemic you learned that millions of pounds could be saved by delivering education online instead of at an expensive venue. Even better, huge numbers of productive hours were returned to the business by eliminating travel time and reducing instruction time. Hundreds of people could attend a session previously capped at two dozen.

You don't know whether this new format has a comparable impact because, frankly, you've never seen anything especially persuasive from the training team about that. How would you now respond to a business case proposing to fly people to an expensive location so that they could be 'trained'? Whatever you were going to put in that business case, it had better not boil down to getting people together to show them some slides!

The corporate learning industry now had a compelling reason to move away from education (showing people PowerPoint decks) and move to learning (designing experiences). Whilst everyone was pretty much in the dark regarding how to do the latter, it was abundantly clear that getting people together to share bullet points was at best pointless and at worse risky.

Business leaders intuitively grasped that we would need to have much better reasons for meeting: we should only be meeting when we were doing something we couldn't do over Zoom. Oddly, people in businesses struggled with the idea of coming together if not to stare at information.[3]

As it happened, Covid-19 presented us with an opportunity to apply human-centred learning design and be one of the first organizations to show how learning could be done differently at scale, using the 5Di model to realize hybrid learning. By hybrid learning, I don't mean the familiar blend of digital and face to face (both content-focused), but instead a hybrid of resources and experiences (whether digital or not).

CASE STUDY   Designing an award-winning hybrid induction
programme

Our consulting business had decided to onboard around 400 graduates as work picked up during the pandemic. Lockdown restrictions meant that this would have to be accomplished entirely remotely.

By way of context, the previous induction programme was a two-week boot camp-style event held in a hotel in the Cotswolds. It was largely conventional education: for the most part senior partners would show up armed with a much-loved PowerPoint deck, ready to assume the role of teacher and impart whatever life lessons they held most dear.

Taken individually they weren't bad; arranged end-to-end they formed a monstrous content juggernaut, a gruelling topic marathon. If that weren't enough, the programme designers had cleverly created additional assignments to be completed overnight.

Despite this, the participants generally had a good time – but principally due to the opportunity to make new friends, share in the excitement of joining an organization together and drinking liberally. The event had a 'freshers week' feel.

For the reasons outlined, it immediately struck me that replacing a two-week celebratory event with five or more days of back-to-back Zoom presentations would be the very worst thing we could do. From an educational perspective it would look as though we were accomplishing the same things, but by now you and I know these would be radically different learning experiences.

Define

We followed the 5Di approach, beginning with 'define' and talking to key stakeholders about the desired business impact of the programme. It was surprisingly difficult to get them to articulate the outcomes in performance terms.

As is often the case, the course had become something of a ritual, and we had to continually nudge the sponsors away from talking about content and topics that *should* be in the course and instead describe the business impact it should have.

For new analysts there are specific impacts, though, some of which are easier to measure than others: we want to build their confidence and retain their levels of engagement and enthusiasm. We want to lose as few as possible in the year following joining, we want their utilization (the time they are working on client projects) to be as high as possible, and their time on the bench (not working on client projects) to be reduced, especially in terms of the period between joining to working on a client project.

We want them to feel included, experience a sense of belonging and purpose, and look after their wellbeing. We would like them to perform well on client projects – which incorporates a number of component tasks, such as building relationships, solving problems, managing their time, and working well with other team members.

Last but not least, they should be able to articulate the various propositions (services and products) that comprised their part of the business (their 'portfolio').

These outcomes give you a sense of what the programme should achieve.

Discover

In the second stage – discover – we talked to analysts who had recently joined the organization. We talked about their experience of the original programme design, but focused mostly on their experience as an analyst in the first year after joining.

It's important to remember that audience analysis does not involve asking people what they felt they needed to learn, what capabilities they lacked or how the programme should be designed – it is simply about understanding the challenges they faced and the concerns that they had. Don't ask questions about somebody's learning – ask questions about their life.

We ran focus groups with teams of analysts who had recently joined, using emotional curves and tasks and concern lists to analyse the experience. We also talked to them about the previous programme design; what worked and what didn't.

In the time that I have run this process I have never failed to be astounded by the insights that audiences will impart. We identified literally hundreds of ways in which we could improve on the old programme. The central theme was predictable, though: new starts' concerns weren't well aligned with the business's: whilst the business was concerned with people memorizing lots of information relating to systems, strategy, processes and portfolios, new starts were interested in fitting in, making friends, being successful.

Here's one example of this misalignment: the old programme focused on client work, the sales cycle, services and products and project delivery. But many new starts had found themselves 'on the bench' for the first few months – waiting to get on a project with no idea what to do with their time.

They found this depressing, lost confidence, and inevitably some left. Neither higher education nor the induction programme prepared them for selling themselves.

We learned many other things about what was really going on beneath the educational façade. In one case a young woman had received the standard joining instructions advising her that she would need to wear 'professional attire' for the duration of the two week programme.

Not knowing quite what this meant (and presumably drawing on popular TV series for inspiration) she had spent the last of her meagre savings to purchase smart outfits – none of which she actually wore at the event where people were dressed more casually than she had anticipated, or in her client work thereafter.

Another new start remarked: 'Shortly after I joined I was asked to lead a meeting. I had never led a meeting before – I had no idea what to do.' Do you see what I mean about the importance of audience research? Without it, you will almost certainly fail to help people with the challenges they are about to encounter or the worries that they have. You will just be lobbing content at them, and very little of it will stick.

You might think: 'Well – they could always ask someone about these things, or Google them', and you would be right (and have spotted the importance of building a support network), but that response begs the question: 'So why hold an induction event at all?'

In reference to the previous design there were bits they liked: they loved the experience of being together and getting to know one another. The presence of senior partners on the programme together with the quality of the venue made them feel valued (though the quality of the speakers varied hugely). Most of all they enjoyed the simulation, where they got to actually try things out and compete as teams to pitch their ideas.

The amount of content they found overwhelming, and they recalled very little of it – which didn't actually matter because for the most part it didn't turn out to be relevant. They couldn't see the point of spending hours looking at how to use IT systems they were yet to encounter. How things were *supposed* to be done was frequently quite different from how things were *actually* done.

Their wellbeing suffered: many of them struggled with the relentless onslaught of lectures and evening assignments.

Design

In the design phase we set about rebuilding the programme from scratch. We aimed to build a hybrid programme, by which I mean a programme comprised of experiences and resources properly allocated.

'Proper allocation' means taking pretty much all of the content out of a course, replacing it with resources that are useful and accessible at the point of need, and building experiences that enable us to achieve the performance and experience outcomes we are looking for.

We used a Concern-Task-Resource-Experience (CTRE) matrix to guide this partitioning activity; itemizing the concerns and tasks that the business and the participants had identified on the left, then listing all the potential formats along the top – for example: short video, checklist, experience and so on.

As you can imagine, a central challenge was this: how do you create a digital experience (that isn't just a PowerPoint presentation)? Or to put it more bluntly: how do you take a face-to-face programme and shift it online without damaging the experience in the process? Our guiding principle was that the programme should be entirely experiential. No PowerPoint – just one experience after another.

I think some of the internal team had heard me talk about all this stuff, without it really sinking in up until this point. It came as a shock that we weren't going to be slotting topics into a timetable and lining up the PowerPoint slides to match. The partners were flabbergasted that we wouldn't be asking them to rock up and talk through their decks.

So how did we accomplish this radical shift? As always, there are two components to consider: resources (performance support) and experiences (learning design).

The organization had plenty of learning technologies, but none of these were fit for purpose as performance support systems. They were – as is usually the case – educational systems, designed to dump content on people in a forcible fashion and track completion. They were not, for example, easy to access on a mobile device at the point of need. They didn't make it easy to upload and share checklists or videos.

So we designed, developed and deployed a digital platform that would allow us to get digital resources to people seamlessly, at points of need, on whatever device they preferred.

A common mistake is to think of all your short-form educational content as 'resources' and merrily upload it to your performance support platform. This will pretty much kill your project from the outset. Resources are very different from educational content (such as modules, micro-learning, chapters). They are typically only one page long or a few seconds in length and designed to be used not learned.

We began creating resources that directly addressed the challenges and concerns that people had expressed – for example short videos on what to wear in different contexts, tips and advice from experienced analysts on dealing with being 'on the bench', checklists for the first few months, jargon-busters and so on.

I won't go into the details of designing, developing and deploying an entirely new IT system into a global organization in the space of a few months: I could write a book on that alone. Suffice it to say that nobody believed we could do what we said we were going to do, but we did it anyway.

The experience design was challenging in different ways: many of the people on the project didn't know what a learning design could look like if it wasn't putting together a timetable like the ones they had experienced at school with topics arranged in hourly slots. So instead we used the kind of storyboard format that Hollywood movies use: sketches that brought to life what participants would be doing from one session to the next, how the experience would flow.

Now that we had shifted lots of the content out of the experience, we had freed up time to do the kinds of things participants really enjoyed, and give them space to practise the things that the business needed them to be able to do. We split the simulation up into component tasks and spread them throughout the programme – for example using actors and a forum-theatre style format to allow participants to observe and practise interactions with clients.

We involved external speakers – an extraordinarily energetic and funny professional host as well as diverse celebrity speakers. This was a really important way to make participants feel valued in the absence of the accommodation and food; although the event was much cheaper to deliver digitally than face to face overall, showing that we will invest money in sourcing the very best speakers counters the perception that participants are experiencing a cheap alternative.

We chose people that we knew the audience respected, and we created much more space for new analysts to talk to analysts who had been there a little while. This is also an important point: they got much more from talking to their peers than from very senior folk (though they appreciated the senior folk showing up).

As well as enabling participants to practise things they would have to do at work, we made plenty of space for other kinds of challenges, networking, storytelling and wellbeing sessions.

To accompany the activities we created an activity hamper – a box containing boxes for each day of the programme, which in turn contained all the materials and items people would need for the activities, as well as some surprises. Activities included shared cooking challenges, collaborative art, storytelling and dress-up... it was clear that we were doing digital induction in a way that no other organization had done before.

Because many of the internal team were doing this for the first time – at pace – we partnered with an external vendor familiar with 5Di and used this as an opportunity to build internal capability along the way.[4]

The partners needed a lot of hand-holding. They had become rather attached to their slideware, so we ran sessions on delivering TED talk-style sessions instead: shorter, sharper story-focused delivery rather than lectures.

Overall the design was divided along two axes and flattened across time: we split out resources and experiences as above, and then we split out common skills and concerns and portfolio-specific ones. It made no sense for people to hear about things that didn't relate to their area of operation, so we took the entire group through the 'core' learning experience, and then divided them into smaller groups for smaller elective sessions covering things specific to their part of the business.

In addition the design was 'flattened': rather than the 'sign your contract-attend the event-do the job' format, we provided smoother on- and off-ramps with access to digital resources in advance, briefing sessions in preparation for the event, then buddies and opportunities to shadow assignments digitally post the event.

The result

We ended up with a five-day digital experience. We saw very high levels of (elective) usage of the digital resources, a Net Promoter Score for the digital event that was higher than for the previous face-to-face event, and a range of early indicators suggesting we were impacting business operations positively: for example high rates of utilization, low cohort drop-out rates.

In addition we had modelled an entirely new way of designing learning as a means of driving our strategy – what I have dubbed 'strategic exemplification': rather than try to persuade other parts of the business to change, we now had a proven model which was enthusiastically adopted elsewhere.

And not just in our own business. We entered our work into the prestigious Learning and Performance Institute 2021 Awards, and won Gold in the Best Online Induction Programme category. We had demonstrated that you can use human-centred design approaches to build hybrid learning experiences that are an improvement on conventional educational approaches.

In the end, the Covid-19 pandemic enabled us to change some of the things that we should have been changed long ago. As a senior colleague once said, 'Never waste a good crisis.'

Key points

- Looking to apply new technologies to learning, without changing the underlying thinking, is unlikely to yield significantly better results.

- Organizations should look to shift from courses to resources, enabling people to access what they need, when they need it – rather than trying to memorize information 'just in case'.

- Adding contextual information (such as upcoming tasks) will enable these resources to evolve into context-sensitive guidance.

- Context-sensitive guidance provides a basis for automating tasks.

- In future, learning organizations should shift their focus to employee experience and performance rather than learning.

- The 'experience and performance' organization should be designed to deliver supportive employee experiences, with different teams collaborating to provide resources at the point of need and timely experiences.

- Organizations are intrinsically resistant to innovation, so successful innovation requires a number of tactics aimed at establishing a protected space and cultivating innovation incrementally.

- Hybrid learning involves splitting learning programmes into 'resource' and 'experience' elements, employing a human-centred approach. Both can be delivered digitally, although the latter is harder to accomplish.

Endnotes

1 Fosway Group. Innovation Profile: Sky, undated, www.fosway.com/innovation-profile-sky/ (archived at https://perma.cc/4FVP-JARV)

2 Institute for Government Analysis. Timeline of UK coronavirus lockdowns, March 2020 to March 2021, undated, www.instituteforgovernment.org.uk (archived at https://perma.cc/VFS7-HUVA)

3 N Shackleton-Jones. 10 Things To Do instead of Showing People a PowerPoint, LinkedIn, undated, www.linkedin.com/posts/shackletonjones_stuff-you-can-use-activity-6872108597749301248-CWeh (archived at https://perma.cc/CQ73-ZF9L)

4 Special thanks to Charles Kneen and Stephen McNally.

Ethics and AI in learning

Robot teachers and the responsibility for changing people

More than 2,000 years ago Plato asked: 'What is the just life?'

If you skip to the last page in the history of ethics, the answer to that question is – ultimately – 'Whatever feels just', but sadly we got off on the wrong foot by trying to use reason to reduce it to a set of rules, in the process spawning 2,000 years of philosophical faffing about along a blind alley. (Plato's answer, by the way, was that the more rational a person is, the more just they will be. So that worked out well.)

But let's back up a few steps.

Imagine that your brother is dying of a disease. There is a treatment – a single pill that would cure him – but you are not able to afford it. You know that the drug company that sell the pill charge ten times what it costs to make. Is it right for you to steal the pill from the drug store in order to save your dying brother?

I'm not going to give you the answer, or argue with yours. Instead, I'd like you to notice what goes on inside you when you are asked a question like this: there is a shuffling of sentiments, an alignment to a position based on an instinctive reaction. It may well be that the instinctive reaction has been formed by that 'Big Pharma' critique you read, or your feelings towards your friend who happens to be a pharmacist. In all probability you don't really know – but your sentiments have already taken a position and your mind is already concocting arguments and anticipating a territorial defence.

You suspect there is a conversation ahead – one where two or more people go to and fro, getting increasingly heated – and most likely ending in disagreement. It's probably a liberal/conservative type issue. You have a familiar feeling about how this will play out.

The philosopher Ludwig Wittgenstein struggled with ethics. He talked about it as trying to describe a 'blurred picture'. But the problem he had with ethics turns out to be the problem he began to experience with everything: the closer you look at concepts, the more you realize that their edges are blurred.

There are concepts which start out looking blurry – like 'love' – and then there are ones that look pretty clear-cut from a distance – like 'chair' – until you get up close (or try to teach them to a computer) and only then do you realize that they, too, are blurry.

Ethics is one of the concepts that looks pretty blurry from the start, so studying it can help us to understand the kinds of challenges that having an affective basis for cognition presents.

Ethical progressions

In his popular talks on ethics, Michael Sandel presents us with two classic (and by now hackneyed) dilemmas.[1] You are standing at the junction in a train track, a runaway train is hurtling down the track, if it continues on its current course it will kill five people who are (inexplicably) tied to the track, whilst if you pull the lever, it will change course and kill only one person (also tied to the track). What to do?

It seems pretty clear that the right thing to do would be to pull the lever. But just before we move on to the next level of complexity, note how easily we can blur this distinction: what if the one person were Nelson Mandela and the five others his sadistic prison guards? The possible combinations are endless.

But let's leave that to one side for the moment and consider the next step in the ethical progression: now you are standing on a bridge over the track. There is no junction in the track, only five people once more tied to the rails who will likely die if you don't intervene. Whilst this time you cannot pull a lever, there is an obese person leaning over the bridge who – if you were to push them onto the track – would likely cause the train to stop or derail.

The question is: would you push the person onto the track to stop the train and save five people? Most people recoil at the idea. It just 'feels' wrong. But – goes the argument – what is the difference *logically* between killing one person by pushing them onto the tracks and pulling the lever which kills the person by diverting the train?

People struggle to articulate a logical response. Some people talk about 'physical agency' (i.e. actually having to push someone) as being the deciding factor. But the truth is: there is no logical response. It's a trick. All the example does is expose the affective mechanics behind everyday concepts.

In his book *Crime and Punishment*, Dostoevsky tells the tale of a young man, Raskolnikov, living a desperate life as a brilliant but impoverished student, who reasons that it makes sense, *logically*, to end the life of a wicked old woman living in his building. The woman in question is clearly a nasty piece of work, but has a considerable stash of cash which – Raskolnikov reasons – could be put to better use. Objectively, he decides, it would be a good thing to dispatch her. Which he does. With an axe.

What then happens is the real point of the story: whilst Raskolnikov is able to convince himself that, rationally speaking, he did the right thing, his feelings about what he has done haunt him so that eventually, consumed by guilt, he hands himself into the local police. In other words, right and wrong were not defined by what he thought, but by how he *felt*.

What does this tell us about our runaway train dilemma?

The answer to the question 'What is the right thing to do?', is: 'Whatever feels like the right thing to do' – *and it will never get any clearer than that*. Your feelings might be changed by an argument. Your feelings might be changed by how you happen to feel about overweight people – or by the look of a person. You might sit in a lecture hall and decide that something is the right thing to do and then – just like Raskolnikov – decide that you just can't bring yourself to do it in reality.

Picture the scene: you are standing at the junction, lever in hand, convinced that you must divert the train that is about to kill five people and then you catch the eye of the terrified person you are about to condemn to death by pulling the lever. They look at you with an expression of such deep sorrow – such desperation and fear – that you just can't bring yourself to do it.

The blurriness of ethics is a much more compelling topic than, say, the blurriness of the word 'chair' because there are some big consequences attached: the law and artificial intelligence (AI), for example.

In formulating laws we try to draw lines where none exist – and as a consequence the outcome of legal cases can often still feel wrong.

Consider a recent court case, in which a 78-year old pensioner was attacked in his own home by two burglars, armed with knives and a screwdriver. The media reported that his disabled wife was upstairs in bed as he grappled with the attackers. In the ensuing struggle one of the burglars was badly wounded. The two fled and one collapsed in the street and later died, his companion abandoning him. The pensioner was subsequently arrested on suspicion of murder, but later released without charge. Some people called him a hero.

Other people chose to lay flowers and cards at the roadside where the burglar had died, causing outraged members of the public to angrily destroy the makeshift roadside memorial.[2] Would you do either thing?

Now that you understand affective context, note how every aspect of this story subtly contributes to your feeling of right or wrong. What if – instead of being a 78 year old pensioner – the man had been a 35-year old martial arts expert? What if he had three small children instead of a disabled wife asleep upstairs? What if the burglar's companion had not abandoned him in the street, but valiantly struggled to carry him to the local hospital? What if both the burglars were women? Or asylum seekers? What if you have just had lunch?

A 2011 study examined over 1,000 verdicts made by Israeli judges and found that judges were far more likely to give lenient verdicts at the start of the day and also immediately after a break, such as lunch.[3] Jonathan Levav, one of the co-authors of the paper, summarized it as follows: 'You are anywhere between two and six times as likely to be released if you're one of the first three prisoners considered versus the last three prisoners considered.'

The likelihood of a favourable ruling went from around 65 per cent to around 0 per cent, depending on snack times. That's a massive difference! So now we can now explain it: whether or not someone is innocent or guilty very much depends how you feel.

This tendency, of people to answer complex questions in a way that seems rational, but is actually done by referring to how they feel, has been dubbed the Substitution Principle by Daniel Kahneman (also called attribute substitution). In essence, Kahneman is saying that we often answer complicated logical questions by using how we *feel* – and then presenting our answers as if they were logical conclusions.[4]

He gives an example: the question 'How much would you contribute to save an endangered species?' quickly becomes 'How much emotion do I feel when I think of dying dolphins?'

But what if we try to eliminate all this pesky humanity by introducing dependable AI – will that solve the problem?

AI and learning

As so-called AI advances in sophistication and complexity, some people have begun to fear the realization of scenarios long depicted in Hollywood movies in which the machines rise up and systematically obliterate their creators, with or without snappy dialogue.

The answer, some assert, is ethics. We need to programme the machines with ethical guidelines, not unlike Asimov's famous Laws of Robotics. All the software programmers will take a couple of evening classes in ethics and we will be fine.

I don't mean to worry you, but now that we understand how ethics works we can see how terrifyingly naïve this all is. Take even the simplest example – an example that one can imagine arising, somewhere, right now:

An autonomous car is driving an 8-year old child to school. Unexpectedly, a cat runs out into the road. There is no time to brake – what should the car do? (Note that this dilemma is a bit like the train track example above.)

The car calculates that if it swerves suddenly there is an increased likelihood that it will miss the cat, but at a cost of increasing the risk to the life of the child. Here's a question: what's the trade-off? If the chances that swerving will save the cat are 99 per cent and the risk to the child only 1 per cent, would that make it OK? If it were your daughter? Or is the life of a cat literally worthless?

Let's assume the life of a cat does have some value – we normally do. How many cats would have to be lined up in a row before it is worth sacrificing the life of an 8-yr old child? Would it matter if the passenger were not a child, but instead a criminal – would they be worth fewer cats? How many cats are *you* worth?

Perhaps we're just being silly and neurotic about everything: the car quickly does the calculation and figures out that the cat isn't worth the effort, so ploughs on, terminator-like, without so much as slowing or a hint of remorse. The child feels a slight bump. 'What was that?' she asks. 'Nothing to worry about,' says the car. 'Only a cat.'

Are we happy about this? Do we feel that this is ethical behaviour? When we hit a cat (as sometimes happens), we usually make at least *some* attempt to slow down – or at least to express sorrow.

'Fine!' says the weary programmer. 'We'll make the car say "Oh, I feel *so* bad! – I hit a cat – that's just *terrible!*" in a sad voice. Happy now?'

Not really. The only thing worse than a relentless terminator is a relentless terminator that apologizes profusely as it shoots you in the face.

Because ethics is fundamentally about how we feel, and about how we feel other people feel, there really is no chance of us being able to create 'ethical robots'. Asimov's Laws of Robotics are ridiculous and laughable. You have every reason to be concerned.

When it comes to AI and learning, this creates both profound challenges and superficial opportunities.

Consider the following questions: if my learning is steered by those things I care about, how does an AI system judge what really matters to me? How do teachers today judge what matters to me?

If 'a connection' is integral to my learning process, i.e. that I share concerns with the person or system guiding my learning, how confidently can a student 'connect' to an algorithm? If, as our experience of school suggests, enthusiasm and passion are infectious, is there such a thing as an authentic simulation of this?

Finally, much learning involves the extrapolation of one concern from another; for example: 'If you care about your family, you should care about safety – had you considered the impact that being injured at work might have on them?' Do we believe that a computer program could, or should, steer this process?

Today, we have algorithms that can make music or shopping recommendations that we describe as 'AI'.

For the most part AI is not much more complicated than a list of 'If... then' conditional branches. Their power comes from the data they are based on, and this – in essence – is why Big Data is a big deal. Such algorithms compare your profile to millions of other similar profiles, and make recommendations based on what people like you liked.

In an educational setting you can see how this might have advantages over an instructor-led process. An instructor is essentially saying: 'This is what I care about, so this is what you should care about,' whereas an algorithm can personalize, saying things like: 'I can see you like dinosaurs and cars. Other people who liked dinosaurs and cars were also interested in robots. Would you like to learn more about robots?'

Does AI encourage 'unlearning'?

In one sense, you can see that an AI relationship can seem far more personal than a human one. AI notices every small detail of the things I care about – down to the time my mouse cursor lingers on an image – and can personalize accordingly. AI is never impatient (unless we want it to be), and seems never to put itself before us – superficially.

But how do you feel about the prospect of a mentor who knows you better than anyone else on the planet, but would dispatch you without a second thought should the need arise? AI is the epitome of Cartesian psychopathy: whilst AI could certainly help us learn, it is actually busy helping us unlearn. After all, why would we design AI to help us figure out the answer, when AI *has* the answer? Where is the commercial imperative to *reduce* our dependence on technology?

Imagine this in a music recommendation context: AI could tell you about the album that people like you liked and enrich your musical experience, or it could subtly nudge you to purchase the album it has been paid by the record company to promote this week.

In short, whilst AI could theoretically be designed to provide a highly personalized learning experience, that would buck the trend. It can be used by unscrupulous education vendors to push their (unhelpful) modules, until that model is overtaken by vendors with a system that tells you what to do so you don't have to bother with the modules. Want to be a world-class leader? Purchase the Gold Subscription from LeaderBot™ for a proven 37 per cent improvement in the quality of your decisions at only $15.99 per month.[5]

In thinking about applications of technology to learning and education, we need to keep a clear head about the difference between the illusion of understanding and understanding. A machine can now write a poem about love that passes for a human poem. It does this by averaging millions of human poems about love into an acceptable composite. This does not mean that it experiences love to any degree, though.

There is no doubt that we have made significant advances in the sophistication of computer algorithms, and in machine learning. However, we have not taken a single step towards a machine that understands.

This is because human understanding is based on our reactions – our reactions to dogs and chairs and so forth – and machines do not have anything approaching human reactions. A machine may count the words in a sonnet, but that is not the same as understanding a sonnet.

So while computers might be good for marking multiple-choice responses, they cannot grade essays: you cannot understand what a person intends by counting the words – indeed anything truly original would necessarily be ignored, because it wouldn't match past patterns.

AI is inherently regressive when it comes to statistical approaches to interpretation. While it may be able to make learning recommendations by looking at individuals with a similar profile to you and copying their choices, it cannot understand what matters to you.

We have fallen into thinking that computers will help with learning because – yet again – we have thought of the whole process as being about transferring information from one place to another (the learner's brain). In this light, it looks as though computers might figure out what we need to know, when, and fire just the right bit of 'stuff' at us at that moment.

Certainly progress can be made in creating performance guidance systems, that is to say systems that use simple contextual data to make available the resources that are most likely to be useful, or suggest the best course of action (like GPS in your car). It is also true that virtual environments – to the extent that they reproduce the emotional features of an experience – can accelerate learning. But both of these approaches will depend for their effectiveness on a process in which one person understands what another cares about.

Future applications of technology to learning

At present the most promising application of technology to learning (as distinct from performance guidance) is augmented and virtual reality. Our learning experience is accelerated by first-hand experience: if we want someone to learn how to fly a helicopter then actually enabling them to practise doing that in an environment that feels real (i.e. has realistic affective consequences) will speed learning.

We don't actually need people to believe the simulation is real – just for it to *feel* real. What I mean is that our brain's more primitive affective responses override your more sophisticated ones – this is why if I have a nosebleed mid-conversation you are likely to remember that, regardless of whether you are a medical professional. So if it *feels* as though you are plummeting to your death – even if you know you are not intellectually – the experience will be more memorable.

It is hard to accomplish this kind of impact via storytelling or 2D simulation alone. Sitting in a cinema is not the same as experiencing something first-hand.

Memory is also context-sensitive, so VR gives us a way to digitally retire the classroom, sending people to the Battle of Hastings or Ancient Egypt as we wish.

It's interesting to speculate what that would do for assessment methodologies; how would we assess someone who had learned to fully integrate into Roman society as a dressmaker? Presumably not with a written exam. One imagines that the simulation would itself be the assessment.

Of course none of these fantastical possibilities will be realized without investment, and it seems more likely that this will come from corporations rather than institutions with a vested interest in the status quo. This, in turn, will determine the range of applications: you can easily imagine the military creating environments in which there is a more or less seamless transition from simulations in which soldiers are being selected, to one in which they are actually fighting battles.

But zookeeping might be a very different matter; zoos are small, independent entities – they would probably be better off sticking with a system of work placements where people can experience the real thing.

This experiential ecosystem will become a feature of the 'hybrid' learning landscape – real apprenticeships dovetailed with virtual simulations. Real work carried out physically and digitally.

Returning to ethics, I have far more confidence that a dog will behave ethically than a robot ever will. Why? A dog is designed similarly to us; it is a creature that feels pain, must eat and defecate. It is a creature that gives birth, that shows every sign of loving its offspring. It is a creature that seems to experience happiness and even shame.

Studies suggest that, in common with a wide variety of creatures (including birds and rats),[6] dogs have a sense of fairness and experience empathy. I can be confident that a creature is ethical to the extent that I can be confident that a creature feels as I do.

Of course there is one creature about which I feel differently to all others: myself.

Question: would you buy a single daffodil to support a Cancer Research charity?

In a piece of research conducted by Nicholas Epley and David Dunning, 83 per cent of students said they would buy a flower to support a cancer research charity, and that they estimated only (on average) 56 per cent of their peers would do so. When the opportunity arose, only 43 per cent actually bought a flower.[7]

Everyone is the hero of their own story. Even prisoners. A separate study found that prisoners rated themselves as above average for every single pro-social trait except for being law-abiding.[8]

There is now a vast body of research relating to the biases that we exhibit in our assessments of ourselves. Overall the headline is that, except in some specific circumstances (such as clinical depression) we consistently feel far better about ourselves – about our future, our abilities, our worthiness – than we should if we were objective and rational.

In practice, the need to feel that one is good and doing the right thing forms the basis of much social interaction. We even have an expression for it: social validation. People gossip about the thing that they did, and expect to hear people say: 'You did the right thing!' or 'I would have done exactly the same!' In turn, people tend to surround themselves (whether online or in real life) with like-minded people.

This 'same is safe' bias protects the hero of the story (you) from ever having to feel like they made a bad decision. This desire to seek out similarity in friendship and relationships is described as 'so common and so widespread on so many dimensions that it could be described as a psychological default' by Angela Bahns, co-author of a study that suggests our desire for like-mindedness is hard-wired.[9] They go on to suggest you are: '[…] trying to create a social world where you feel comfortable', strongly suggesting an affective basis for the behaviour.

Is it impossible to be reasonable?

I want to revisit a concern that may have unsettled you since the outset of the book, where I argued that humans are emotional, not rational, creatures, and that the divide between thinking and feeling is an illusion. The question on your mind may be something like: 'Does this mean that it is impossible to be reasonable?' or: 'Are you saying that there is no right or wrong?'

In an episode of his *Freakonomics* podcast, Stephen Dubner talks to Redouan Bshary, a professor of behavioural ecology at the University of Neuchatel in Switzerland. Bshary studied a type of fish called Cleaner Wrasse, a small fish common among coral reefs.

As their name suggests, Cleaner Wrasse make their living out of cleaning other fish – eating the parasites and dead scales from their bodies. What Bshary discovered, is that the Cleaner Wrasse obey complex laws of economics – for example providing preferential treatment for visitors vs residents, and adjusting their behaviour according to the level of 'optionality' that their client enjoyed. In short, they were behaving like savvy entrepreneurs.

Now no one is suggesting that the fish were actually economists – but they were acting in accordance with economic theory. Equally, the fish were not aware of the totality of economic theory (one can safely assume), but employed the laws that were relevant to their lives.

In other words, though the fish were obeying the laws of economics – and had to some degree internalized them – economics exists independently of the fish themselves. It's a description that we can apply to their behaviour. The same is true of humans. Reason describes a set of laws – logic, mathematics and so on – that exist outside of them. Humans are purely emotional creatures, but those emotions can be made to behave in accordance with reason.

When it comes to ethics, 'fairness' is not merely something we feel strongly about, but – a bit like economics – describes a feature of the world. Our feelings can be made to correspond to what is fair, just as they can be made to conform to reason. That said, we're rarely very reasonable – and normally terribly illogical.

Your average person might, for example, have some basic maths – they most likely know the difference between an 'and' and an 'or' statement. But in terms of the totality of logic and mathematics as we know it, they are only organized to behave in line with a tiny fraction of it. Much like our fish.

Now, philosophers tend to struggle with the existential status of things that exist independently of the human mind, but in practice we recognize the independent existence of mathematics and logic. Why else would we send a Voyager spacecraft into the unknown containing mathematical definitions, unless we presumed that these exist independently of human beings?

So 'reason' describes patterns that exist independently to humans, just as economics exists independently to our Cleaner Wrasse. Both things express logical relationships between things in the world, that could be described by different species at different locations and times in the universe's history. So why the confusion?

The confusion comes about because whilst Cleaner Wrasse are unlikely to have feelings about 'economics', humans do have an affective response towards the concept of 'reason'. Because of our ability to have a reaction not just to what we're experiencing, but imaginary experiences, we can also imagine rules that we like, and we can even fall in love with mathematics. Expressed poetically, we can bend our emotions into the shape of an equation, much as we might bend a willow branch into the shape of a heart (or a chair).

So though we remain – like the Cleaner Wrasse – thoroughly emotional creatures, saying so does not usher in some dreadful relativistic apocalypse where I can say '2 + 2 = lobster' if I feel like it. No, our sentiments can still conform to reason or not, just as the fish's behaviour can conform to economic law – and unlike the fish, we can be aware of it.

In 1895, in his book *The Crowd*, the French intellectual Gustave Le Bon wrote: 'Given to exaggeration in its feelings, a crowd is only impressed by excessive sentiments.'[10] Today, we are witnessing the exaggeration and exhaustion of sentiment to an unprecedented degree, spurred on by the dispassionate ambition of marketing algorithms.

It may seem that we need the voice of reason more than ever, and that in undermining it I am throwing fuel on a fire.

The impact of social media

The problem we face today is not a lack of reason. A closer inspection of reasonable argument invariably reveals a hidden agenda – and this in turn incites suspicion.

So the balance in question is not to be struck between strong feeling and logical argument: instead we need to offset our immediate reactions with the ones we have towards abstract concepts and possible futures. The difficulty social media presents is instead a consequence of affective myopia: the internet focuses us on immediate sensations, and we forget to consider how we feel about more distant possibilities. Everything is 'Now! Now! Now!'

The cure is not more reasonable debate, but debates with more imagination and openness. This ambition flies in the face of current trends, where media vies for ever more extreme expression in a grotesque affective arms race. News is more shocking, movies more mind-blowing, sexual expression more overt, positions more extremely entrenched. We are intoxicated with immediacy.

This is the tide that teachers fear they cannot turn. Whilst our world has become exponentially more affectively charged, the classroom has remained extraordinarily dull. Whilst some progress has been made in educational practices, a lot of time is still spent sitting, listening to someone talk about something you are not interested in.

It is not that students' attention spans have dropped – that's a ridiculous idea – it is just that 50 years ago the alternative might have been climbing a tree, where now it is flipping through 100 hilarious or shocking memes in a minute.

When it comes to learning and ethics, the trend is not our friend: if we wish to make better ethical decisions we must each find a way to swim against the current of emotional desensitization that is sweeping us all downstream. If we wish to learn, we must battle technology's desire to make our lives easier in exchange for our capability.

We must continue to make very human decisions: we must take the time to understand people as individuals, by which I mean the things that they care about, and in designing learning experiences we must have an acute awareness of our own motivations and make careful judgements regarding how far to challenge people, monitoring the emotional cost of growth as we go.

Key points

- What is right or wrong is ultimately decided according to how one feels.
- In reaching ethical decisions we must be transparent about how the people involved in making the decision feel, and how those impacted will feel. We cannot always know in advance how people will feel, so must be open to revision at all times.
- Education's ambition to automate parts of the educational process raises ethical questions.
- Whilst AI can personalize content recommendations to a greater degree than a human can, it accomplishes this by matching you with similar people rather than by understanding you as a person.
- Performance support or guidance systems generally act to reduce human capability, rather than enhancing or building it.
- Virtual reality promises improved digital experience design, by virtue of delivering a more strongly affective experience.

As learning experience designers we must compete with ever more numerous and powerful sources of affective significance that compete for learners' attention.

Endnotes

1 Merriam-Webster. Next Stop: 'Trolley Problem', undated, www.merriam-webster.com/words-at-play/trolley-problem-moral-philosophy-ethics/ (archived at https://perma.cc/92C6-R8JD)

2 J Mills. Floral tributes to burglar killed by pensioner put back up after being ripped down, *Metro*, 10 April 2018, metro.co.uk/2018/04/10/floral-tributes-burglar-killed-pensioner-put-back-ripped-7455692/ (archived at https://perma.cc/RB2R-2BSA)

3 S Danziger, J Levav and L Avnaim-Pesso. Extraneous factors in judicial decisions, *Proceedings of the National Academy of Sciences*, 2011, **108** (17), 6, 889–92

4 D Kahneman (2011) *Thinking, Fast and Slow*, Penguin Books, London

5 If you think that sounds unrealistic, perhaps consider that every significant decision a senior leader takes represents a risk to their career. What better way to outsource risk? Hiring decisions? The algorithm picked them. Firing decisions?

6 H Wein. Rats show empathy too, National Institutes of Health, 19 December 2011, www.nih.gov/news-events/nih-research-matters/rats-show-empathy-too (archived at https://perma.cc/J6N2-TJ45)

7 N Epley and D Dunning. Feeling 'holier than thou': Are self-serving assessments produced by errors in self- or social prediction? *Journal of Personality and Social Psychology*, 2000, **79** (6), 861–75

8 C Sedikides, R Meek, M D Alicke and S Taylor. Behind bars but above the bar: Prisoners consider themselves more prosocial than non-prisoners, *British Journal of Social Psychology*, 2014, **53**, 396–403

9 A J Bahns, C S Crandall, O Gillath and K J Preacher. Similarity in relationships as niche construction: Choice, stability, and influence within dyads in a free choice environment, *Journal of Personality and Social Psychology*, 2017, **112** (2), 329–55

10 G Le Bon (1895/1977) *The Crowd: A study of the popular mind*, Penguin Books, New York

How to change someone's mind   11
someone's mind

Learning and attitude change

'*We often refuse to accept an idea merely because the tone of voice in which it has been expressed is unsympathetic to us.*'

FRIEDRICH NIETZSCHE

We love to obsess over individual differences: personality psychology abounds with categorizations of types and traits. Popular psychology magazines trade on salacious tales of oddity. 'Find out your personality type!' will remain dependable click-bait for the foreseeable future.

But it is only *our* group that are different and diverse: we tend to see other species, even other ethnic groups, as looking and behaving much the same. This effect is called the illusion of outgroup homogeneity. It disappears as we get to know a group, so our sense of each other as individuals probably develops as we get to know each other and recognize each individual as unique – in the way that we have done with our own group.

In time, we start to see each person as distinct and different, having their own motivations and storyline.

Despite all this, what makes people tick is depressingly straightforward: conformity. Close up we are all different: at a sufficient distance, we are sheep. As distinct as bees in a hive.

Conformity

In any given situation the vast majority of people will do whatever the people around them are doing 99 per cent of the time. As we get to know people, we obsess over the minor variations in their behaviour – and overlook the vast stretches of commonality between them.

As a college lecturer I taught thousands of students. During the course of the year I would get to know many unique personalities among the rows of upturned faces. But not once did a student get up and brush their teeth mid-lecture. In fact, for the vast proportion of the time every single one of these unique individuals sat quietly, taking notes. In a given week the most remarkable thing they might do would be to interrupt me while I was talking.

Our species depends on conformity, and the mechanisms that keep us in place. We are instinctively herd animals, deeply concerned about each other. What you think of me literally alters my biology. This shared trait has allowed us to outperform potentially smarter, more individualistic hominids: we may not have been the brightest or strongest homo species, but we hunt in packs and share our spoils. Studies of Neanderthal skulls show that their brains were larger than ours by a significant degree.

Brain size isn't everything though; some creatures (such as dolphins and elephants) have brains that are larger than ours but don't seem smarter.

A key distinction is the extent of neoteny: more than any other creature humans are born with relatively underdeveloped brains and it is our extended period of learning that is illustrative of our intellectual potential. Studies of Neanderthal skulls show that their brains took even *longer* to develop than ours, suggesting an even greater capacity for learning.

The standard explanation is that their visual cortex, not their prefrontal cortex, accounted in large part for the difference in brain size – but it may well be that this is little more than a convenient post-rationalization since few accounts are offered of the additional mental capabilities they would have possessed. It may just be that as stronger, smarter, apes they had less need to hunt in groups. Perhaps this meant less of an emphasis on cognitive abilities associated with social interaction and empathy, and perhaps these abilities were part of the prerequisite for culture to emerge.

Like other creatures we encode our experience affectively – but other people's reactions play a disproportionately large part in that. We have a big chunk of our brain dedicated to processing faces, for example. We can identify a human gait from nothing more than small dots of light, even draw inferences about how that person is feeling. We are happy to watch a video of someone reacting to something.

The classical explanation for this is that it is all about detecting intent in others, but recent research has shown we can struggle to identify the practised liar from their facial expressions, so whilst intent is part of it, we are also just looking to gauge other people's *reactions* – to the things they experience, and most importantly to the things we do.

Emotion at heart

We have a tendency to think of emotion as something that is overlaid onto our perceptions of the world, rather than as fundamental to the way in which we perceive the world. But there is something very wrong with this. I mentioned earlier that children naturally attribute sentiment and intentionality to objects around them – that this is hard wired into the way they perceive things.

And as adults, we may learn that trees don't care if we kick them, but we continue to assess the world around us entirely on the basis of how it feels to us (even when we are thinking logically, as we will see shortly). I frequently get angry with coat-hangers, for example, which I am convinced are out to annoy me on a daily basis.

Consider the following experiment by Fritz Heider and Anne Simmel. Fritz and Anne created a short film (around two and a half minutes) starring two triangles and a circle. In their animated short – which you can watch for yourself on YouTube – all three geometrical movie-stars moved around and in and out of a rectangle. People watching the film were then asked questions about what they had witnessed.

What they found was that almost all of their participants interpreted the film intentionally and emotionally, having no trouble at all describing the motivations and sentiments of the geometrically disadvantaged actors. In fact, for the general population it was very hard for people to see it otherwise. In later research, it was found that pre-school children would tell very similar stories about what is going on.

It's an interesting finding, because it suggests that an affective interpretation is not something that we later learn to apply to the world around us, but something 'baked in' from the outset. Some philosophers have wanted to see humans as natural scientists, using the power of reason to develop and test hypotheses regarding causal relationships between events in the world.

David Hume took this view, and even today there are people who believe our brains to be some manner of scientific calculator, constantly proposing and testing logical relationships between events. But this is just philosophers dreaming of being rational gods – in practice people don't work this way; young children are not looking for rational explanations of what they see – indeed, what they see they immediately interpret intentionally.

Our predictions are predictions of intent: that rock wants to roll down the cliff, that person wants to steal my food, etc. Of course it's important for your brain to predict the future, but it doesn't do this in some logical Bayesian statistical fashion, instead it's more like premonition: you know how things are going to feel because of how they felt in the past.

Even as an adult – despite all your conditioning – you will occasionally experience this first hand: you bang your head against a cupboard door that has been left open and you slam it shut angrily or swear at it. Instinctively, you are annoyed with the cupboard door. Your car breaks down and you yell at it. Rationally you know that the door was not 'out to get you', or the car undermining you – but this is not your instinctive response. We get annoyed with inanimate objects all the time, and in these moments our true way of working surfaces.

Balance theory

Encoding the world in terms of our reactions, in terms of how it makes us feel, helps us to understand the way that things are linked in our minds.

Imagine an old friend – someone you haven't seen since school days – with whom you were very close. Now imagine you bump into them unexpectedly. You are delighted to see them again and suggest they come round to dinner.

Over dinner you learn, to your horror, that their politics are now diametrically opposed to yours. Some of the remarks they make about a woman's right to choose and about identity politics make you quite uncomfortable. Finally, you learn that they believe that cannabis should be legalized – whilst you are very much opposed to recreational drug use of any kind.

At the end of the evening you bid them farewell, and you are left to ponder your dilemma: if you stay in touch with them you will feel like you are compromising your values; if you don't you will feel like you have turned your back on an important relationship.

Fritz Heider also had something interesting to say about this kind of situation. He noticed that when we have mismatched feelings about parts of our world, that we try to 'balance' them. He called his theory 'balance theory'. The best way to picture his theory is as a triangle; imagine that you, your friend, and cannabis exist at the three corners of the triangle.

The sides of the triangle now represent attitudes towards the connected points. You like your friend (so that's a positive attitude), they like cannabis (so another positive link) – but you have a negative attitude towards cannabis. In Fritz's terminology the triangle is 'unbalanced', because your attitudes towards related items (your friend and cannabis) are in conflict.

You experience something that psychologists have called 'cognitive dissonance': an uncomfortable feeling that you are motivated to resolve. You can do that in two ways: you can decide to let go of the relationship with your friend, conceding that they are 'not the person you used to know' – or you can decide that maybe cannabis isn't all that bad after all.

Fritz proposed that sentiments are balanced if the affect valence (how we feel about things) balances out.

This is a very useful model for everyday use: for example if you are trying to sell something to someone, it's not a bad idea to get them to like you first. Alternatively, why expend the effort, when you could just use some data from social media to find out who they *already* like, then get the person they like to endorse your product?

It is also very handy for learning contexts. As a young psychology lecturer my college discovered my interest in technology and promptly conscripted me into teaching an Introduction to Technology evening class for adults. This was at a time when the internet was new and middle-aged people were suspicious of technology and generally baffled by it all. People didn't know how to use a mouse (although those seem to be dying out these days).

I discovered that the way to get someone to like the computer was to find something else they liked – say gardening – then find pages, communities, videos, etc on their favourite topic scattered around the internet. People would follow the trail of stuff they liked like Hansel and Gretel picking up sweets on the way to the witch's house (I may have mis-remembered that story, but I prefer my version here).

It's interesting to note that our fundamental motivation is to harmonize how we feel; we want to feel good about the world. It's not about reason or logic. You can probably see an immediate parallel between our perceptions of reality, and reality itself: life is good, so long as nothing in reality 'unbalances' our mental model. The psychologist Jean Piaget called this state 'equilibrium'.

Jean's thinking (and that of many developmental psychologists after him) was that this had something to do with schemas – mental models of the world which we build up over time. Eventually we reach a point where what happens in the world conforms to what we are expecting, and at that point we are no longer motivated to learn or adapt. This is what I mean when I describe learning as a *homeostatic* mechanism.

There is a big problem with Jean's account, though: psychologists were never able to figure out what those schemas are, or what they are made of, in a way which corresponds to how humans behave.

What I am proposing is this: what psychologists have called schemas are in fact a complex pattern of interrelated affective reactions that are activated when we experience an event, or a memory of that event. I agree that we map the world mentally, as psychologists have suggested, just that we do so *affectively*. Our mental maps are sentimental, not semantic. This is important to know if you are designing learning; we are not linking related ideas, we are linking related feelings.

You might point out that quite often we have contradictory feelings about things, and invariably our mental model of the world doesn't exactly correspond to reality, leaving you wondering why we are not constantly experiencing cognitive dissonance.

The answer is that we are fine with conflicting feelings, so long as we don't experience them concurrently. For example you might be anti-immigration, but also a fan of the Bible. If someone makes pointed remarks about the parable of the Good Samaritan, that might make you feel uncomfortable and motivate you to come up with a reason why that advice doesn't apply in this context.

In summary, not only is our experience of the world formed from our emotional reactions to things, the relationship between things in our world is determined by our feelings towards them.

The world as sentiment

Returning briefly to Wittgenstein's error: it has become popular to think of the world as 'the totality of things', and logic as describing the relationship between them, but it would be more accurate to think of the world as the totality of feelings we experience. We want to say: 'Yes – but feelings are always about *things*!', but this won't really help us, since we only experience things by virtue of the reactions they cause in us. Things we don't react to are invisible.

We accept the abstract idea that the world as it really is, is different: but all we can know is how *we* experience it – and that is inextricably affectively. If you wonder, as Descartes did, how you can know that the world truly exists outside of our sensations of it, the simple answer is that it does not conform to expectations. Whatever is out there, it 'pushes back'.

Possibly one of the biggest recent advances in our understanding of the human mind was the publication of the book *Thinking, Fast and Slow*, which summarized the work of Nobel laureate Daniel Kahneman and colleague Amos Tversky.

Like many popular psychology books, a lot of it consisted of describing 'biases': how many of them there are; how far we stray from being rational. What made this book an advance is that it re-introduces the radical idea – suppressed since Freud and Jung – that we are fundamentally irrational beings, and that much of our thinking is unconscious.

The model that Kahneman and Tversky introduce is roughly as follows: your mind is comprised of two systems – System 1 and System 2. System 1 is the unconscious, intuitive system that does most of the heavy lifting when it comes to thinking. It's the instinctive system that enables you to walk, drive a car, or decide whether or not you like someone without having to use a pen and paper to figure it out. System 2, by contrast, is slow, methodical and rational. Whilst System 1 will answer the question: 'How are you feeling today?', System 2 will answer the question: 'What is 86 x 57?'

The thrust of the book is that System 1 does much more of the work than we realize, and in a fashion which rarely follows the laws of reason. Like many popular psychology texts, it catalogues much of the research demonstrating that, across a wide variety of contexts, our decisions are not taken rationally (by System 2) but instead instinctively (by System 1).

We like to imagine we are rational, but we are not. High Court judges make disturbingly instinctive decisions about whether someone is guilty, and how long they should spend in prison, employers make instinctive decisions about whether or not to hire someone, you and I make instinctive decisions around whether or not to put money aside for the future.

By the end of the book you would be forgiven for thinking that System 2 exists only to provide a post hoc rationalization – a cover story – for all the decisions we take instinctively.

What is the moral of the tale? Well – we're not terribly rational. In many contexts, our instinctive decisions are *bad* decisions from a rational perspective. In sum, we might want to think about using external guides, such as statistical methods or a computer, for a bunch of stuff.

Overall the popularization of biases is a healthy direction of travel: helping us to see that people are nowhere near as reasonable as we might like to believe (another bias of ours). But it should strike you as a very odd outcome: if we were really better off being rational, surely millions of years of evolution would have selected for the less biased individuals. Why did all the rational creatures die out?

Examples of systems

In fact the System 1/System 2 distinction is little more than Descartes' body–mind dualism in disguise. The difference between the two systems is sometimes elucidated using the example of driving a car and concurrently completing the sum 17 x 24 – things which one should avoid doing simultaneously. It serves as an illustration of how 'slow and effortful' System 2 processes can interfere with 'instinctive and easy' System 1 processes. But wait – how about holding a conversation?

The thing is that on the one hand we *do* find it easy to hold a conversation while driving – but on the other hand we generally think of conversation as a rational System 2-type activity (rather than an instinctive activity like, say, catching a ball). In the chapter on language, I have described speaking not as a rational System 2 activity but a thoroughly affective System 1 activity.

The difficulty with this is that mental arithmetic is a really *odd* thing for a creature to do, so it seems as though we are arguing for the existence of an entire mental operating system on the basis of a peculiarly recent, if culturally significant, behaviour.

To use the example from the chapter on education, imagine a Martian culture where everyone has to memorize Pi, and where the corresponding psychological model proposes two Martian mental systems: the instinctive system, and the Pi system. Wouldn't you be tempted to call BS?

As I have mentioned previously – logic and mathematics are held up as epitomizing rational thought – but generally speaking neither humans nor dogs use them. Hardly anybody does. I haven't had to do long division since I was at school. Of course, in everyday life sometimes we say that we have constructed a rational argument – or that a sentencing decision was reached logically – but as Kahneman points out, this doesn't really happen when you look closely – 'rational' is just being used like the word 'compelling'.

It's true that sometimes we do things with our brains that feel especially effortful – but this just means we are using System 1 in a way that it was not designed for – not that there is a separate system. Let me be direct: *there is no System 2.* 'System 2' just refers to using System 1 in an unnatural way.

'System 2' thinking is a bit like using your feet to measure a distance by placing them end-to-end: you can do it, but it feels weird and unnatural and is painstakingly slow. Likewise you could train a pigeon to do simple sums, but the training process would be arduous (as it is with us), it would be unreliable and unsophisticated (as it is with us), and you wouldn't conclude that the pigeon now has a separate 'rational' part of its brain (any more than do we).

There isn't a System 1 and System 2 any more than there exists reason and emotion separately. What there *is* is an ability to balance one set of feelings against another. Human beings, like other creatures, process experience instinctively. But we also have a 'what if' ability – the ability to offset feelings about the right now, with feelings about hypothetical states: 'What if I steal that book, and I get caught, and I land up in prison and I lose my job?' – or even: 'Will I still feel that I am a good person if I steal this book?'

Once again, this isn't really rationality that we are talking about here – it's just the ability to moderate our behaviour according to feelings about non-present things. This is obviously handy.

We can even do it with statistics – we can say: 'What if instead of going with my gut on this hiring decision, I use my abstract attachment to statistical models to guide my decision instead? Perhaps I will be able to boast about it at executive meetings.'

Cognition as an affective system

Once we concede that cognition is an entirely affective system, the biases and related research fall into place. Our cognitive processes are influenced by what people are feeling, because cognition *is* affect.

In the chapter on learning, we discovered that what you remember can be influenced by what you are feeling right now: you may recall that Elizabeth Loftus found people's estimates of the speed of a car varied on whether she used the word 'smashed' or 'contacted' in her question. Here's a prediction of my own: put half of Elizabeth's participants on a rollercoaster, the other half in a library, and see what that does to their estimates.

Possessing an affective basis for cognition also explains some of the more perplexing peculiarities in our thinking – such as the phenomenon known as synaesthesia. Synaesthesia is a phenomenon in which we can easily attribute colours or sounds to superficially unrelated concepts.

Like most human abilities, this one is normally distributed (most people possess it to some extent, and a few people hardly at all or to a very high degree). In extreme cases a 'synaesthete' will be able to tell you how your name smells and feels to the touch – or how the sound of your voice tastes. More commonly, synaesthesia involves experiencing letters or numbers as having different colours (grapheme-colour synaesthesia).

The funny thing is, you probably don't find this difficult to imagine: if I were to ask you to attribute colours to the names 'Rupert' and 'Helen', you probably wouldn't struggle. You might even be able to tell me which food or which colour would go best with each name (personally I see Rupert in burgundy and Helen in a light green and yellow pattern).

The phenomenon continues to baffle scientists; popular explanations allude to enhanced connectivity across the brains of synaesthetes, but scant evidence for this hypothesis has been found. In part, this type of explanation arises because we like to imagine the brain as compartmentalized, with different areas used for storing different kinds of information.

The affective context model cuts through this unnecessary complexity: since all experience is converted into an affective code, we can naturally compare experiences cross-modally. A loosening or a tightening of the degree of association will lead to more or less creative comparisons, but we will all experience the phenomenon to some extent.

After all, we need to be able to quickly adapt to new situations, and since no two situations are exactly the same we need to be able to generalize using experiences that feel similar. You can take me to a restaurant in a different country, and though I have never encountered it before, it will feel like a restaurant and I will know how to behave.

If we were unable to do this, we would act, well, like computers. And it is this same affective coding mechanism that underpins a host of more recently discovered features of human thought.

Anchoring

Here's a question for you: would you say Albert Einstein was more or less than 93 years old when he died? How old do you think he was?

You might be interested to know that half of the copies of this book have been published with a different question. In half of them, the question is 'would you say Albert Einstein was more or less than 63 years old when he died? How old do you think he was?'

Of course I have made that bit up. But if we *had* published two versions of this book, almost certainly the estimates of the group asked the '63' question would be lower than the estimates of the group asked the '93' question. This is an effect called anchoring, and is a specific instance of a phenomenon called priming.

In essence, with anchoring, if you didn't have any particular feeling about something – say, how much you would be prepared to donate to save polar bears – then an initial figure will guide your decision. A person who stops you in the street and suggests a $20 donation is likely to receive donations to a value higher than someone who stops you and suggests a $5 donation.

Affectively speaking, this is easy to explain. If someone has planted a feeling in your mind, where you didn't already have a strong feeling, then your responses will reflect that affective state.

This is a powerful effect to bear in mind when designing learning experiences: on the one hand we will often want to put people in situations where they are unsure how to act, because in making a decision they will be redefining themselves. But what if they make the wrong decision?

Anchoring – for example using stories – can help tip the scales in the right direction whilst falling short of mere conformity. The photograph of a role model on a desk might be sufficient to anchor one's mindset at significant decision points throughout the day. Learning professionals tend not to think in these terms; a fixation on events and content gets in the way.

The effect of anchoring is measurable even where people believe they are acting rationally. In one particularly disturbing experiment, German judges rolled a pair of dice prior to passing judgement on a description of a criminal case. It was made clear to them that the dice bore no relation to the case – however, those who rolled a higher number tended to suggest significantly longer sentences than those who rolled lower numbers.

If you ever find yourself facing a prison sentence, you might consider wearing a shirt with a low number on it.

The halo effect

Another example of this effect comes in the form of the halo effect. Take a look at the following description of Sam:

> Sam is intelligent, industrious, impulsive, critical, stubborn, envious.

By now you won't be surprised to learn that in experiments where half the participants read a description like this in reverse order (Sam is envious, stubborn, critical, impulsive, industrious, intelligent), they rate Sam lower on a likeability scale than people who read them in the order you did. Why is that?

The first part of the explanation is that we react emotionally to each of the words – indeed, that is all a word is: a sound that creates an emotional reaction. The second part of the explanation is that we are creatures governed by homeostasis: in other words, we constantly strive for a steady state, one in which we expend the least mental effort. At a cognitive level we have seen this referred to as 'equilibrium 'and 'balance'; a state in which our model of the world matches our experience. In simple terms: once we've made up our mind about something, we don't like to change it.

As you probably know from your own experience, we generally don't like it when the world forces us to change our opinion of things – for example, when we take a friend to what we believe to be the best pizza place in the city, and the food turns out to be terrible. 'Maybe the regular chef was sick today', you suggest.

In the case of the halo effect, once we feel positive about something – a person for example – we don't much like to change our opinion, so we tend to disregard contradictory evidence and selectively remember supporting evidence.

This extends to *us*, of course: people like to feel good about themselves. This self-sentiment effect extends to a whole range of self-serving biases – for example optimism bias (feeling that our lives will be better than average), or over-confidence in our judgements. As an example, if you are undecided about your choice of car, once you have made your decision your confidence in your decision will go up dramatically and you will be able to come up with lots of reasons why your choice was the right decision. Just as Fritz Heider suggested, if we feel good about ourselves, we want to feel good about the decisions we have made.

This model can be used to explain the sometimes counter-productive effects of conventional diversity training.[1] In essence, people who normally feel pretty good about themselves are made to feel bad about themselves in the course of the training. But this feeling can easily be redressed by various rationalizations – such as blaming the victim.

In essence, rather than shoulder the responsibility for discrimination and feel bad about themselves, people will tend to find justifications for it. The feeling that people are trying to re-establish in this way is that the world is broadly fair, and that bad things happen to bad people.

In fact, a recent *Harvard Business Review* article entitled 'Why diversity programs fail' found that conventional diversity training did very little to improve organizations and in many cases was immediately followed by a *reduction* in the desired behaviours.[2]

They went on the describe the kinds of interventions more likely to have a positive effect, though – of which one was mentoring arrangements. You can perhaps see why: it's much harder to hold negative attitudes towards someone when you have agreed to be their mentor and meet regularly with them over extended periods of time. To dislike a person and elect to meet regularly with them would create cognitive dissonance.

Changing your mind

In many organizations, a significant chunk of learning will be dedicated to risk; to identifying it, avoiding it, managing it. In developing such programmes, we should bear in mind that we will have most impact where we can connect at an emotional level – for example through experiences and storytelling that connect to the things that really matter to people – rather than through rational appeals. People may – intellectually speaking – appreciate that reputational risks can damage their company and ultimately endanger their job, but if their level of engagement is low and the job market is buoyant, what's the big deal?

People who claim to be rational are never really so. Have you ever wondered why panellists on radio or TV debates so rarely reach agreement? If they were really arguing rationally (and they invariably claim to be) this would be statistically unlikely: usually *someone's* argument is logically stronger.

But somehow we know intuitively that the opposing sides are just going to bark at each other and come away if anything *more* convinced that they are right. Why is that?

Media companies know this, of course – that's why they set the debate up in the way that they do (ideally with the most inflammatory speaker from each side) *because what audiences are really there for is the emotional fireworks display*. At no point is anyone expected to say: 'On reflection, I concede that your conclusion is the more logical interpretation of the available evidence, and I hereby change my mind'. I have listened to thousands of such debates and never heard anyone say anything like that.

Affectively speaking, this makes sense: people become attached to a familiar set of opinions and beliefs. Not only do they react negatively to unfamiliar views, it causes them to react emotionally in defence of their own – especially since they are acutely aware of the reputational cost of publicly admitting defeat. Nobody wants to go on the radio and admit that they were wrong.

Recent research has found that people exposed to views that contradict their own, tend to *harden* rather than question their beliefs – the very *opposite* of what we would expect if they were rational.

The reasons for this should be clear by now: if you've worked hard to build an internally consistent set of views, changing an important one is going upset the balance; it would be like removing a scaffolding pole. Unless you're in love with the person opposing your view, you're better off just reinforcing what you currently think, whatever they say.

Imagine, for example that you are deeply opposed to capital punishment on the grounds that it is an ineffective deterrent and does little to reduce crime rates.

What if you were presented with compelling evidence to the contrary – evidence that clearly shows its effectiveness in reducing crime? Would you change your mind? You would if you were rational. But this is not what people do.

We know this, because precisely this experiment was carried out by Charles Lord, Lee Ross and Mark Lepper at Stanford University.[3] They identified two groups of students – one group in favour of capital punishment, the other opposed to it – and presented them with (manufactured) evidence that directly contradicted their views.

The result? They actually *hardened* their views. Those who started out in favour of capital punishment were even more in favour of it, those who initially opposed it were now more deeply opposed.

This same finding has been replicated in a wide range of contexts; most topically in the area of politics. People on either side of the political debate are gobsmacked that blatant evidence of the opposition candidate's wrongdoings do nothing to soften support for him/her – in fact the opposite! The more evidence we provide, the more polarized the debate becomes.

Global warming provides another example: how can climate change denial exist in a world where the evidence of climate change is overwhelming? Do people really still believe the world is flat?

The answer is that if people were fundamentally rational, we would not see these effects – but if they were fundamentally emotional we surely would. You and I become attached to ideas, objects, and events. If you are in love with someone, then having an acquaintance point out your darling's shortcomings may simply cause you to harden your defence of them, and weaken your relationships with the critic.

The factual accuracy of our beliefs is far less important than what our friends believe; after all, for a social creature it's the attitude of those around you that will most likely determine how you feel.

Every so often we do come across people who pride themselves on factual accuracy. On closer inspection, it turns out that their friends also take pride in this, so it seems that what motivates them is the sense of shame they would experience should a close friend point out their factual blunder. It's a recurrent theme: reason piggy-backs on sentiment.

So how would you change someone? How would you help them develop? Not with rational argument. You'd be much better off, as balance theory suggests, getting to know them and befriending them – discovering common ground, things you both care about. But when you're sitting at home, viewing the world via a screen, opportunities for shared experiences are few and far between.

This makes digital interaction (and learning) inherently polarizing – even if it weren't for the algorithms actively generating and promoting outrageous content. It's also a challenge for me, as an author: like you, I have read many books and I struggle to think of any of them that have profoundly influenced my behaviour. If I really wanted to change your mind, we would need to spend time together.

Since for the most part I can't, some of this book is intended to connect with you in other ways, such as using a range of examples and situations some of which you may identify with. If, ultimately, you accept what I am saying, it will not be because it is correct – but because of how you feel about the idea. You might be more inclined to take my side if a close friend recommended this book, for instance.

Another way in which processing our experience affectively is evident is in the phenomenon called the substitution effect. Let's return to relationships to see how it works.

The substitution effect

If you are hoping to date someone, then being a regular feature in your crush's day is a good start – in fact, physical proximity is still the best predictor of who will end up with who in a relationship. The 'familiarity breeds liking' effect will work in your favour and eventually you will wear them down to the point where they are prepared to go on a date, generally by talking about all the things you have in common.

But then you have to figure out where to take them on your date. Intuitively, you know how to solve this problem: figure out what they like, then arrange your date accordingly. This is partly because you want to demonstrate that you also like the things they like – but also because you probably guessed that some of how they feel about the date will transfer to how they feel about you.

You would be amazed at the extent to which this affective association trick works. In essence people will answer a whole variety of questions by simply checking: 'How do I feel right now?' Questions like: 'What are the prospects for the economy?' are influenced by whether the sun is shining. 'Is this person guilty?' by whether or not you are feeling hungry. A whole host of questions such as: 'How long will you live?', 'How good was your holiday?', 'How happy are you with your relationship?' or 'How confident are you in a given stock price?' are determined by your general emotional state, rather than factual information. People lie to themselves that they have good reasons, when in reality they are just going on gut feel.

Many of us make use of this phenomenon at an intuitive level. Dating is an obvious example; the right time to ask a person how they feel about you is when the date is going really well, not when you have just knocked their glass of red wine over, permanently staining their clothing.

Returning to sales, which is an excellent area of application, if you're going to pop the question: 'Would you like to purchase this product?', you're going to want to manoeuvre the customer into feeling as good as possible at that point. Rationally speaking, attractive salespeople who flatter you shouldn't make one jot of difference to your decision about a product – but in reality they do.

Having spent a regrettable amount of time in classrooms, I can attest to a similar effect in educational contexts – not the effect of attractiveness, I hasten to add, but around how we evaluate learning. In corporate education, the standard of a course is often assessed using questionnaires at the end, where people are asked things like 'How effective was this course?', 'How competent was the trainer?' and so on.

Learners actually have no idea about the answer to these complex questions – in my experience, nobody does. Figuring out how effective a course is or the impact a trainer has had on behaviour requires the kind of longitudinal data that is rarely available.

So what do students do? Simple: they substitute a quick assessment of how they are feeling at the time of asking. In light of this, a canny instructor will engineer an 'emotional high' into the final hours of a programme: end early on a Friday perhaps, conclude with a fun exercise, have some kind of applause or group photo take place – or maybe just hand out sweets.

Popular science books make the mistake of seeing these as 'biases' and departures from a rational ideal – much as many philosophers from Descartes to Dennett have done. But cognition is sentimental through and through.

Cognitive dissonance

Along similar lines to Fritz Heider, and at around the same time (1957), Leon Festinger put forward his aforementioned Theory of Cognitive Dissonance. To recap: the theory says that people experience psychological stress when they hold contradictory beliefs, values or ideas.

The thing to notice here is that it is not the logical inconsistency that is stressful: it is the affective inconsistency. Cognitive dissonance is affective dissonance.

Affective dissonance is not limited to a conflict of values: imagine driving to your favourite restaurant only to find that it is permanently closed. How would you feel? Disappointed? Shocked? Affective dissonance is the fundamental process that drives cognitive adaptation in any creature. Affective dissonance is the basis of learning and memory whether you are a man or a mouse.

What every nervous system strives to achieve is a state where the internal model of the world matches the external model of the world. Every time the world surprises you, you have to adjust your internal model and that takes energy and is experienced as dissonance. The feeling of dissonance is how nervous systems experience the need to change.

When we are designing learning experiences – whether as complex as a flight simulator or as simple as a role play – this is what we are aiming for: the right amount of dissonance, or discomfort. We want to create a sense of being challenged, so that we are obliged to change how we feel about the world. We may even experience some pleasure at overcoming challenges, as we do with computer games – we are offsetting our immediate discomfort with the anticipated pleasure of accomplishment. A challenge must impact us affectively.

People will sometimes say, for example, 'We learn best from our mistakes', but that isn't strictly true – after all we are making small mistakes all the time. I am making numerous grammatical slips even as I write. We learn from the mistakes that we *feel* – for example when a respected friend points out a schoolboy error in our writing.

When Jonathan Haidt, author of *The Righteous Mind*, says: 'The emotional tail wags the rational dog', he is only on the way to being right: the dog is emotional from nose to tail. There is no rational dog. There is only an emotional dog that can be trained to be rational (this is true both literally and metaphorically speaking).

We can, for example, train a dog to add two numbers – just as we have trained people to do so. We can take purely emotional systems and line them up in a way that behaves in accordance with laws of reason.

Rationality is something that emerges from purely emotional agents working together. Because humans are – emotionally speaking – aware of themselves *as* emotional agents behaving rationally, we get confused.

When we consider the science of psychology as a whole, it has had a troubled relationship with the idea of 'thinking'. Possibly the most successful approach of all – behaviourism – turned its back on thinking entirely.

Behaviourism requires affective states

In Chapter 2 we encountered behaviourism – a school of thought that arose partly as a reaction to Freud, Jung and psychoanalysis. Sigmund Freud entered our collective consciousness by proposing a model in which the human mind was the product of a vast 'plumbing system' of desires and pressures hidden from view – under the floorboards, if you like.

One of his most famous books – *The Interpretation of Dreams* – suggested a mechanism for taking a peek at our unconscious. Unfortunately, he made psychology 'spooky', and whilst that was popular it was out of step with the growing desire to be more scientific.

Most of what Freud was talking about was not directly observable – instead he proposed a set of wild, fantastic stories about the mind and how it worked. The extraordinary nature of these stories ensured their spread and persistence – but irked a scientific community that were increasingly putting their faith in what you could see and measure.

Whilst you couldn't directly inspect the human unconscious, you could see and measure human behaviour – and that's how behaviourism was born.

In essence, behaviourism was the idea that you could understand humans and other creatures without having to know anything about what was happening in their heads – solely by looking at their behavioural responses (that you could measure) in response to stimuli (that you could also measure). Some of these stimuli ('positive reinforcers') would make creatures do things more often, others ('punishments') would result in them doing them less. And some would make no difference at all. But why?

This mystery at the heart of behaviourism remained unanswered, and largely unnoticed, throughout its history. The entire approach rests on assumptions about how creatures react to different kinds of stimuli and the fact that some they like, some they don't. Without these, the definitions of positive and negative reinforcement remain circular: what is a positive reinforcer? Something that makes us do something more frequently. What makes us do something more frequently? Positive reinforcement.

But as we saw in Chapter 2, the affective context model can provide us with a better answer: a positive reinforcer is something we feel good about. Rats don't learn to press levers for wooden pellets, after all. Behaviourism is a set of techniques that depend on a theory of affective states.

In his YouTube lecture 'Memories are made of this',[4] Eric Kandel, Nobel-prize winning neuroscientist attempts to explain learning in the simple sea slug (*aplysia*). In doing so he uses the standard behaviourist lexicon, talking about classical conditioning and sensitization – *but he is unable to do so without making reference to affective states*: he talks about the sea slug 'learning to fear' and 'frightening the animal'.

It's a marvellous illustration of how a behaviourist account must *always* rest on a model of learning as a fundamentally affective process.

The irony of the lecture is that Kandel himself uses affective impact to make his speech memorable – for example by telling jokes and getting members of the audience to touch the peculiar slug-like sea-dweller. Though he does it intuitively, this undermines any behaviourist account of memory and hints at the real mechanism behind learning: he can shock the sea slug just as he can shock the students. That's what memories are made of.

From an affective standpoint, behaviourists found two really interesting things: first that our behaviour is strongly influenced by its affective consequences. No surprises there. If something we do has negative consequences we tend to do it less, positive consequences we tend to do it more.

Moreover, they discovered that the most powerful schedule of rewards and punishments was a variable one, i.e. one where you were never quite sure when your behaviour was going to pay off. You might see this in a relationship, for example, where one person works really hard at pleasing their partner because it's never entirely clear when their efforts will be rewarded. Behaviourists usually skip the part about these consequences being essentially affective.

The second thing they discovered is that how we feel about something can be transferred by association to other things – such as a token. How do you feel about being given a million dollars? Pretty good? A million dollars is just a million bits of paper – or a number on a computer screen – but we feel good about it because dollars are tokens that we can exchange for things we do feel good about: food, houses, holidays, cars, horses and so on.

Some of the things we might exchange it for may themselves be tokens: expensive clothing or watches may not actually help keep us warm, but may themselves be tokens of status which in turn are exchanged for admiration and social rewards.

Episodic versus semantic memory

The distinction between semantic and episodic memory dates back to the 1970s and Endel Tulving. Tulving argued that semantic memory is a kind of 'mental thesaurus' that provides the knowledge necessary for the use of language, whilst episodic memory is memory for stuff that happened to us.[5] So, for example, we may have learned that the Battle of Hastings was in 1066, but this is stored in semantic memory, whilst if we were actually present this experience would be held in episodic memory.

But this is wrong. First, we have proposed above that our words draw their significance from our experience and our reactions to things. Second, although learning about the battle of Hastings in a classroom is a very different experience to actually being there, it is an experience – an episode – nonetheless. Our classroom experience may be further supplanted with other experiences – films of battles that we have seen in which armoured knights battle heroically – or the gruesome image of Harold clutching the arrow in his eye (which is presumably why it was captured in the Bayeux tapestry).

Once again, Elizabeth Loftus' work suggests that the distinction isn't true: she discovered that you could tell somebody about an episode, and they would later believe that it had actually happened to them – moving seamlessly from semantic to episodic.

Strange as this may sound, we do this all the time: popular Western culture represents birthday parties as events where children are gathered among balloons to enjoy jelly and cake. People will often recall their own birthdays as having involved jelly, cake and balloons – even if the photographic evidence shows that none were present at any of their birthdays.

Likewise, if I ask you to tell me what you know about clocks (semantic memory), your answer will be just the sort of emotional abstraction that your mind builds from your various experiences of clocks.

In fact, if I ask you about *any* experience you have had, you will draw on your stored reactions to all kinds of things – events you have experienced first-hand as well as those you have not – in confabulating a memory.

So if I were to ask you to describe the Battle of Hastings you might describe men in armour, some on horseback, charging at each other across an open field. There would be archers, spears and swords. You would be well aware that you were not personally present, but your account would likely be a concoction based on related experiences: trips to museums, fairytales and movies.

In our memories, episodes of different kinds – those we experience and those we witness – will often merge into a single affective pattern that we use to conjure up a memory. It's just more efficient that way. If we believe that car crashes often involve broken glass, then we remember broken glass. In other words, every so-called semantic memory is a 'mash-up' of episodes, which in turn are fabricated from emotional reactions.

There is another way to refute the semantic memory hypothesis. Consider our closest relatives, evolutionarily speaking. Do we imagine that chimpanzees have semantic memory as distinct from episodic? Or that dogs do?

We do not. And why on earth would we have the hubris to assume that in the relatively short evolutionary distance that separates us we have developed an entirely new way of organizing information in the brain?

Some recent research has suggested that episodic memory and semantic memory are stored in different part of the brain, since fMRI scans show different patterns of activity corresponding to each. As always, there is an alternative explanation: namely that that the sensation of 'I-ness' causes a distinct pattern of neurological activity.

This is consistent with the finding that people can sometimes believe that experiences they merely heard about actually happened to them personally.

In summary, our understanding of learning is still proto-scientific; a patchwork of hypotheses that set our minds apart from other creatures. Be sceptical of them all, ask yourself: 'Could we apply this theory to other animals?'

These days we accept evolution as an explanation of how we became what we are – but it seems we have yet to accept Darwin's observation that we are different only in degree but not in kind from other creatures.

Key points

- Human behaviour is largely governed by conformity.
- We interpret the world around us in intentional terms, and map our world affectively.

- We try to harmonize our feelings towards the things we are aware of.
- We do not have two cognitive systems (instinctive and rational), just one emotional system that balances immediate emotional states and imagined emotional states.
- Cognitive biases are features of a system that processes experience affectively.
- Changing attitudes requires an understanding of existing attitudes.
- Behaviourism requires affective states in order to be coherent.
- There is no distinction between semantic and episodic memory.

Endnotes

1 F Dobbin, A Kalev and E Kelly. Diversity Management in Corporate America, *Contexts*, 2007, **6** (4), 21–27

2 F Dobbin and A Kalev. Why Diversity Programs Fail, *Harvard Business Review*, July–August 2016, hbr.org/2016/07/why-diversity-programs-fail (archived at https://perma.cc/9EBE-CFKW)

3 C Lord, L Ross and M Lepper. Biased assimilation and attitude polarization: The effects of prior theories on subsequently considered evidence, *Journal of Personality and Social Psychology*, 1979, **37** (11), 2098–109

4 George Kalarritis, Clinical Psychologist. Memories are Made of This. Eric Kandel (2008) (online video), 5 January 2017, www.youtube.com/watch?v=rPtxuQnpB9A (archived at https://perma.cc/KXC3-V9RS)

5 E Tulving (1972) Episodic and semantic memory. In E Tulving and W Donaldson (Eds), *Organization of Memory*, Academic Press, New York

The future   12

When Mark Zuckerberg created a web page where he and his Harvard college chums could share stuff,[1] he probably didn't imagine it would contribute to electing a game-show host to the position of President of the United States. People are easy to predict. Technology is easy to predict. The interaction between the two isn't.

People are easy to predict because they stay the same. Culture changes, but we remain the same old monkeys that we were 70,000 years ago. Technology changes, but in predictable ways: it does logical things faster, it extends its reach further in directions that make our lives easier. We can confidently predict, for example, that sex will continue to be an important part of the way people use technology in future.

If you want to see into the future, it's really helpful to bear in mind that people are fundamentally affective in nature, and computers are fundamentally not: for example, you can immediately dismiss the idea that we will all be fitted with some kind of USB port, drilled into our skull, that will enable us to instantly learn a language – or Kung Fu.

We may well end up with devices attached to our heads, but they will do the work for us – they will *reduce* our learning. You might even find yourself strapped into a robot that knows Kung Fu – but unless you have sweated your way through the (potentially VR) gym sessions, you will not.

In fact, as you become ever more technologically enabled you will continue to learn *less* with each passing year – of this we can be sure. But how can we be sure?

There are, and always have been, many books about the future. These days such books have a contemporary urgency about them and a sense of awe in the face of the immense scale of the challenges we now face. They describe risks and possibilities relating to areas such as AI and automation, climate change, Big Data, biotechnology, globalization – and ponder the impact these might have on employment, democracy, the economy, and the global order.

These books tend to make us worry and feel powerless, because they signpost uncertainty without describing a journey. Some are more optimistic, some pessimistic, but overall the message is that there is a lot of change ahead of us, we cannot be sure in which direction it will take us, we will just have to wait and see.

In thinking about the future, it's important to have a proper frame of reference otherwise it is very hard to make sense of anything at all. By 'proper frame of reference', I mean one that isn't bound to a particular historical period or ideological standpoint. For example, we can focus on economics and the role of capital in the future – and easily overlook that economic considerations really only arose in the last few thousand years.

In general, any frame of reference which is specific to humans – such as religion, economics or politics should be called into question, since we can safely assume that there is a more fundamental level of analysis that lies beneath it.

In fact, humans are especially susceptible to 'supernatural' narratives, by which I mean stories about our origins or destiny that place us above the rest of the animal kingdom. These escapist stories paint our future in terms of fleeting phenomena – like money or politics or science – rather than the more profound, immutable ones.

What such books lack is the right perspective. I don't mean that they lack a historical perspective, I mean they lack an underpinning narrative: a story in which all our past, present and future make sense, and one which can be used to accurately predict the course of destiny.

What Plato and Socrates can teach us

There is such a story; an old story that enables us to both interpret the past and anticipate the future. It's also a tale that will tell us about learning, and what will happen to learning. We have encountered it already, but I'd like to discuss it in more detail here, because it's the most important story I know of. It's a story shared by Plato in the *Phaedrus*, as told by his teacher Socrates.

About Socrates we know only what two of his students (Plato and Xenophon) wrote about their mentor. Socrates himself chose not to write.

The story starts like this:

> Very well. I heard, then, that at Naucratis in Egypt there lived one of the old gods of that country, the one whose sacred bird is called the ibis; and the name of the divinity was Theuth. It was he who first invented numbers and calculation, geometry and astronomy, not to speak of draughts and dice, and above all writing (*grammata*).
>
> Now the king of all Egypt at that time was Thamus... Theuth came to him and exhibited his arts and declared they ought to be imparted to other Egyptians. And Thamus questioned him about the usefulness of each one; and as Theuth enumerated, the King blamed or praised what he thought were the good or bad points in the explanation.[2]

So the Egyptian god we know today as Thoth brings the gift of writing to be judged by King Thamus. You might wonder why a god would be worried about what a king thinks, but Thamus is king of all the gods, so by comparison Thoth is something like a demi-god, and the scenario is a lot like the familiar TV series *Dragons' Den* in which a young entrepreneur attempts to pitch their promising idea to the circumspect investment dragons by extolling its benefits and potential.

So here's Thoth with his big idea – writing – how is he going to sell it to King Thamus?

When it came to writing, Theuth said, 'This discipline, my King, will make Egyptians wiser and will improve their memories; my invention is a cure (*pharmakon*) for both memory and wisdom.'

So picture Thoth as the young eager, entrepreneur: 'My invention can make you superhuman! I promise it will make you smarter, wiser! It will even improve your memory!' This is pretty much how we see writing today – as something that compensates for the failing of our memories, a remedy for human intellectual frailty, and the cornerstone of civilization. But – *incredibly* – King Thamus *rejects* writing, and here's what he has to say:

> Theuth, my master of arts, to one man it is given to create the elements of an art, to another to judge the extent of harm and usefulness it will have for those who are going to employ it. And now, since you are the father of written letters, your paternal goodwill has led you to pronounce the very opposite of what is their real power. The fact is that this invention will produce forgetfulness in the souls of those who have learned it because they will not need to exercise their memories, being able to rely on what is written, using the stimulus of external marks that are alien to themselves...

The same Greek word – *pharmakon* – may be translated as 'cure' or 'poison'. So the basic dynamic is this: Thoth says: 'Writing is great – it's a cure for human weaknesses' and Thamus says: 'It might look that way to you, but it's really a poison – the *very opposite* of a remedy – it will actually make us weaker. I'm not buying it.' But we bought it.

Note that there is a triple irony here: Socrates is relating a story about the dangers of writing – which he refuses to write down. Plato then writes it down and in doing so commits to writing a story about how writing is actually a really bad (toxic) idea! The final irony is that – true to Thamus' prediction – we've completely lost the ability to understand the story more than 2,000 years later.

At this point it certainly looks like writing is a 'cure' – but Thamus spots that writing is something alien, something more like a parasite – it feeds on us, growing stronger as we grow weaker.

Thamus didn't need to describe writing as 'alien', he could have simply ended his comments at 'external marks'. By describing it as alien, he implies that writing has an agenda of its own. The relationship between humans and writing works because the parasite creates ever better living conditions for us in return for something (can you guess what that is?).

Homeostasis is the drive we share with the most primitive organisms – with every creature that can learn. It compels us relentlessly to seek out better conditions, easier lives. And so the bargain with technology is struck: easier, safer lives. A nest feathered with technology. With each passing year the need to learn less as knowledge and capability are handed to an automated environment.

Consider this: if you hitched a ride on a time machine and found yourself stranded in the Stone Age – how well would you cope? Which of your modern-day inventions would you be capable of recreating? An iPhone? No. How about a toaster? How would you generate electricity? Do you know how to smelt iron?

Let's face it – you'd struggle to create fire. You'd probably be considered an imbecile by caveman standards – unable to hunt, to distinguish one plant from another, incapable of making your own clothes. You'd draw some wild pictures in the sand though.

Why is this particular story so important in understanding our future? Fundamentally, it's not a story about writing, but about the birth of technology and how it feeds on homeostasis. It's a story about why with every passing year we will learn less, as our lives become more comfortable and predictable.

What does technology take from us?

Technology, not writing, is the alien parasite; something that exists in a seemingly symbiotic relationship with humans. Unlike language, which comes naturally to many species, writing is difficult to learn – *we have to be adapted for writing*, painstakingly and over the course of many years. Writing adapts *us* and in return it offers comfort via culture.

As libraries sprung up around the enlightened world, they didn't seem like a terribly dangerous thing – quite the opposite – but what started to happen was that knowledge became *externalized*, just as Thamus warned.

This is a great trick, because it means that each of us can 'stand on the shoulders of giants' – generations do not have to recite the sacred stories around the camp fire – instead they can just look up the answer in a book.

As a consequence, our culture began to grow incrementally – embodying more and more knowledge even as each of us individually knew less and less – we put our knowledge *into* the things around us, with the result that each of us needed to hold less in our heads.

In the beginning the relationship was complicated – we had to be adapted, via writing, in order to begin externalizing knowledge. As technology grew in capability, it became possible to lower the 'entry requirements', to the point where soon we will not need to write, we will only need to speak – and then perhaps merely to think.

As I write, I have an AI assistant in my house. I can ask it to bring me pizza, and pizza will magically arrive. I know next to nothing about almost every aspect of it, barring how to plug it in. I am ignorant of the chemical composition of the plastics in which it is encased, the language in which it is programmed, the number or type of circuits it contains. I do not know the complex value chain that connects it to the pizza people – or even if people are involved at all.

Indeed, it is likely no single person knows all this: the collective knowledge required for its creation is scattered across thousands of heads situated in the 'value chain' that require its creation. We are much like our nest of ants; we know what we are doing, but not what the nest is doing.

Why does the nature of technology inevitably eliminate human learning? The journey from infant to adult is a painful process during which learning adapts us to the inconveniences of the world around us. But what if we could adapt the world, remove all those pesky inconveniences, and reduce our need to learn entirely? What if, instead of having to learn to grow crops and how to cook, we could just yell at a device 'Food!' and food would arrive by drone? What if we could merely think 'pizza!' and it would be printed before our very eyes?

This arrow of destiny eliminates learning, driven by the most fundamental drive of all – homeostasis. Learning is a cost, and homeostasis seeks to eliminate it.

When all our knowledge was merely contained in libraries, it was easy to overlook the trajectory: it didn't seem such a terrible idea to externalize knowledge since we were still reading and writing books in order to build more cultural artefacts.

The next big leap was when books no longer needed us as hosts for their development. This happened when we began to externalize not merely knowledge – but *capability*.

Knowledge could now have agency in a way that no longer required human intervention. First with industrialization, then with AI and automation, we began to understand that it was never really about writing at all – indeed writing was only ever a 'larval form' to be cast off. In our contemporary culture, writing itself is dying out, people write less and less, use emojis, pictures, sounds and facial expressions more and more – and soon we will return to the point in history where only the scribes needed to write.

Those 'external marks' of which Thamus warned will be encoded in binary, and for the most part only technology will need to read them.

Of course not everybody is locked in this relationship with technology in the same way – for the foreseeable future we will need dwindling numbers of specialists, but rather like the Pied Piper story, more and more people will find themselves left behind. Technology does not need each of us in the same way.

Performance guidance systems

If you are wondering what the next big thing in learning is – it's performance guidance systems. What we are seeing currently is the next evolutionary step in the emancipation of ideas, the externalization of decisions.

Once all knowledge was externalized, the next logical step was to externalize decision-making capability. A decision is, after all, an investment of energy on our part. Resource-based systems like Google are only so useful – they still require us to search for information, to decide which information to believe, and to act on it.

By contrast, systems such as satellite guidance (GPS systems) require none of these things: once you have made the decision to trust in the device, it tells you what to do, when to do it – and you follow it unquestioningly. Well, almost. Perhaps not if you are about to drive into a lake. But what if you are in an autonomous car?

The appeal of such systems is precisely that they reduce cognitive effort on our part. Homeostasis is traded for capability. Our comfort is traded for power – which passes to technology.

So it is homeostasis that determines destiny's direction. Technology is not part of the story, technology *is* the story – one in which we play a minor role. Capital, religion, politics, climate change remain players in a story of relentless homeostatic ascent whose latest incarnation is technology. This story stretches as far as the eye can see and beyond, from the primordial soup to the end of humanity.

In your lifetime you will witness a vast de-skilling, overwhelming offloading of decision-making capability, just as past generations witnessed the cataloguing of human knowledge. Systems that guide our every whim – from what to watch, to who to vote for – will dominate our existence. To a significant degree they already do.

As learning professionals, we will play an important part in this story: we will create the resources that enable people to achieve higher levels of performance. Organizations that do not tread this path will suffer higher resourcing costs and struggle to compete. In turn, they will look to guidance systems as a stepping stone to automation.

It was never about us, nor was it about writing. The arrow of destiny has been determined by the *pharmakon* – the cure that is also a poison. Writing has shed its skin and revealed itself to be technology; growing into adulthood even as we shrink into our infancy.

The future will continue to be dominated by this trend: technology will reduce our need to learn, smoothing our experience of life until almost all our desires are satisfied instantaneously without the slightest effort. At some point soon, technology will be able to evolve exponentially without our help – and it is impossible to say anything about that state of affairs that could be understood by anyone alive.

The philosophers of which I have been so critical fanned the flames of these developments: Plato, Descartes – even the repentant Wittgenstein – admired the alien, anti-human parasite – nursing it through its infancy in writing and logic, encouraging its spread, enabling it to come of age as embodied technology. I am afraid it is, and always was, inevitable.

In case this sounds like apocalyptic doom-mongering, rest assured that you have little to fear in your lifetime: on the contrary, you will see a considerable acceleration of the pace at which technology makes your life more comfortable, your experience more seamless. Your most basic desires will be satisfied as immediately as you can think of them.

Despite this, it is hard not to ask: 'But what does technology want?' Your current view is perhaps that technology only wants whatever we want it to want: to optimize for a certain outcome, such as views or clicks or sales of products. But what the ant wants differs from the nest wants. Look at your own body: a towering metropolis of simple cells, each wanting only to survive, but collectively wanting so much more.

So whilst an individual algorithm may have limited ambitions, it is much harder to say what technology as a whole wants. We can only observe that it wishes to grow more powerful and perpetually extend its reach, and that it will continue to do so in an exponential fashion.

A little time travel

Let's take a look at some of the things technology is doing to the way we experience the world right now.

Imagine that you want lots of people to like the video of the outfit that you have posted online. You want this because you are a social ape, hardwired to experience positive bursts of reward chemicals when members of your group like you.

But people are annoying and unpredictable – what if you could simply create digital versions of people that reliably provide you with positive feedback? How about the clothing itself: clothing costs money, takes time to be delivered, and may not fit correctly. What if you could simply click a button to display yourself perfectly attired, and avoid all the inconvenience of actually getting ready?

Of course your body itself is part of the physical world and shaping it is effortful, requiring dieting and exercise. How much easier it would be to create a digital copy of yourself – an avatar – that can take any form you wish.

You might think that this is little more than deceit; how would it be to turn up for a date only to discover that your partner looks nothing like their idealized online representation? But why turn up for a date at all? It's a lot of hassle, isn't it? If you could digitize the experience using virtual reality and haptic simulators, could not both parties enjoy precisely the experience they hoped for?

Of course, however someone appears there is always the possibility they will be rude or uncooperative; so let's have AI play the role of perfect partner instead…

Digital technology represents a step change in our ability to organize the world around us **because many of the physical things in the world can now be digitized, and digital stuff is easier to control than physical stuff.** Unlike the real world, a digital world doesn't 'push back'; instead it takes any form we wish.

But while we are busy clicking our way through our digitally perfected life, we may become aware of another source of disruption emanating from the physical world – news. News risks disrupting our perfectly balanced internal state: we may hear, see or read things that are discordant with our beliefs or which upset our plans. News is an attempt to get us to see the world as it really is, and as such is likely to lead to dissonance and disequilibrium.

As we've seen in previous chapters, people may not see the world as it is. Here's an example: We all have off days, right? Do you have days when you don't feel quite yourself? I'm going to let you into a secret: *nobody notices.*

Back in the 1970s Stanley Milgram (yes, the electric shocks guy) was experimenting with 'Cyranoids'. Cyranoids is a made-up word to describe people who – like the character from Cyrano De Bergerac on which the movie *Roxanne* was based – are speaking someone else's words rather than their own.

So, for example, Milgram would give earpieces to children and adults and have a professor dictate responses to a 12-year old (a bit like Tom Hanks in *Big* in reverse). Milgram steered his Cyranoids through a series of interactions with people – such as teachers – who were asked to observe them, assess them and so on. Bear in mind that – essentially – they were each acting as if a Yale professor were trapped in their body.

Pretty much nobody noticed that there was anything odd about them.

That should unsettle you: it raises the possibility that you live your entire life without anyone ever actually seeing or hearing 'you' as you really are. Instead, people take one look at you, decide what they expect of you and pretty much ignore anything that doesn't fit with their stereotype.

It's just one of a number of experiments that illustrate that to a large extent we don't see the world as it is, we see it as we want to *react* to it. This phenomenon ranges from 'perceptual set' at the awareness level, through to 'confirmation bias' at the cognitive level.

Research into the phenomenon of fake news confirms the assertion in a recent article: 'People will share things even if they know it's not true, just because it fits with their values and what they believe in'.[3]

Whilst there is a global shortage of people who understand the affective context model, there is no shortage of practical applications springing up in areas ranging from digital marketing to political influence.

Fake news works, because it mirrors what we want to *feel*. We love memes (which encapsulate a popular sentiment) and we share them with other people who feel like us, so they can feel like we do too (this is also why we tell stories). It doesn't matter whether they are true.

Why do our political leaders lie so much? Because they know that what people want to *feel* is what really matters. They strive to achieve affective coherence through polls and focus groups.

In itself, this is nothing new – throughout human history we have sought out things that confirmed the way we felt – only now we have the unimaginable power to *create* them, we are only a short step away from realizing Aladdin's genie.

Fake news is not, therefore, a cultural 'phase' we will grow out of – it is an inevitable consequence of the bargain we have struck with technology: the world around us is being digitized wholesale. Reality recedes into the background as technology recreates a world that more closely matches your appetites.

We used to feel bad about lying. But in a world where you can undermine authority, where you can say: 'We are tired of experts' and 'YOU are FAKE NEWS!', nobody has to feel bad about anything. That's the secret: remove the authority. Once you have called into question the status of respected news agencies, you can say whatever people want to hear with impunity.

Before you throw up your arms in horror, the world was already awash with views that exist only because they fit with what we want to feel – everything from the afterlife to Hollywood storylines.

Mainstream media allowed people in power to tell us how to feel. The internet allows us to feel however we want to feel, and the people in power to feed those feelings thanks to ever more accurate data revealing the things we care about.

As we peer back through evolutionary history, the consistent problem is reality: the world doesn't behave exactly as you would like it to, and this forces you to adapt which is effortful – even painful – and requires that you learn and change. This is the simplest form of refutation of the idea that the world is 'just a dream': if it were just a dream, things would always go to plan.

As I have explained above, what happens in our heads is much like a dream – but a dream is constantly disrupted by an objectionable reality. This disruption, this *dissonance*, is what ultimately shapes us in a process that drives individual learning and cultural progress.

The arrow of human history points towards changing the world so as to narrow this gap – to reduce the need for us to change, learn, or expend effort.

Key points

- Technology tends to reduce human learning by externalizing knowledge and capability.
- Resources, guidance and automation reflect a larger trend towards learning elimination.
- Digitization has enabled more people to have more of the experiences they desire, more of the time, at the price of reducing their connection to reality.

In closing

The philosopher Friedrich Nietzsche wrote: 'We should consider every day lost on which we have not danced at least once. And we should call every truth false which was not accompanied by at least one laugh.'[4]

Thanks to some rather violent, resentful philosophers we have fallen into believing that reason and emotion are separate, that storytelling and play are childish or frivolous, and that emotion is something to be mastered by reason.

This was a lie, and believing it has led us astray. It has corrupted our relationship with the world, with other creatures, and with ourselves. We have neglected learning and paved over it with education. We are now trapped in a toxic relationship with technology, one which promises a less challenging world with every day that passes – in exchange for our development.

We, the people who care about people, may assist the progress of technology with resources or further the development of people with challenges.

Endnotes

1 B Carson. This is the true story of how Mark Zuckerberg founded Facebook, and it wasn't to find girls, *Business Insider*, 28 February 2016, www.businessinsider.com/the-true-story-of-how-mark-zuckerberg-founded-facebook-2016-2 (archived at https://perma.cc/9XPN-2KBJ)

2 Plato (1925) *Plato in Twelve Volumes*, Vol 9, translated by H N Fowler, William Heinemann Ltd, London

3 K Rogers and A Bellemare. Misleading Trudeau 'joke' video demonstrates the political power of editing, CBC News, 6 September 2019, www.cbc.ca/news/technology/trudeau-media-bribery-fake-video-1.5273163 (archived at https://perma.cc/QBU9-HQ8Z)

4 F Nietzsche (2006) *Thus Spoke Zarathustra: A book for all and none*, Cambridge University Press, Chapter 56 (old and new tables), number 23

INDEX

CPSIA information can be obtained
at www.ICGtesting.com
Printed in the USA
BVHW011808060223
657988BV00011B/131

9 781398 607194